AF522623

VALUES
ATTITUDES AND PRACTICES

VALUES
ATTITUDES AND PRACTICES

By
Dr. A. Gayatri Ganesh
M.Sc., M.A., M.A., M.Ed., Ph.D., PGDGC
Deptt. of Education
Sri Venkateshwara University
Tirupati (Andhra Pradesh)
(India)

DISCOVERY PUBLISHING HOUSE PVT. LTD.
NEW DELHI-110 002

Published by:
Tilak Wasan

DISCOVERY PUBLISHING HOUSE PVT. LTD.
4383/4B, Ansari Road, Darya Ganj
New Delhi-110 002 (India)
Phone : +91-11-23279245, 43596064-65
Fax : +91-11-23253475
E-mail : parul.wasan@gmail.com
discoverypublishinghouse@gmail.com
web : www.discoverypublishinggroup.com

First Edition: **2012**

ISBN: 978-93-5056-128-7

Values—Attitudes and Practices

Printed at:
Shree Balaji Art Press
Delhi

PREFACE

"The end of all education, all training is man-making."

Education in general and value education in particular occupies a prestigious place in the modern context of the contemporary society. Education is supposed to be a powerful instrument of change and has a progressive impact on human behaviour, but in actual practice it is doing very little to cultivate moral, social, cultural and spiritual values in our youth and to promote national consciousness in the country.

Consequently the problem of value oriented education of the youth has assumed increasing prominence in educational discussions during recent times. Parents, teachers and society at large are concerned about values and value oriented education.

Teachers in fact are the designers of the future of the students. Teachers are the dynamic forces to inculcate education in students. Directly or indirectly they influence their students, hence teachers should present themselves as ideals. Considering the very role of teachers in imparting value education a research is conducted on the attitudes towards values and value practices of prospective teachers and this book helps to know more about them.

Dr. A Gayatri Ganesh

CONTENTS

INTRODUCTION

> "No system of education, no syllabus, no methodology, no text book can rise above the level of its teachers. If a country wants to have quality education it must have quality teachers"—
>
> *V.S. Matthews.*

Deterioration of values and thereby deadening of the learning experience is a worldwide phenomenon. Despite its several thousand years old value-based cultural tradition, India is also subject to massive erosion of values. That is why political and economic corruption, scandals, scams, anti-social and anti-national activities are on the rise in the present national scenario. The rapid degradation of values in the Indian context has posed a heavy challenge before higher education.

Degradation of mind and morals in the higher educational institutions is leading to value crisis. The National Policy on Education 1986 called for fostering social and moral values as an integral part of the process of Education. The institutions of higher education have to foster community values suitable to the changing society.

Education plays a vital role in weakening value crisis and strengthening values from the grass root (lower) level. The ultimate aim of education is the total development of personality of the individual. Balanced development of cognitive, affective and conative domains is of utmost importance for fruitful life. To have a happy and successful life, the educational system should give top priority to the inculcators of values. It is high time to evaluate the present value system prevailing among students and explore the ways and means to internalize the most important values in students. As the crux of value orientation is the teacher, he is an important source of values. He has to arrange curricular and co-curricular activities that may inculcate values in students. Even though, many factors such as family, friends, mass media, socio-economic factors, curricular and co-curricular activities are helping to form certain values in students yet the influence of family and teachers on students is the highest.

MEANING OF EDUCATION

The development of any nation depends mainly on the standards of its educational institutions. Education is the most powerful and effective instrument for inducing radical changes in the behaviour of students. Education is the process through which an individual is developed into individuality and a person into a personality. Education should be individualized and personalized to the utmost and should constitute preparation for self-learning.

According to the Indian philosophers, education is defined as follows: Mahatma Gandhi defined education "as an all-round drawing up the best in child and man—body, mind and spirit."

Swami Vivekananda perceives education "as the manifestation of divine perfection already existing in man "Education, he said, "Should aim at man-making". By man making he implies the formation of character, increase in the power of mind and explanation of the intellectual capacities.

According to Grambs, J and Morris (1964), Education is the process by which an individual is enabled to function according to the expectations of his society as well as according to the units of his capabilities. Rosenkranz (1964) agrees with him by saying, "Education can only develop and unfold, it cannot create anything new".

"Education, according to Indian tradition is not merely a means to earn a living, nor it is only a nursery of thought or school for citizenship. It is an initiation into the life of spirit, a training of the human souls in pursuit of truth and the practice of virtues". Therefore to mould the people along the above desired lines, the state has to depend on education, especially on Value Education, as the pursuit of truth, goodness and beauty comes from values. Value education has its impact upon national integration and international understanding at large.

The word education has a very wide connotation. It is hard to define. There is no single objective, which can cover the world of life with its various manifestations. The two poles of our concern; the temporal and the world of spirit are widely apart. Philosophers and thinkers from Socrates to Dewey in the West and from Yajnavalkya to Gandhi in the East have defined education in accordance with their philosophy of life, with the result of that there emerged divergent concepts and definitions of education. The concept of education is like a diamond, which appears in different colours when seen from different angles.

SIGNIFICANCE OF EDUCATION

Education is a never-ending process intricately interwoven with life, enriching the individual with a variety of experiences kindling the flames of knowledge through constant probing into the mysteries of life. The 'life adjustment' approach is one of the priorities of education now popular with the modern professional educator, who advocates that the individual should fit snugly into the existing social set up. Looking at the situation today, teachers agree that a thorough re-examination of the philosophical postulates is necessary in the interest of restoring human values in education.

It is the education that creates civilization and culture. A child learns many things when he grows into a man and he teaches many things to others. This process of learning and teaching began with the creation of the world and it will go on till the existence of the world. The education plays an important role in the development of the world. The development of the society and the world, therefore, depends on education and the society and the world will continue to develop for so long as there is education, learning and teaching through the educative process.

In any modern society it is the educational system that can guarantee the effective functioning of the socio-economic system. Education plays an important role in the economic and social development of the country, in the building of a truly democratic society, in the promotion of national integration and unity and above all in the transformation of the individual for endless pursuit of excellence and perfection.

Education is a powerful instrument of national development—social, economic and natural. The highest priority should therefore be accorded to the development of national system of education which will accelerate transformation of the existing system into a new one based on the principle of justice, equality, liberty and dignity of the individual enshrined in the constitution of India; provide adequate and equal opportunity to every child and help him to develop his personality to its fullest; make the coming generation conscious of the fundamental unity of the country in the midst of her rich diversity, proud of her cultural heritage and confident of her great culture.

In developing countries like India, the educational system has a pioneering role to play in shaping the nation's future. Education has an immense effect on the political, economic and social development with the increasing recognition by all the countries. Despite our achievements in the past 40 years of independence, by way of preserving democratic institutions, doubling food production, building an extensive industrial base and by expanding educational facilities large masses of our people live in abject poverty. Humayun Kabir (1959) rightly emphasized that "A nation, however rich in national resources, cannot prosper unless its human resources are properly developed", and such a development is essentially, a function of education.

The essence of education lies in stimulating the growing generation with a consistent, compelling and creative system of values around which cultural heritage, both spiritual and material of the community is transmitted, to the tender souls so as to develop them into civilized, creative and productive members of a progressive society.

VALUES

Meaning and Concept of Values

Values permeate the whole of human existence and are a major factor in determining what sort of human beings they are and how one will behave. The word value is derived from the Latin root, 'Valerie' meaning to be strong and vigorous. 'To be of Value' is to have a certain virtue.

Our values or principles or beliefs serve as guidelines to help us make decisions about actions, behaviours and life choices. They reflect what we value and how we feel about the rightness or wrongness of things. As a general rule, when we act in accordance with our own values, we tend to feel good about our actions and ourselves. When we act in a way that violates our values, we tend to feel badly about it. Our values are influenced by many factors, including our experiences, perceptions, parents, friends, school and religion. No two people share exactly the same set of values. Values may change over time. As we have new experiences and receive new information, we may re-evaluate our values and modify them. What we think is right or wrong in any given situation may change when we find ourselves actually in that kind of situation. Values lack universal definition but they have been interpreted in different ways.

Values are described as the socially defined desires and goals that are internalized through the process of condition, learning and socialization. Values are goals set for achievement and they motivate, define and colour all our activities cognitive, affective and conative. The concepts of values are closely associated with the concept of man.

According to Sheppard B. Clough (1960), values have been variously viewed as preferences, criteria, objects and possessions, personality and status, characteristics and states of mind that are absolutes, inherent in objects present in man and stages of mind and identical with behaviour.

According to Carl Rogers in 'Freedom to Learn' (1969), valuing is the tendency of a person to show preference.

Value Classification

Values are classified into different ways. Indians classified values as *chaturvarga* 'the four supreme ends' *viz.*, Dharma, artha, kama and moksha.

- Considerations of righteousness, duty and virtue is Dharma.
- Other activities by which a man tries to gain materially is called artha.
- Kama includes organic or health value.
- When a man enunciates all these activities and devotes to religious or spiritual activities to liberate oneself from worldly life it is called moksha".

Spranger in terms of pure or ideal types of men describes six main types of values which appeal to people in varying degrees and around which they build unity of their lives". These six basic types of men are as follows:

- The ideal or theoretical type for whom the primary value is discovery of truth;
- The economic man values what is useful and is rather practical;
- The aesthetic man sees the highest value in form and harmony;
- The social man places a great value on affiliation and love;
- The political man places great value on power. His primary focus is on power, influence and active competition to expand power;
- For the religious man the highest value may be called unity. He seeks to comprehend and relate himself to higher value experiences through his religious philosophy;

The nine values *viz.*, Social, Religious, Economic, Democratic, Knowledge, Power, Hedonistic, Aesthetic and Health which are presently taken for the study are defined as follows:

- *Social Value:* Social value refers to those values which are other oriented, they are concerning to society; which are cherished and practiced because of our association with others. The social values necessitate the interaction of two or more persons and they are always practiced in relation to our neighbours, community, society, nation and world. Social values may be defined in terms of charity, kindness, affiliation, love and sympathy for the people, efforts to serve God through the service of mankind, sacrificing personal comforts and gains to relieve the needy and the afflicted of their misery. One gets social values from friendship, love, family and participation in good activities.
- *Religious value:* It is defined in terms of faith in God, attempt to understand Him, fear of divine wrath, act according to the ethical codes prescribed in the religious books. The outward acts of behaviour

expressive of this value are going on pilgrimage, living a simple life, having faith in the religious leaders, worshipping God and speaking the truth. If a person considers an object divine, it is said to have a religious value and its experience is called religious experience, which may be spiritual or divine.

- *Economic value:* It means that an object commands a money price and stands for the desire of money and material gains. A man with high economic value is guided by considerations of money and material gain in the choice of his jobs. His attitude towards the rich persons and the industrialists is favourable and he considers them helpful for the progress of the country.
- *Democratic value:* It is characterized by respect for individuality, absence of discrimination among persons on the bases of sex, language, religion, caste, colour, race and family status ensuring equal social, political and religious rights to all, impartiality and social justice and respect for the democratic institutions.
- *Knowledge value:* It stands for love of knowledge of theoretical principles of any activity and love of discovery of truth. A man with knowledge value considers knowledge of theoretical principles underlying a work essential for success in it. He values hard work in studies, only if it helps to develop the ability to find out new facts and relationships and aspires to be known as the seeker of knowledge, for him knowledge is virtue.
- *Power value:* It is defined as the conception of desirability of ruling over others and also of leading others. The characteristics are the person prefers a job where he gets opportunity to exercise authority over others, prefers to rule in a small place rather than serve in a big place, that the fear of law of the country rather than the fear of God deters him from having recourse to unapproved means for making money and that he is deeply status-conscious and can even tell a lie for maintaining the prestige of his position.
- *Hedonistic value:* It is defined as the conception of the desirability of loving pleasure and avoiding pain, for a hedonist present is more important than future. A man with hedonist value indulges more in pleasure of senses and avoids pain.
- *Aesthetic value:* One realizes aesthetic value when one perceives an object as a unified expression of meaningful feelings. The aesthetic experience is a special kind of experience and is an interaction between an object and a subject. The subject that is the person contributes sense organs and also depends on his past experiences for appreciation or dislike of objects. Generally, aesthetic value is characterized by appreciation of

beauty, form, proportion, harmony and love for fine arts *viz.*, drawing, painting, music, dance, sculpture, poetry and architecture, love for literature, love for decoration of the home and the surroundings, neatness and system in the arrangement of the things.

- *Health value:* It is the consideration for keeping the body in a fit state for carrying out one's normal duties and functions. It also implies the consideration for self-preservation. A man with high health value really feels sorry if through some act of negligence impairs his health, he considers good physical health essential for the development and use of his abilities.

Attitudes Towards Values and Practices of Values

Attitude

Attitude is a dispositional readiness to respond to certain situations, persons, and objects in a consistent manner, which has been learned and has become one's typical mode of response.

Attitude is the predisposition or tendency to react specifically towards an object, situation or value, usually accompanied by feelings and emotions (Good, 1973).

Attitude is a person's tendency to feel about and act towards certain people, situations, objects, ideas, etc. in a particular manner (Derek Rowntree, 1981).

Attitudes Towards Values

They may be defined as the tendency to respond favourably or unfavourably/positively or negatively regarding a particular value.

Characteristics of Attitudes

- Attitudes have a subject-object relationship.
- Attitudes are learned and acquired dispositions, they are not innate and inherent in an individual, and consequently they may be differentiated from physiological motive.
- Attitudes are relatively enduring states of readiness to respond to a certain stimulus.
- Attitudes have motivational-affective characteristics.
- Attitudes are numerous and varied as the stimuli to which they refer.
- Attitudes range from strongly positive to strongly negative and they involve direction as well as magnitude. The positive and negative attitudes may involve intense feelings and vary from large negative to the increasingly positive values.

Formation of Attitudes

Like all other features of mental life, attitudes also grow and develop. Following are the four common processes involved in the making of attitudes:

- The integration of experiences;
- The differentiation of experiences;
- Trauma or dramatic experiences;
- The adoption of the available attitudes.

Factors Involved for the Formation of Attitudes: Two factors are involved for the formation of attitudes:

- Factors within the individual himself viz., physical, intellectual, emotional, social, ethical and moral factors.
- Factors within individual's environment *viz*., Family and social. Social environment includes school, religious groups, social clubs, and mass media.

Importance of Attitude in Education

- Attitude is formed through our education and experience. So the teachers' responsibility is to create proper attitudes in the students towards different objects and ideas.
- Teachers must be careful so that no undesirable information and experiences are given to the pupils.
- Often friends and classmates influence to form wrong attitudes in them which cannot be changed so easily. So, before such permanent attitudes are formed, association of pupils concerned should be immediately changed.
- More over, books, periodicals, journals and political addresses by leaders may form perverted attitudes, in such cases; the teacher should hold out the total picture of the situation before the students and encourage proper reasoning and thinking.
- The teacher should try to create favourable attitudes towards curricular and co-curricular activities of the school in the students.
- The teacher should also be conscious of his own behaviour so that no negative attitude develops against him/her.
- Through different social and cultural functions, the teacher should encourage the students to form ideal attitudes towards different communities.

Practice

Practice is defined in terms of individual behaviour, of what the individual does. It is customary, typical and habitual. Practice is the behavioural manifestation of the knowledge of an individual in using a value.

Chaplin ((1975) described practice as the repetition of an act or behavioural function for the purpose of improving the function.

Practice of Values

It may be defined as the habitual formation of a value and that is repeated till it becomes customary. Value practice is the product of interaction between attitudes and personality.

Educationists recognize that value practice is a process that should be set in motion from the very first years of the child. The vastness of the problem and its spread make it difficult for the educationists to take any concrete steps to change parental attitude to child rearing practices, which would make a significant contribution to value practice. The problem of value practice is faced with a number of independent variables inter-acting on each other, which can be enumerated as under:

- The home and the family;
- The value system of the community to which individuals belong;
- Religious institutions, professional organizations and social groups in which individuals live and grow;
- The ideals which leaders of public opinion project before the people through their speeches, action, behaviour and example;
- The professional conduct followed by prestigious groups such as doctors, engineers, industrialists, etc;
- The ideas preached through their exams, practice and precept by teachers of all grades;
- The ideals put forward by the public media such as press, cinema, radio and T.V., in many of which today there is an over-emphasis of sex and crime.

Thus, value practice is a training given for a lifetime. It is an investment in attitudes, principles, convictions and values pay dividends in all living experiences.

The secret of teaching values is to inspire and kindle the quest among the students by means of one's own example of character and mastery of knowledge. Human values being skills can be learned with hard work, perseverance and practice. These skills can only be taught in an atmosphere where the student's basic needs for safety, belongingness, love, respect and self-esteem are taken care of.

Education and Values

The major purpose of education is to a shape the personality of the child in such a way that the individual becomes a better learner, a better person, a better worker, not only in terms of knowledge, understanding and skills but also in terms of values and motives which give meaning and significance to one's behaviour.

The aim of education is growth and development of intellectual, moral, ethical and psychological dimensions of an individual which can aid the school in the greatest of all constructions and in the building of a free and powerful character. Only knowledge of the order and connection of the stages in psychological development can ensure this. Education is the work of supplying the conditions, which will ensure the psychological foundations to measure in the freest and fullest manner.

For Dewey, John (1966) the central purpose of education is to enable human beings to make the necessary adjustments to meet the constantly changing environment and the most important adjustments to be made in the ever-changing circumstances of society.

Krishna Murthy Jiddu (1981) defines the aims of education as "To make a true and happy contended individual capable of facing the problems of life; to develop the power of critical thinking and analysis; to develop alertness by a keen sense of observation and attention; to help discover the reality *i.e.* 'What is' and to help the child not to imitate or be guided by norms but to learn to be himself and realize truth and reality."

According to Huxley Jullian (1964) education should be humanized to redeem our society from the evil effects of widespread corruption, selfishness, exploitation, authoritarianism and nepotism. This calls for the infusion of human values in their operations.

Sources of Values

The system of values can be treated from the following sources of understanding

1. *Cultural Background*

Our values are usually grounded in the core values of our culture, which reflect culture's orientation to five basic problems *viz.*,

- Beliefs of child rearing and social control.
- The attitude to take nature as fatalistic or seeing it as a challenge to be conquered in the interests of man's comfort.
- The question whether man should live for the present or the future.
- The kind of activity most valued; and the kind of inter-personal relationship whether it is competitive or cooperative.

2. *Scientific Background*

It helps us to make value judgments only to the extent that we relate it to value assumptions. New information on the scientific front need not pose a threat even if it requires a change in the present frame of reference.

3. ***Religious Background***

In its pursuit of truth religion is also concerned with values. Many basic values are common to all religions.

4. ***Life Experience***

Many values originate out of the experiences of the individual and those of his fellow men. Men constantly keep on determining what values they must follow to find happiness and fulfill their destiny as human beings.

These source orientations are conformed by Radhakrishnan (1950) who observed, "Values in education although they find their source in philosophy, have a second source in society, the people, their culture and their ideals".

Teacher's Role and Influence on Values

The teacher occupies a pivotal role in imparting moral instruction. If the teacher merely meets the students in the classroom there cannot be adequate interaction to make moral instruction meaningful. A tutorial house and a counselling system is a must. An understanding of the attitudes, emotions, feelings, values and motives of the pupils is equally important. "Moral growth of the child consists of development through a number of definite stages associated with age groups. Moral character is to be conceived not in terms of conformity to specific virtues but in developmental terms. The teacher should organize his teaching in such a way that it matches the moral level of the children".

Hirst (1970) rightly states "In moral education as in any other area of education what is asked of the teacher is a total commitment to the development of the rational autonomy in both thought and action."

Next to the parents, the teachers have an important and effective role in the inculcation of values amongst children. The behaviour of the teacher therefore becomes important for actions speak louder than words. If the teacher has good habits, good manners, courteous words and has ethical, social and spiritual values the children will by love and imitation adopt these values. So, teachers in order to develop values will have to use many charts, film strips, tape recorders and other aids. Besides these, role-playing techniques and dramatization have also to be used. When teachers face the lack of that aids the standards of education will suffer and indirectly the process of value orientation also will suffer.

When a student respects and admires a teacher he learns far more from him than the subject matter. He tends to take the teacher's attitudes as well. Some times emotional learning from the parent or the teacher seems greater at moments when no teaching was intended. The teacher must cultivate in the child the quality of sincerity of purpose in whatever the child undertakes.

The teacher should not treat the child harshly for the undesirable impulses and habits. When a child commits a mistake, one must see that he confesses it to the teacher spontaneously and he should be made to understand his mistake with kindness. A fault confessed must be forgiven. When a child asks a question he should not be admonished. Curiosity cannot be postponed and in such a way as to make the answer comprehensible to the student's mental capacity. Whenever there is a disagreement on any matter, as a decision to take, or an action to accomplish, one must not stick on to one's own conception or point of view.

Education itself is a value infused process, in which the teacher makes value decisions on how to relate to students, maintain classroom control, select material, evaluate results and perform various other duties. It is also necessary that if the school were to produce people who become self-actualized then the teachers themselves should be self-actualized persons. This poses another problem, which becomes more acute in the face of the paucity of teachers and their caliber. The teacher's role is to help every student to:

- Become aware of the values he has learned.
- Make him understand the reasons for his beliefs.
- Make him aware of how to use his values when faced with choices.
- Understand to relate choices with consequences.
- Understand what value alternatives exist for other.

Need of Value Education

Hemming James (1969) opines that since men depend on one another in society there must be some rules that every body conforms to. These are the moral principles and hence must be some foundation for the same. These moral principles must be derived from something *viz.*, the well-being of the individuals and the ability of the individuals to grow and fulfill themselves.

Rogers Carl (1969) says "There is a great deal of concern today with the problems of values. Youth all over are deeply concerned and uncertain of its value orientation. Values associated with various religions have lost much of their influence. The reasons are that the world culture seems increasingly scientific and relativistic and the rigid absolute views on values which come to us from the past appear anachronistic".

Tarkunde (1978) opines, "Value education enables the skills to live in society as a fully functioning individual and to lead a happy satisfied and contended life. It is by perfecting skills like self-help skills, social skills and ethical skills, the child gains self-confidence and is accepted by the group. The group acceptance helps the child to develop his personality without any feeling of inadequacies".

He further observed, "The true education lies in enlightenment from within. Only when the enlightenment of inner truth enkindles the heart from within, the knowledge from schooling transforms itself into wisdom of perfection. To achieve this, the children need to be introduced to human values and be helped to develop a priority of values which would determine their behaviour".

Students should not be afraid to disagree with a viewpoint. Value education must spell out fundamental goals and general principles, rather than at the level of specific prescription. The cultural diversity of the group is also used as an excuse not take up value education. It is felt that value education is the privilege of the parents and often this contradicts the principles taught in state run schools and private schools and hence value education should be taken up by schools.

There is a negligence of moral and spiritual values, which the Indian Education Commission (1964-66) laments in the words, "At a time when the need to cultivate a sense of moral and social responsibility in the rising generation is paramount, education does not emphasize character formation and makes little or no effort to cultivate moral and spiritual values, particularly attitudes and values needed for a democratic and socialistic country". Today the situation is no better except that the need for value education is gradually being felt in wider circles. In India there is a fear that any kind of religious education conflicts with the secular ideal. Moral education as a school subject is viewed with suspicion let it turn out to be religious education. It is not surprising that despite several recommendations to the effect that provision must be made in educational institutions for the inculcation of moral and spiritual values, several state school systems have chosen not to deviate from status quo.

Emphasis on Value Education in India—Committees and Commissions

University Education Commission (1948) headed by Dr. Radha Krishnan considered the issues pertaining to the inclusion of religious and moral education in the educational content at the university stage. It was of the opinion that the great virtues of loyalty, courage, discipline and self-sacrifice may be used for good or bad ends and as such spiritual training is included. Religion cannot be imparted in the form of lessons. It is a permeate influence, a quality of life, and an elevation of purpose. It held that no one could be made moral or spiritual, unless these qualities are native to and inherent in man. It recommended that while in schools stories, which illustrates great moral and religious principles are used, in college classes ideas, events and leading figures associated with religious movements should be studied. Religious instruction must bring awareness of the great historic insights. In order to ensure absolute religious neutrality of the state, what is good and great in every religion must be presented.

The Secondary Education Commission (1952) headed by Dr. Lakshmana Swamy Mudaliar converted the school stage. It considered the healthy trends arising from three sources:

- The influence of the home, which is the dominant factor;
- The influence of the school through the conduct and the behaviour of the teachers themselves and the life in the school community as a whole;
- Influence exercised by the public of the locality and the extent to which public prevails in all matters pertaining to religious and moral codes of conduct.

No amount of instruction can supersede these three essential factors. It can be supplemented to a limited extent by properly organized instruction given in schools.

Kothari Commission or The Education Commission (1964-66) headed by Prof. Kothari observed, "A serious defect in the school curriculum is the absence of provision for education in social, moral and spiritual values. A national system of education that is related to the life needs and aspirations of the people cannot afford to ignore the force of religion." It therefore recommended that a conscious effort should be made for the development of social, moral and spiritual values with the help of the ethical teachings of the great religions.

Curriculum for the Ten Year School (1975), the framework of the curriculum was developed by NCERT in 1975. It emphasized "The values enshrined in our constitution point towards the development of a pluralist open society and a state which is a secular democratic and socialistic in nature". The school curriculum should be related to national integration, social justice, productivity, and modernization of society and cultivation of moral and social values. It recommended that all subjects should be taught in such a manner as to foster the spirit of scientific humanism.

Linked with the process of character-building is the cultivation of such qualities as compassion, endurance, courage, decision-making, resourcefulness, respect for others, team spirit, truthfulness, faithfulness, loyalty to duty and the common good. The student should be able to understand the value of national and civic property and take care of them. He should have a clear grasp of the principles of democracy, secularism and socialism.

The Document Education for People (1978-79) prepared under the chairmanship of justice Tarkunde suggests programmes to bring about educational transformation. The report states that "The value system underlying education should emphasize social objectives, co-operation and team work, complementarily of intellectual and manual work, development of skills and building of character. The ethics of the existing system is highly authoritarian where values such as equality, love or truth, or spirit of enquiry cannot be fostered. Great emphasis will have to be placed on promoting a scientific outlook on life and the basic values of pursuit of truth, equality, freedom, justice and the dignity of the individual".

Seminars on Value-oriented Education at Simla in May 1981 suggested that an increasing stress is being laid on the formulation of objectives at uniting science and humanism, ethics and aesthetics and material welfare with spiritual welfare. It recommended inter-alia that value orientation should be the central focus of education and the teachers should be given the necessary training in the effective methods of development of values among students and teachers.

At the same time the Government of India constituted a working group to review the teacher training programmes with a view to promote value education, with Mr. Kireet Joshi as the chairman. The committee recommended as under:

- Provision for Value Oriented Education should be made throughout the country with due regard for flexibility of approach;
- It should be regarded essentially as an education for becoming and self-developing;
- Value-orientation should be the main focus of education;
- This Value-orientation should not only be for the children but even parents should be involved in it;
- The learning process itself has a great bearing on the Value-orientation of the children;
- There is a need for producing literature especially designed for the Value-orientation of the children;
- All teachers in the school should be regarded as teachers of value education and all subjects should be used for inculcation of right values;
- There should be an integrated approach in the Value oriented education programme;
- There should be foundation courses both at the secondary schools and university aiming at giving the children basic knowledge about India;
- Pilot projects for school improvement should be taken up;
- There is a need for establishing a resource center for literature on Value-oriented education;
- Special schools, designed for Value-oriented education, should be established;

- Special teacher orientation programmes should be taken up at the state level;
- Some studies of schools, where value education is being imparted successfully should be taken up.

New Educational Policy (1986) defining the goals of Education, stresses that emphasis must be laid on the socio-economic well-being, competence and creativity of the individual, which encompasses:

- Physical, intellectual and aesthetic development of the personality;
- Inculcation of scientific temper, democratic, moral and spiritual values;
- Development of self-confidence to innovate and face unfamiliar situation;
- Fostering a healthy attitude to dignity of labour and hard work;
- Creation of an awareness of the physical, social, technological, economic and cultural environments;
- A commitment to principles of secularism and social justice;
- Dedication to uphold the integrity, honour and foster the development of the country; and Promotion of international understanding.

TEACHER

The teacher occupies a pivotal position in the system of education. In the 13th chapter of the 'BHAGAVADGITA' the characteristics of a real teacher are laid down as follows: absence of pride, free from hypocrisy, non-violence, forgiving nature, straightforwardness, service of the preceptor, purity of mind and body, steadfastness and self-control. In line with this, centuries ago in this land of Vedas the teacher devote all his time for the upliftment of his pupils in all directions—knowledge, morals, values etc. He was called the *'Guru* or *Acharya'*.

There was close relationship between the teacher and the taught, a relationship that was found more on love and affection than on authority. It was so intimate, that one was giving shelter to the other, whenever there was a need. The famous Sanskrit verses which the teacher and taught recited together tell the essence of their mutual relationship.

"Sahanavavatu

Sahanabhunaktu

Sahaviryamkaravavahai

Tejasavinamavadhitamastu

Mavidvisavahai"

Which means May He Project us both; may He save us both; may we do together great deeds; may our learning be taught; may we not hate each other.

Place of Teacher in Any Educational System

According to the Department of Teacher Education, the educationists, teachers, administrators thought that a teacher should know the objectives before the nation in terms of the economic, social, political and cultural growth, which should engender in him the ability to train present generation of students into enlightened citizens of India.

A teacher should have good information about Indian thought and culture from ancient times to the present, which will help to have an adequate and healthy personal philosophy of life. He should have a clear perception of the importance of his job for the nation and should take consequent pride in the teaching profession. A teacher should have healthy emotional development and cheerful disposition. If a teacher is joyful he will rejoice in life with all its variety. A teacher should be well informed, curious and alert. He should not only have a thorough knowledge of the subject taught or skills imparted by him but also habits of wide reading including current journals and magazines.

"Of all the different factors which influence the quality of education and its contribution to national development; the quality, competence and character of teachers are undoubtedly the most significant." Kothari Education Commission (1964-66).

The importance of the teachers in the educational programme of a country is too great. The greatness of a country does not depend on lofty buildings, gigantic projects and large armies but on the quality of its citizens. If a nation has young men of sterling character and unimpeachable patriotism, she is found to make a rapid progress in all fields. Young men are entrusted to the care of the teacher and it is therefore the sacred duty of the teacher to impart the right type of knowledge and make them good citizens. It is the teacher who impresses his children with his personality.

The framers of Second Five Year Plan in India observed, "At all times the teacher is pivot in the system of education". This is especially true in the case of a nation in its transition. The Secondary Education Commission (1952-53) also points out that every teacher and educationist of experience knows that even the best curriculum and the perfect syllabus remain dead unless quickened into life by right methods of teaching and the right kind of teachers. For imparting good education a good teacher is needed. All other things relates to infrastructure are secondary.

The teacher, a national integrator as he is, is the backbone of society, particularly so in the remote villages. He stands as an outstanding figure among the illiterate and semi-literate families. He is their friend, philosopher and guide. The teacher actively shares the responsibility of reconstructing a social order, with all cherished values and traditional beliefs, which are being eroded by the surge of new ideals and practices. He acts as a social reformer and counsellor to the community.

The role of the modern teacher is not confined to teaching alone. He/ She is expected to participate in the development programmes of the community life. The question arises as to how this could be integrated with the teacher education programmes. Mudaliar Commission (1952-53) report stated rightly, "We are convinced that the most important factor in the contemplated education reconstruction is the teacher—his qualities, his educational qualifications, his professional training and the place that he occupies in the school as well as in the community". On similar lines Kothari Commission (1964-66) stated that, "Nothing is more important than securing a sufficient supply of high quality recruits to the teaching profession, providing them with the best possible professional preparation and creating satisfactory conditions of work in which they can be fully effective".

Importance of Teacher and Teaching

Teacher plays an important role in the field of education. Today's education is child-centred. But the child-centred education cannot be successful without the teacher. The teacher is the maker of the future of the child. The children of today are the citizens and leaders of tomorrow. It means that the teacher is the maker of the leaders or the rulers of the nation.

The co-operation of teachers is necessary for the management of the educational institutions. Without the co-operation of the teacher, the management of the institution will not be perfect. Many social, cultural, educational and athletic programmes are organized in the institutions. It is the teacher who makes necessary arrangements for these programmes and functions. The teacher also arranges function for the prize distribution. Importance of teacher in extra-curricular activities is great.

Like a master architect, the teacher has a very thorough knowledge of all the details essential to his work. He knows the real nature of the objectives of his work and the ends to be attained. Besides an understanding of the nature of the outcomes desired, he understands the nature of the different kinds of learning experiences necessary to attain them. He also knows how to use effectively the best teaching techniques and devices available. He guides learning and gives suggestions and directions to the students in order to make them able to attain the desired knowledge.

In any system of education, teacher has a pivotal role to play. The responsibility of making the education work successful lies with the teacher. He is undoubtedly the key point in all educational programmes and the quality of education depends on the quality of teachers. In good olden days 'GURU' was considered indispensable. As long as learning was considered desirable, the disciple was with the GURU only. In the modern concept of education, child is the center of all educational activity and learner achievement is considered as the indicator of quality. Learning is a continuous phenomenon. The learner has the potential to explore, investigate and innovate, therefore he requires challenging situations. 'Learning' to be which was the key word till 20th century is now replaced by "Learning to learn". Providing challenging situations to the learner is the job of the teacher in the present age. If this is taken care of, learning continues forever. This approach requires lot of preparation, high degree of competence and commitment on the part of the teacher. In other words, the teacher today is required to be able to cope with the aspirations of rising generations of youth and the changing needs of the society playing a multidimensional role.

Teaching has been one of the oldest and most respected professions in the world. When a systematically organized human society come into existence the need to mould its children on proper lines arose requiring persons who could perform this role that is teachers. The task of shaping the future citizens is a noble one and so the teacher has always occupied a place of honour and reverence in the Indian society over the ages. The preparation of teachers has changed with the passage of time and with the changes in expectations of the society. Thus, the success of any educational reform depends upon the quality of teachers and in turn the quality of teaching depends to a large extent on the quality of teacher education. Teaching has always been considered to be essential for preservation and development of all intellectual life. Among other agencies, teachers are considered to be the major transmitters of accumulated knowledge and experience of human race from one generation to the next. The very foundation of the social order rests on citizen who are taught and trained in the classroom with or without walls. Teachers, thus, determine to a great extent the character and destination of a nation.

With a view to realize Truth, Goodness and Beauty, man has created different arts. Technique of Teaching or Art of Teaching is one of them. The importance and utility of technique of teaching is great because this art gives birth to other arts and develops them. It is due to the art of teaching that our civilization and culture grows from generation to generation and it has become potential. It is through the art of teaching that man is able to call himself civilized and cultured.

The Concept of Teacher Education

Teacher education has been defined as, 'All formal and informal activities and experiences that help to qualify a person to assume the responsibilities as a member of the teaching profession and to discharge his responsibilities more effectively'. The concept of 'Teacher Education' is not new. However, scholarliness was considered the sole criterion for becoming a teacher. The concept that teachers are born and not made was also prevalent in olden days.

It has been aptly remarked, "If you educate a boy, you educate one individual. If you educate a girl, you educate the whole family and if you educate an individual as a teacher, you educate the whole community."

The contention that teachers are born, not made, can be true only in a few rare cases. It is also not contended that training, by itself, is sure to make a good teacher. But it is generally observed that a teacher with training becomes more mature and confident to perform his task more efficiently. Proper training and education enables the teacher to have knowledge of how children grow, develop and learn how they can be taught best and how their innate capacities can be brought out and developed.

According to Monroe Encyclopaedia of Educational research, "Teacher education refers to the totality of educational inputs, which contribute to the preparation of the person for a teaching position in schools". But the term is more commonly employed to designate the programmes of courses and other experiences offered by an educational institution for the announced purpose of preparing persons for teaching and other educational services.

Kilpatrick, W.S. the famous American educationist once remarked, "One trains circus performers and animals, but one educates the teachers", consequently the new term 'Teacher Education' has been adopted replacing the term 'Teacher Training'.

Teacher Education now includes every aspect of the student teacher's personality. We may define teacher education as such institutionalized educational procedures that are aimed at the purposeful organized preparation or further education of teachers who are engaged directly or indirectly in educational activity as their life work. This concept of teacher education does not exclude members of other professions who prepare for teaching as secondary or supplementary activity.

Teacher Education is not mere pedagogy or acquisition of a training qualification. It is preparation of persons for family, for society and for the country. It is nurturing of creativity, inculcation of commitment and generation of a strong will to contribute at the highest level of efficiency through a value-based approach. Teacher education is a process of unearthing the treasure within every teacher and subsequently within every learner in each and every learning center. It is the process, which makes the individuals realize the magnitude and potentialities, which, if nurtures and inculcated in the right direction, could make significant contribution to the identified sectors.

Need and Significance of Teacher Education

The quality of a nation depends upon the quality of its citizens, the quality of citizens depends upon the quality of their education; the quality of education depends upon the quality of teachers; and the quality of teachers depends upon the quality of Teacher education among many other factors.

The 21st century has been acknowledged as the century of learners and teachers, and we have to demonstrate that every teacher every day is performing the miracle of teaching. The learning society offers many and varied opportunities for learning at school and in economic, social and cultural life. The teachers are now required to update their knowledge. The teacher will have to be essentially a learner and the learner in his turn will also act as a teacher.

Teacher Education is needed for kindling the initiative of the teacher, for keeping it alive, for removing the evils or 'hit and miss' process, for according a process, for according a professional status to the teaching profession and above all for making the optimum use of time and energy of the teacher and the taught.

Kothari Education Commission (1964-66) observed: "A sound programme of professional education of teachers is essential; for the qualitative improvement of education. Investment in Teacher Education can yield very rich dividends because the financial resources required are small when measured against the resulting programme in the education of millions".

The link between national development and education is rooted in the concept of the educational process, essentially as 'Human Resource Development' accepted world-wide, especially during the last few decades. It was very much in keeping with this concept what the National Education Commission popularly known as Kothari Education Commission (1964-66) states: "The destiny of the nation is being shaped in our classrooms". It is obvious that the class-room teacher who directs, controls and guides classroom operations is in-charge of building the nation's destiny by gradually transforming the children under his charge into enlightened citizens, who later through their vision and selfless work contribute to have all-round benevolent progress of the nation which not only should hold its head high in the comity of nations of the world but also become the harbinger of a healthy, vibrating and dynamic New World Order granting peace, progress and prosperity for all.

Such being the case, every nation must realize the highly noble and onerous responsibility on the heads of its teaching fraternity and should be equipped with knowledge, skills, interests and above all divinely oriented human values directed towards the noblest of visions for the future of mankind as a whole, subjecting all narrow links and desires to disappear in the interest of creating a Heaven on Earth where all are equal in terms of opportunities and self-realization to the optimum of their potential. 'Teaching as a profession is not only vocation, along with myriads of vocations, but in depth and reality it is the 'mother of all other professions'. Hence, while designing and implementing a professional course for teachers, it is necessary to lay down the foundations of all aspects of human resources for all areas of national development and not just one area of 'class-room' teaching of 'academic subjects' of a syllabus and handling of a few co-curricular activities in addition.

In the light of this basic need, teacher education, as it stands today in India, is in dire need of rejuvenation, not just of a tinkering with a topic here and a topic there, or the provision of gadgets like 'computer' and other hardware and software, but a total overhauling of the entire system. This is reflected in five significant aspects in the National Policy on Education (NPE), 1986 and Programme of Action, 1992; namely:

(i) Education as investment for the present and future;

(ii) Five-fold role of teachers (teaching aids preparation, extension, research and management);

(iii) Value development to deal with value crises in society;

(iv) Merit as the only basis of recruitment of teacher and to meet all these four;

(v) Overhauling of Teacher education.

National Policy on Education (NPE), 1986 calls for the overhaul of Teacher Education as the first step towards educational reorganization. In this context effective Teacher Education becomes a core condition to ensure high proficiency and quality school education. In other words effective school education anticipates effective Teacher Education.

PERSONALITY OF TEACHERS

The importance of the teacher is as clear as the presence of the Sun. Since Vedic period, teachers played an important role in the society. Some research studies have been conducted in India during the last few years on teacher's personality. From that, it is evident that personality determines the performance of a teacher.

The task before the teachers in modern society is very formidable and complex. The teacher has not only to equip the child with the tools of learning but has also to impart various skills as well as abilities so that the child is able to adjust himself in the rapidly transforming society. Further, the teacher has also to play a role by which he is able to help the child actively and intelligently participate in the cultural revolution of today. For this reason the teacher's personality to which one could refer. But one can conjecture and point out certain personality traits, which the teacher should have so that those traits of his personality help him to play important and helpful role in his professional task.

Different Psychologists Define Personality as follows:

Cattell (1962) Personality is that which permits a prediction of what a person will do in a given situation.

Eysenck (1970) Personality is more or less stable and enduring organisation of a person's character, temperament, intellect and physique which determines his unique adjustment to the environment.

Guilford (1959) An individual's personality then is his unique pattern of traits. A trait is any distinguishable relatively enduring way in which one individual differs from another.

Allport (1961) Personality is a dynamic organization within the individual of those psycho-physical systems that determine his unique adjustment to his environment.

Warren's Dictionary (1934) "Personality is the integrative organisation of all the cognitive, affective, connective/connative and physical characterization of an individual as it manifests itself in focal distinction from others.

Hartman (1979) Personality is the integrated organization of all the pervasive characteristics of an individual as it manifests itself in focal distinctiveness to others.

Personality is the whole individual considered as a whole. It is the most characteristic integration of an individual's structures, modes of interests, attitudes, behaviour, capacities, abilities and aptitudes. Personality may be considered as the sum of activities that can be discovered by actual observation over a long enough period of time to give reliable information. It is the reaction mass as a whole.

Personality is a word that signifies the personal traits and patterns of behavior that are unique to the individual. You experience these traits and patterns of behavior as your own; others observe them directly or through your communication with them. Personality includes attitudes, modes of thought, feelings, impulses, strivings, actions, responses to opportunity and stress and everyday modes of interacting with others. When these elements of personality are expressed in a characteristically repeated and dynamic combination, we have what is called a *personality style*.

In order to understand personality and its proper connotation it is to be taken up from biology, sociology, psychology and allied science. In fact, personality is formed out of biological, sociological and psychological elements and so all these sciences contribute to the proper assessment of the meaning of personality. What is the attitude of a person towards society, what is the shape of physical, psychological, moral and emotional development of an individual as an integration of all traits, which determine the role of the status of the person in society? Personality might be therefore, described as social effectiveness. It is difficult to summarize the studies involving personality because it is difficult to compare the variable and the instruments for measuring personality except in a crude way. However, the research on personality traits of student-teachers revealed diversified conclusions.

It is reasonable to presume that, attitudes towards values, their practices, personal and personality traits of an individual help to determine their behaviour and teachers are not an exception. Moreover, personality factors influence the attitudes and practices of values. Hence the present study is undertaken to fulfill the need and is designed to identify the personality characteristics related to attitudes towards values and their practices among B.Ed. students, in particular.

B.ED. COLLEGES

In the past Basic Training Schools, later Teacher Training institutes used to play an important role in producing required teachers for elementary schools. In the place of T.T.Is a new type of educational institutions called DIET has been conceived with in the NPE and POA as one of the major steps towards the effective teacher education at the primary level. Later educational institutes called Colleges of Education have come into existence and there are nearly 400 B.Ed. colleges in Andhra Pradesh.

The present study entitled, *"A Study of Attitude Towards Values and Their Practices in Relation to Certain Personality Factors"* is a survey type research. The investigator collected the necessary information and made a statistical analysis and has drawn inferences so that the educational training can be, modified to overcome the shortcomings and to strengthen the system in general and value system in particular.

REVIEW OF RELATED LITERATURE

A Summary of the writings of recognized authorities and of previous research provides evidence that the researcher is familiar with what is already known and what is still unknown and untested. It gives us the relevant material published in the problem area under study. The topic for the present study being "A Study of Attitudes towards Values and Their Practices in relation to Certain Personality factors among B.Ed. Students in Andhra Pradesh", the review of literature is concerned with the following headings:

- Studies on Values and Value Education.
- Studies on Values related to Teaching Community.
- Studies related to Influence of Personal and Demographic variables on Values and Teacher.
- Studies related to Personality traits and Values.
- Studies related to Personality traits and Teacher.
- Studies that have relevance for the present study.

In the history of psychometry it was, at one time 'believed that social attitudes contained some essence that could not be identified and measured. People were sure that in making the attempt the psychometricians would measure only the trivia', Thurstone (1959; p.182). Since Thurstone made this observation sometime at the close of the twenties of the century considerable development has taken place both in the concept of values and its measurements. Now, values are considered to be different from attitudes and beliefs. They constitute a motivational dimension. Although, social psychologists differ in their definitions of value, most of them believe that value is a concept of the desirable ends, goals, ideals or modes of action, which make human behaviour selective. Since Thurstone averred that values could be measured by means of psychometric methods with the help of a suitable non-physical metric, several attempts have been made to measure values. The efforts of Precker (1952), Gordon (1956), Morris Charles (1957), Rosenberg (1957), Dennis (1961) and Super (1961) are noteworthy.

In this country, most of the researchers have adapted Allport-Vernon-Lindzey (1951), 'The Study of Values' either in English or the regional languages. Notable are Ojha (1984), Ahluwalia (1997), Verma (1986). Other tests on values are developed by Upadhyaya (1978), Aggarwal (1979), Chauhan and Arora (1981), Aggarwal (1986) as reported by Bhargava (1997). The need of a tool to assess human values in the indigenous cultural milieu has been felt for a long time in India. The present tool "Attitudes towards Values and their Practices" is an attempt in this direction.

STUDIES ON VALUES AND VALUE EDUCATION

Bertera, Francis John (1979) studied the value change in graduate school. The main objective was to investigate the value hierarchies of graduate school students. 68 graduate school students of psychology formed the sample. The Rokeach value survey was the instrument used to investigate the value hierarchies. The hypotheses of the study were:

(i) The ranking of the terminal values such as a sense of accomplishment, freedom, happiness, mature, love, pleasure, inner harmony and wisdom is significantly higher in a high socializing group versus low socializing group;

(ii) The ranking of the instrumental values such as logical, imaginative, intellectual and independent is significantly higher in a socializing group.

The findings revealed that all the hypothesis in their null form was accepted. However, the two groups showed high similarity to psychology graduate students.

Jayaswal (1982) viewed that inculcation of values like social, moral and spiritual, which can transform a child to human adult. The essential activities described suggest bringing out a value-based education policy, acquainting the children with cultural heritage and spiritual greatness of India and teachers need to shoulder the responsibility of imparting value-based education. All the teachers have to work together for developing moral, social and spiritual values. They need to be acquainted with the techniques and strata gives of value education.

Annamma (1985) carried out a study on 'Values, aspirations and adjustment of college students'. The main objective of this study was to gain an understanding of students through a study of their values, aspirations, adjustments, opinions and practices. The researcher had taken 734 boys and

743 girls in the first and final year classes from 10 colleges for the study. Thus first and final year college students' framed the sample of the study. The Mathew Materialism–spiritualism scale, a problem checklist and Aggarwal data questionnaire were used as tools for data collection. ANOVA was employed to study the relationship of variables. The major findings were:

(i) Students have stable value system;

(ii) Rapid changes in culture do not alter basic life values;

(iii) No difference is noticed between boys and girls;

(iv) Residential location did not show any significant relationship to spiritualism;

(v) Father's educational level and occupational level were not found to be significantly related to spiritualism.

Theodore, Alexander Philip (1986) undertook a study on 'Attitudes concerning values and value education held by students and faculty members at the University of South Alabama'. The major findings were:

(i) Both the groups feel the need to promote value education;

(ii) Both the groups supported the use of various value education techniques in college;

(iii) Students and faculty members did hold certain types of values to be important.

Baythi (1987) conducted a study to examine the relationship of education with values and types of values constitute the core of this article. It is asserted that both are inter-related. Instrumental, intrinsic and aesthetic values are defined. Secular, humanship and moral values are discussed. Theology of education, in respect of humanistic values is emphasized. Field types and other community activities should be organized for imparting and strengthening moral education.

Khanna (1993) conducted a study to compare the students of general stream to the students who are undergoing teacher training on the five human values of truth, righteous conduct, peace, love and non-violence under similar environment. It was found that teacher-training group has scored higher on two values, namely truth and love than the general group.

Padhan (1993) conducted a study to find out the relationship of 10 values with moral judgement and socio-economic status. It was found that moral judgements were positively correlated with religious, social, democratic, knowledge and health values but negatively correlated with economic, hedonistic, power and family prestige values and the socio-economic status was positively correlated with social, economic, knowledge, power and family prestige values.

Padhan, Gopal Chandra (1994) conducted a study to find out the possible relationship between moral judgement and each of the ten personal values of the PVQ. Findings of the study revealed that, there was significant positive correlation between moral judgement and religious values of the subject. A significant positive correlation was found between moral judgement and social values of the students. There was no significant correlation between moral judgement and aesthetic value. There existed a significant positive correlation between knowledge value and moral judgment of the subjects. There existed a significant positive correlation between hedonistic value and moral judgement of the subjects. There was a negative and significant correlation between moral judgement and personal values. There existed a negative correlation between moral judgement and family prestige value of the subjects, which was also very low. The correlation between moral judgement and health value was positive and significant.

Aluja, Fabregat (1996) studied the relationship among attitudes toward social values and personality factors. Subjects were 43 male (mean age 23.6 years) and 137 female (mean age 24.21 years) university students. Information on socio-demographic variables, attitudes toward social values was obtained by questionnaire. The results were evaluated according to sex; conservative or liberal social values.

Broadly, Carl Amos (1998) conducted a study on 'Values, knowledge and competencies that are important for youth development professionals'. The purpose of the study was two fold:

(i) To identify the list of values, competencies and knowledge components that members of an expert panel of youth development professionals believe to be necessary to successfully with non-formal youth groups and volunteers that impact these youth.

(ii) To develop a taxonomy (a list of job components) that a majority of the nation's youth serving agencies and organization can adopt as their professional research and knowledge based.

Participants were surveyed using a modified Delphi technique in three rounds of questionnaires to arrive at a consensus on what they as professionals viewed as essential and important to their day to day work. The nine items that youth development professionals deemed essential to their job were:

(i) Respect

(ii) Honesty

(iii) Interpersonal communication

(iv) Positive youth development

(v) Ethics in working with youth

(vi) Confidentiality

(vii) Accountability

(viii) Biased free approach

(ix) Continuous life long learning

Susan, Jacob and Anupama Shah (1998) studied the selected desirable characteristics and values of home science students in the state of Gujarat. The main objective of the study was to find out the differences in the characteristics and values among the respondents from different universities. The sample consisted of 600 final year students of under-graduation from 15 colleges offering Home Science Programme under 10 different universities, Gujarat. The tools for the study consisted of a questionnaire, a standard scale, a checklist, rating scales and situational tests. The statistical methods such as percentages, ANOVA and correlation were employed for the analysis of data. The findings were:

(i) The respondents with high academic achievement had higher level of all characteristics and values than the low achievers;

(ii) The respondents with mothers having higher level of education had higher level of self-esteem, fearlessness and values for gender equality and feminism than their counter parts;

(iii) The respondents belonging to high SES group had higher level of self-esteem, fearlessness and values for gender equality than their counter-parts;

(iv) The respondents with higher vocational aspiration had higher level of independence, self-esteem, fearlessness, leadership and values for gender equality, vocationalism and collectivism than the respondents with low vocational aspiration.

(v) The respondents with high family climate had higher level of all characteristics and values.

A comparative study of value perceptions and normative rule compliance of Malaysian and American secondary school students was conducted by Barone, Thomas Nicholas (1998). American and Malaysian education are increasingly concerned with the moral orientation of young people. The purpose of this study was to examine the norm conformity and value acceptance of Malaysian secondary school students. It was hypothesized that Malaysian students would demoralize great norm conformity and value acceptance as compared to American students. Since Malaysian students are taught values formally through moral and Islamic education. It was further hypothesized that with in each county female student would be characterized by greater norm conformity and value acceptance when compared with male student. Norm conformity and value acceptance of students were measured by the responsibility, socialization, self-control and norm favouring scales of California Psychological Inventory. Further, a value/behaviour questionnaire was administered to students in both counties, which measured the adherence to values based social norms. Further, to understand the nature of rule compliance and value perceptions of secondary school students and teachers in both counties are interviewed. It was found that Malaysian students had higher norm conformity and value acceptance for American students (significant for all scales). For gender, significant differences were found in these scales measured collectively in Malaysia but no gender differences were found for American students. The results of the values/behaviour questionnaire showed that although there were differences by county, most students reported adherence to positive social norms. Finally, some data obtained from the role/behaviour questionnaire triangulated with the results of the students and teacher interviews, which focus as value perceptions and the role of the teacher as a moral agent. Unlike Malaysian students, American students were not sure if teachers should teach values. Students in both counties also felt that the teacher/student relationship was governed by implicit values of justice, fairness and respect. Student also felt that good teachers could teach positive values and American student felt they could go to good teacher for advice with moral dilemmas.

Berman, Alan, M. (2001) made a study on the process of exploration in identity formation. 215 university students completed questionnaires concerning identity style, critical problem-solving competence and exploration of and commitment to the four ideological domains of politics, religion, occupation and values. Results showed that cognitive competence exerted a small but significant effect on variation in the formation of identity.

K.M.Chetty (2003) made a study on perspectives of Value-oriented Education and concluded that through both teaching and practice the teacher should aim at transforming student's individuality into personality.

Shamshuddin, SK. (2005) made a study on academic achievement and prevalent values of D.I.E.T Students. Findings revealed that Religious, social, democratic, economic, knowledge, hedonistic and health values exert significant influence on academic achievement.

Rabindranatha Reddy (2006) made a study on Sri Sathya Sai System of Education *A Model to Follow,* and gave a detailed account of Practices of Human values in the Sathya Sai Institution. He stressed on Education for Human Values (EHV) curriculum. In India, independent research studying the impact of EHV in the eighteen schools adopted by the Institute of Sathya Sai Education at Mumbai showed that along with practice of human values taught, there was also academic performance.

Ramachandra Reddy and Manchala, C. (2006) made a study on Values and Teacher Education System and concluded that value inculcation should not be an additional subject. It should permeate all works and activities in educational institutions like a Guardian Angel. Values therefore have to be inculcated through deliberate effort and not left to chance. Values have to be both caught and taught.

Rangaswamy, G. (2006) made a study on moral judgement. Findings revealed that sex and intelligence have significant relationship with regard to moral judgement scores.

STUDIES ON VALUES RELATED TO TEACHING COMMUNITY

Spaights (1967) found that the academic record of students intricately involved in their behavior with the teacher. But almost all the studies agree that a teacher's behaviour is the major deciding factor in creating a pattern of behaviour in the class.

Varma (1972) had undertaken a study of 'Relationship between the parents of interpersonal relation and the value of teachers and students in secondary schools'. The major findings were:

(i) The value system of the teachers and students were found to be quite different from each other and the teachers were found to be more concerned with their status and power and less with knowledge and social virtue;

(ii) The friendly interpersonal relation between the pairs of individuals was found to be unrelated to the value systems of the paired members;

(iii) The unfriendly interpersonal relation between the pairs of individuals was not found to be related to the value systems of paired members;

(iv) The role of a value, in its individual capacity as a correlate of interpersonal relations, was found to be depend on its own native such as affiliate or competitive, and on its position in the value system of the group;

(v) A competitive value was found to be a correlate of paired friendly relations when it was low, average and not high. An affiliate value was found to be correlate of pair's friendly relations when it was high or average and not low;

(vi) Dominant values did not differentiate between high and low SES groups;

(vii) The popular teachers were found to be helpful and cooperative in achieving the students' goals and making their school life a pleasant experience, while the unpopular teachers were likely to produce the reverse effect.

Kulshresta (1979) conducted a study on the emerging value patterns of teachers and new trends of education in India. The study aimed at measuring various types of teachers' values in the present socio-cultural environment of schools in India. A Scale of Teachers Values (STV) was constructed and was administered on 700 teachers teaching secondary and higher secondary classes in U.P. The investigator himself with the help of various persons filled the information, wherever needed; interviews and observation techniques were also employed. The value patterns were studied under the following broad categories:

- Humanitarian
- Social
- Professional
- Progressive
- Aesthetic
- Economic
- Authoritarian
- Non-social
- Traditional
- Non-professional
- Non-aesthetic
- Extravagant.

The investigator found that teachers were more interested in humanitarian value than the other values.

'A study of the prevalent value system of the secondary teachers of the high schools in South Gujarat' was conducted by Patel (1979). The major findings were:

(i) On social, political, economic and religious values the older teachers scored significantly higher than the younger teachers;

(ii) On aesthetic and democratic values, the younger teachers scored significantly higher than the older teachers;

(iii) On theoretical, ethical, philosophical and scientific values, there was no significant difference between the two groups;

(iv) On religious and aesthetic values, the female teachers scored higher than the male teachers;

(v) On political values, the male teachers scored higher than the female teachers;

(vi) The rural teachers scored significantly higher on social, political and economic values than the urban teachers.

(vii) On aesthetic value the urban teachers scored significantly higher than the rural teachers.

Wiron, Donglar (1982) made an attempt to study the teaching of values to the college classrooms; faculty and students perception at three contrasting institutions. The objective of the study was whether institutions of higher education had a responsibility to teach values in the college classrooms as distinct from teaching only the information necessary to master content are obtained in employment. This research was based on 161 personal interviews with freshmen, seniors and professors at three institutions of higher learning in the state of Utah. Students and faculty were presented for distanced models for dealing with values in the college classrooms. They were asked to identify the model they believed were in use at each institution and compare them with models they thought to characterize teaching at each institution. The major findings were:

(i) The responses or the selected freshmen, seniors and faculty to those questions were remarkably similar on almost all questions;

(ii) No significant differences were found for any demographic or academic factor, including affiliation with the regionally dominant Mormojz church;

(iii) Students and faculty were satisfied with the teaching of values taking place at appropriate level at all institutions;

(iv) No congruence between what was taking place and what they believed ought to be lacking place;

(v) At each institution the value advocacy model was prepared by a majority of the respondents.

Zuberi (1984) made observations of live interactions and on the existing status of the teachers with regard to the values they hold, the temperamental traits they possess, the degree of adjustment in job they feel, the needs they express and the academic achievement they have at the time of investigation. The study found that no significant differences among the three groups of teachers on values except the religious value, which was found in teachers. In relation to need and teaching behaviour, the teachers were not found differentiable on any need variable except need autonomy. The results obtained indicated that temperament and teachers behaviour were not differentiable on any of the temperamental traits studied. In case of academic career and teacher behavior, the former was found not to affect the latter. The findings of the study demonstrated that the teacher's classroom behaviour precisely sets the 'Tone' for classroom instruction.

Verma and Tyagi (1988) made an attempt to find out whether the sex differences exist in the values of senior secondary school teachers. The findings indicted that male teachers were significantly higher on economic and political values and lower on social values as compared to female teachers.

Nayyar, Surindar Mohan (1989) attempted to find out values cherished by student teachers belonging to various castes and communities. Moreover, the investigator wanted to study the mental makeup of student teachers from various community groups in terms of open-mindedness and closed mindedness. Findings of the study revealed that the most important teacher values according the student teachers from all categories were justice and fair play, discipline-role of the school as a change agent, naturalism, honesty, morality and pride in the cultural heritage in India. The correlations between the teacher value scores and the open-mindedness and closed mindedness were not significant in these groups. There was no significant correlation between the teacher value scores and the socio-economic status scores.

Neeta Khanna (1993) compared the students of teacher training stream with the students of general stream on the five human values of truth, righteous conduct, peace, love, and non-violence under similar environment. The results revealed that there are significant differences between the two groups of students on two of the five values, namely truth and love. The inspection of the mean scores shows that the teacher training group has second higher on these two values. The difference of the mean scores of the two groups on the remaining three values namely righteousness, conduct, peace and non-violence are not significant. Although the hypothesis of significant value differences between the two groups of students has been partially confirmed, it may be said that while the teacher trainees show a clear advantage on the values of truth and love, their mean scores on the remaining three values depict a tendency to be higher. One may surmise that some additional exposure to teacher training curricular or greater contact with school situation is likely to develop all the five values significantly ahead of the students of general education streams.

Murray, Joseph Jr. (1995) had undertaken a study of the moral aspect of leadership in an urban school context. This study investigated morality in the practice of school leadership by posing two research questions:

(i) What are the values and morals that are expressed in the language/ actions of the school community?.

(ii) Are the right features of critical pragmatism evident in the discourse of administration, teachers and students in an urban school setting?.

The analysis included interviews of school administrators, audio taped interactions of a principal and faculty and student interviews from a large southern urban school context. The findings demonstrated the multiplicity of values in these urban schools. Administrators expressed caring, justice and moral responsibility. Student values related to justice achievement, behaviour and society. In the interactions, actions were guided by personal, professional and pragmatic values in one situation and educational and democratic in another. The features and process values of critical pragmatism indicated a distinct climate for change. The analysis demonstrated that democratic school communities were interpersonal and situational that communications were align with organizational goals rather than individuals needs and that aesthetic discussion of school life were rare. This study concluded that morality in the practice of school leadership is shaped by moral values engaged in democratic processes. Morality affects practice within the context of specific interactions around educational issues. Interactions must involve truthful, honest, communication and fair treatment of adult and children. School leaders must consider the multiplication of values, voices and venue to develop more dynamic and moral strategies of school leadership.

Leonard, Pauline Elavine (1997) studied the dynamics of school culture through an examination value orientation. It was guided by multi-perspective (*i.e.*, District, School, teaching teams, Individuals) conceptual framework for examining four major aspects of school culture *viz.*, Educational purpose, curriculum orientation, educational professionalism and leadership. This qualitative study entailed five weeks of participant of evaluation in an urban multi-cultural elementary school. During this time, each of two teachers was separately observed for two-week periods while other school members were observed throughout the duration of the investigation. Semi-structured interviews were conducted with 19 participants and informal interaction within and among other participants were recorded for analysis. This interactive process uncovered communication inconsistency and analysis, which led to further revelations concerning teachers underlying basic assumptions about education. The data revealed that some of the basic assumptions were compatible with the cultural manifestation in the school, while others were in apparent direct conflict. Examining both the similarities and variation in core values provided insight and understanding of school's culture.

Assor, Avi (2000) made a study on value accessibility and teacher's ability to encourage independent and critical thought in students. He examined whether teachers educational values predict their behaviour and students attributes when these values function as chronically accessible, positively valenced categories, which are linked discriminately to perceptions of specific behaviors. The Encouraging Independent Thought (EIT) test was utilized. 52 teachers were administered a sorting task and questionnaires assessing the variables of interest. Several months later, the 1,614 students (in grades 3-6) of these teachers completed questionnaires assessing teacher behaviorus and students attributes. Discriminant accessibility of the value of EIT in teachers predicted two value consistent teacher behaviours, showing tolerance for independent and critical students' opinions and showing interest in and respect for students ideas—as well as two students attributes: assignment of little importance to the value of conformity and sense of acceptance by classmates. The findings demonstrate the theoretical usefulness of the notion of discriminant accessibility of value and suggest that, as part of teacher education programme, it is important to strengthen teachers' inclinations to examine the contribution of concrete actions to the realization of abstract values.

Ramesh, H. (2002) made a study on Professional ethics for teachers and concluded that teaching profession is a responsible profession and values like mutual dependence, co-operation, realization of one's duties and responsibilities should be developed right from the early stages.

Barone, Thomas. N (2004) made a study on Moral dimensions of teacher-student interactions in Malaysian secondary schools. The purpose of this study was to examine the norm conformity and value perceptions of Malaysian secondary school students. To measure adherence to value-based social norms, a values behaviour questionnaire was administered to approximately 400 Malaysian adolescents. The results showed a self-reported high degree of conformity to social norms. In order to increase understanding of the moral dimensions of schooling, semi-structures interviews were conducted with teachers and students, which gave voice to teachers, and students as moral agents. The results indicate that some students view school rules as too rigid and undermining the moral development schooling is trying to promote. The research also shows that the implicit values of respect, justice and fairness are central in Malaysian students' relationships with their teachers. This research shows teachers and students as active constructors of moral meaning and recommends that policy-makers, when thinking about moral education reform, consider these views.

Talwar, M.S. and Sheela, G. (2006) made a study on moral judgement of pre-university students in relation to moral judgement of their teachers. Findings revealed that moral judgement of students is highly correlated to that of their teachers.

STUDIES RELATED TO INFLUENCE OF PERSONAL AND DEMOGRAPHIC VARIABLES ON VALUES AND TEACHER

Chandra kumar and Arokiaswamy (1974) conducted the study to verify gender influence over the value orientation of the college students, findings of the study show that:

(i) The female students had little better value orientation than the male students;

(ii) Gender did not influence the values orientation of the college students;

(iii) There was no consistency in the preferences and values on gender in all three years.

Patel (1981) study revealed that with the increase in age, the students became more society oriented. Girl students of both grades scored high on moral values. A good majority of students liked to be active in aesthetic art oriented activities. On social, national and moral values, the students with lower income scored high than the students with higher income.

Anatharaman (1981) aimed to study the effect of sex, social class and locality on values. In the end, the researcher found that the male students have more theoretical and practical values. Upper class subjects have more religious values. Subjects from urban locality have lesser theoretical and more aesthetic values.

Saraswat (1982) made an attempt to examine the relationship of self-concept measures with adjustment, values, and socio-economic status of boys and girls. It was found that boys and girls differed significantly with regard to possession of values.

Adhikari (1986) studied the importance of values in relation to SES of rural students. Results indicated that the boys of high SES had higher theoretical value than of middle and low SES. No significant difference was observed between low and middle SES boys where as girls did not show any significant difference in theoretical values on varying SES. The rural girls and boys had some economic values irrespective of their SES. The aesthetic value of rural boys was higher than low SES in companion with that of a high and middle SES, whereas no significant difference was observed with the aesthetic value for girls. The social values of boys were found to be same in all three groups, but these were significantly low, in low SES girls than in high and middle SES girls. The political value for girls and boys were the same in all the three groups.

Kalia and Mathur (1986) conducted study on 'Value preferences of adolescents' studying in schools with different socio economic environments. Results pointed out that adolescents studying in high SES schools were more theoretical in comparison with those studying in moderate SES schools and low SES schools. Adolescents studying in low SES school were more economic in comparison to adolescents studying in high SES schools and moderate schools. Adolescents, studying in high SES schools and moderate SES schools were similar in aesthetic, political and religious values among adolescents studying in high SES schools, moderate SES schools and low SES schools.

Sibia, Sukhvinder (1990) attempted to study the value pattern of children at piagetian concrete and formal stages of development. Age was found to be very important factor influencing the value pattern of the children.

Chand (1992) conducted study to examine the personal values of adolescent boys and girls in relation to SES. Findings revealed that there was no significant correlation between SES and religious, democratic, economic, knowledge, hedonistic, power and family prestige values.

Datta (1992) conducted a study to assess the distribution of value pattern and compare the distribution of values among scheduled caste students in relation to aspiration, adjustment and academic achievement and need pattern with non-scheduled caste students. Variations with regard to possession of values were found with regard to caste on theoretical, economic and aesthetic values. No relationship was found between possession of values and achievement of the students.

Sati (1992) compared the needs, values, aspirations and adjustments of SC and Non SC secondary schools in relation to their academic achievement. Sample of the study consisted of 200 students from each group. The findings of the study revealed that the Sc boys and girls did not differ in their values and educational aspirations SC students had higher theoretical, political, order, autonomous, affiliation, nurturance and endurance needs than non-SC students. High achieving SC boys had higher theoretical values than low achieving boys though low achieving boys had higher economic values.

Sharma, Meenu (1992) made an attempt to compare male and females on different levels for their socio-economic status, value and attitude towards the nation. It was found that male and female teachers of different levels differed in SES but they did not differ on value orientation and ATN. To some extent, value orientation was related to ATN and SES was also finding to be related.

Singh (1997) conducted a study to find out the values of urban and rural adolescents both male and female. The findings showed that urban students had higher mean score under theoretical and religious values where as rural students had higher mean scores on social and aesthetic values. The male students had higher mean scores than female students in theoretical and economic values.

Bajpai, Sunil (1998) investigated the sex differences in value pattern of tribal students. The major findings were:

(i) The non-tribal adolescents were higher in theoretical, religious and aesthetic values than tribal adolescents;

(ii) Social values of tribal adolescents are higher than non-tribal adolescents;

(iii) In theoretical and economic values the tribal boys are having higher values than tribal girls whereas the girls have higher social and religious values.

(iv) Non-tribal girls have higher economic, aesthetic and social values than non-tribal boys.

(v) For theoretical, political and religious values, non-tribal boys have slightly higher values than non-tribal girls.

Ali and Karunanidhi (1998) conducted a study to examine the influence of religiosity, age and gender on values. It was observed that the effect of high and low religiosity groups on values was significant with regard to gender and age of students.

Taj (1998) studied the influence of social class and modernization on the personal values of Hindu and Non-Hindu students. Results of the study revealed that social class and modernization had an impact on the personal values of students. Some of the background variables such as religion, type of family and size of family had also considerable effect on the personal values of students. It stressed that development and enrichment of values should be accorded due to attention in our school curriculum.

Yadav (1999) made a comparative study of urban and rural science students in order to find out the values like ideological, economic, social, political, religious and aesthetic as classified by Spranger. The findings revealed that there was no significant difference between rural and urban science students in ideological, economic and religious values whereas significant difference existed in social, political and aesthetic values. It is suggested that policy makers and teachers must concentrate on promoting these values in students.

Rajasekhar Reddy, T. (2002) made a study on attitude towards value-oriented education in primary school teachers. Findings showed that urban primary school teachers obtained higher mean scores than the rural primary school teachers.

Rajini, M. (2003) made a study on promoting values in teacher trainees. Findings revealed that there is significant impact of gender and locality of students studying in D.I.E.T. Colleges in possessing attitudes towards values.

Talwar, M.S. and Sheela, G. (2004) made a study on moral judgement of pre-university students in relation to Socio-economic status. Findings revealed that students from low economic status are obedient.

STUDIES RELATED TO PERSONALITY TRAITS AND VALUES

Bhagavathy (1977) did an analytical study of personality, intelligence, values and problems of adolescent girls. The investigator has given the following findings:

(i) Significant differences were seen in the personality variable and intelligence (both verbal and non-verbal) between the four deviant and one normal group studied;

(ii) The five groups could be differentiated on the number and nature of problems in the areas of health, family, personality, social, educational, vocational, financial and religion.

An investigation into the values, aspirations and personality traits of adolescents of Rajasthan was attempted by Bhatnagar (1979). The major findings of the study were:

(i) Student's leaders and conformists gave highest preference to power value followed by hedonistic and economic values whereas religious, social and knowledge values marked lowest; delinquents preferred hedonistic value, while power value was given second place;

(ii) Most adolescents gave top priority to scientific fields, student leaders and conformists gave second priority to the study of arts subjects whereas, delinquents ranked commerce as second choice;

(iii) All the adolescents wanted to see their country free from poverty and preferred peace and morality to material prosperity;

(iv) All the adolescents aspired for friendship with other nations and for world peace;

(v) The overall adjustments of student leaders were significantly better than the adjustment of conformists and delinquents;

(vi) Student leaders and conformists had the healthiest attitude towards parents but delinquents did not see their parents as sources of affection and protection;

(vii) All adolescents expressed unfavorable attitude towards other generation;

(viii) Student leaders had a favourable attitude towards their peers, including girls;

(ix) Delinquents expressed fear of failure in examination and lack of interest in studies student's leaders were more optimistic about their academic future and aspired for achieving high standards.

Singh (1980) investigated on sex role preference in children that is between boys and girls, upper caste and lower caste, role of personality of parents in the developments of sex-role preferences in their children by taking sample of 325 children and parents. The tools administered were Appropriate Sex role Scale and Masculinity and Femininity Scale. His study revealed that 5 year girls and boys are most feminine and masculine than 3 year old girls and boys. Upper caste children are more conscious of their appropriate sex role than lower caste children. If father dominates, boys dominate, mother dominates, girls play masculine role. That means personality as variable showed significant effect upon the development of sex role preference in children.

Zamen (1982) conducted a study on religious, moral and social values of class XI students and to find their relationship with character traits and personality adjustments. Findings of the study revealed that there were differences in the values held between urban and rural students, between students of two sexes and among the three communities, viz., Hindu, Muslim and Christianity. All the three values had greatest influence on character traits and lowest on personality adjustment. It was found that social and moral values influenced the personality traits much more than religious values whereas all the character traits (Congeniality, Helpfulness, Kind-heartedness, truthfulness and dutifulness) appeared to be significantly influenced by values. The study suggested that the development and strengthening of health, social, moral and religious value system among students should be a very important function of the secondary schools which would help in solving problems of students' unrest and discipline.

Scott, Evert Laurel (1986) did a comparative study of personality, values and background characteristics of artistically talented, academically talented and average, 11th and 12th grade students. 363–11th and 12th grade students formed the sample of the study. The study of the values and a background questionnaire by the researcher were employed to collect the data. In addition to that 16 Personality Factor Questionnaires were also used. The major findings were:

(i) Both males and females in the artistically talented group are significantly different from the academically talented and/or the average groups on a number of personality and value variables;

(ii) The artistically talented group reported significantly more positive attitude towards art education and were more likely to report that their families demonstrated an interest in art and would support their child's choice of an art related career.

Sombhi (1990) attempted to find out effectiveness of value-oriented education provided in three different institutions on students value patterns and selected personality variables. The findings of the study revealed that students studying in Sri Sathya Sai higher secondary school have the highest number of desirable values and superior to other two groups of students marks this value patterns and personality traits. The differential impact of schooling is attributed to the conscious effects made in institutions like Sathya Sai Higher Secondary School and missionary schools. It was found that no deliberate attempts were made in central schools to nurture desirable value pattern and personality traits among students.

Aluja, Fabregat (1996) studied the relationship among attitudes toward social values and personality factors. Subjects were 43 male (mean age 23.6 years) and 137 female (mean age 24.21 years) university students. Information on socio-demographic variables, attitudes toward social values and personality traits was obtained by questionnaire. The results were evaluated according to sex; conservative or liberal social values; and the personality traits of conformity, neuroticism, extraversion and emotional strength. The sixteen personality factor questionnaire (16PFQ), the conservatism-Liberalism Inventory and the Eysenck Personality Questionnaire were used.

Solis Camera, R. Pedro (1999) made a study on Conceptual Analysis of Competitiveness: Its Relation with the Mexican Personality. The relation of sociocultural values, personality traits, competition and love of money in Mexico was studied. Human subjects included 20 normal male and female technical school students and 40 normal male and female university students. Data on socio-demographic variables, sociocultural values, personality traits, competitiveness and love of money were obtained using the Life Philosophy Questionnaire, the Transcultural Work Attitudes Questionnaire and a semantic differential questionnaire. Three work factors (work compromise, high competition and social professions) and 4 life values factors (active-affiliation, internal-external, audacity-caution, autonomy-interdependence) were identified. The role of success and failure were also determined. Factorial analysis and other statistical tests were used.

Chaturvedi, Archana (2001) made an attempt to find out personality traits, normal values and national awakening among the students studying in different culturally based schools. The findings of the study revealed that the leadership ability of the students in western oriented schools was highest, whereas the Hindu, Christian and Muslim school students were at the second and third positions. The students of Saraswathi Shishu Mandir scored higher on moral values. Students of western culture and Christian culture schools were in second and third positions. In national awakening programme students of Hindu, Western, Christian and Muslim culture obtained the first, second, third and fourth positions respectively.

Roccato Michele, Gattino Silvia, Patris Elena (2001) studied on personality, values and political orientation. They studied the relation of personality factors, political affiliation and values in 281 male and female university students (aged 19-34 years) in Italy. The Social Dominance Orientation Scale, the Libertarian/Authoritarian Scale, the Life Events Scale and a political opinion scale were used. An ANOVA and other statistical tests were used. Based on the results, a model of psychosocial predictors of political orientation was developed. The results suggest that subjects who participate in sports and religious groups or who have little interest in politics tend to be politically oriented toward the right while those who are more interested in politics or belong to non-humanities field of study tend to be politically oriented toward the left.

Wolfradt (2003) made a study on Personality, Values and Belief in a Just World (BJW). This study investigated the relationship between general belief in a just world (BJW) and different values (conformity, security and self-direction) as well as personality traits (Five-factor-Model of Personality) among 104 college students and 108 professionals. Previous findings have shown that BJW is positively related to the value domains conformity and security as well as to extroversion and negatively to neuroticism and openness. In this study, a negative correlation between BJW and openness to new experience was found. Furthermore BJW correlated positively with security and conformity. A cluster analysis on BJW and the value domains revealed three types: value-conscious (high in all values and low in BJW), dependent-just (high in BJW, security and conformity, low in self-direction) and self-directed (only high in self-direction). Value-conscious and dependent just participants showed higher scores on conscientiousness, whereas, self-directed participants scored higher on openness. Further research should take into account the individual function of BJW and values for personality function.

Rangaswamy, G. (2006) made a study on moral judgement in relation to certain personality factors and found out that there is significant relationship between the personality factors E, G with moral judgement scores.

STUDIES RELATED TO PERSONALITY TRAITS AND TEACHER

Ryans (1960) research exemplified the transition from research paradigms that focused almost exclusively on teacher Personality Traits to those that directed inquiry towards the investigations of both teacher attitudes and behaviour. He used a scientific approach called the critical behaviour in teaching to study the characteristics of teachers. A large-scale research study on the characteristics of teacher by Ryan not only assessed teacher personality characteristics but also broadened the way to think about the teaching learning process by focussing on the observable behaviour of teachers in the classrooms. Ryan's research exemplifies the transition from research paradigm that focussed exclusively on teacher personality traits to those directed inquiry towards the investigation of both teacher attitudes and behaviours.

Bhagoliwal (1962) made an extensive study on "Personality Characteristics Associated with Teaching Effectiveness Seen Through Rorschach Technique". The sample was 264 teachers (120 male and 144 female). The findings of the study:

(i) More effective teachers characterized by their superiority over less effective with respect to their overall intellectual level;

(ii) More effective teachers characterized by having more of creative potential indicated by imaginable resources;

(*iii*) Inner control was better in these teachers and these people were having fairly higher level of differentiation and integration in their cognitive and perceptional functioning.

The Madsley Personality Inventory was given to first year university students over 3 years by Savage (1962) and the scores on this were related to academic performance at the end of their first year. The results showed that Australian University population had higher mean neuroticism and extroversion scores than the norms of the tests. ANOVA and correlation techniques showed that high scores on both factors were negatively related with academic performance.

Getzel's and Jackson's (1963) broad findings consistently revealed that good teachers possess positive personality characteristics and interpersonal skills.

Anderson and Brewer (1965) studied the influence of teachers' classroom personalities on children's behavior, particularly at the primary and elementary school levels were. In order to obtain objective measurement of teachers classroom personalities and concomitant children behaviour, 26 teacher behaviour categories and 29 children behaviour categories were developed by which both teacher pupil verbal and non-verbal behaviours might be categorized.

Saxena (1969) made an attempt to study the attitudes and personality of teachers. He used Cattell's Contact Personality Factor' (Form 'A' Hindi Version) on 139 teachers in U.P. in relation to their teaching competence. A coefficient of correlation of +0.60 with factor 'H' and +0.42 and +0.36 with factor 'A' and 'H' respectively were obtained. With high teaching competence, these correlations were +0.60, +0.42 and +0.36 respectively, which show a curvilinear relationship. It shows that a very high score on factor 'H' is typical of less component teachers and only a moderately high 'H' is characteristic of a more successful teacher.

Levine (1971) analyzed the intelligence, personality characteristics and motivation of pre service and in service teachers and compared them with persons working in the other fields. These two differ according to the sex, level of teaching, area of specialty and perhaps more significant of all institutional affiliation.

Kaul (1972) made a factorial study of certain personality variables of popular teachers in secondary schools. His objective was to differentiate the personality traits of popular and unpopular teachers. He used Cattell's 16 PF questionnaire. He came to the conclusion that the effectiveness of popular teachers was with respect to attitudes toward teaching, public examination results of their students and the appraisal of their work as teachers respectively.

Tripathi (1972) administered the 16 PF test (Form A) to 52 teacher-trainees and 52 experienced teachers to compare the personality profile of working teachers and teacher trainees. The technique of profile matching was employed for smooth comparisons between the two groups. Only SEVEN factors (A, E, F, G, I, L, Q4) out of 16 personality factors distinguished the experienced teachers easily. These teachers were conscientious, persistent, sensitive, effeminate, suspecting, jealous, sophisticated and polished. The experienced teachers were significantly lower from the general population on factors A, E, F and Q4 were aloof, stiff, submissive, softhearted, glum and serious respectively.

Chhaya (1974) compared effective and ineffective teachers with respect to personality adjustment, teaching attitude and emotional stability. Eighty effective and 100 ineffective teachers were selected from 20 randomly selected schools of Kanpur district. Effectiveness and ineffectiveness were known on the basis of high school examination results (Board of Examinations of 1968, 1969 and 1970). She came to the conclusion that effective teachers had significantly better personality adjustment and favorable attitudes towards teaching. They were less interested in teaching than ineffective teachers, emotionally stable, more authoritarian and extrovert. She found that sex and age of teacher were significantly related to his/her effectiveness.

Goyal (1974) studied some of the personality correlates of creativity in secondary school teachers under training. He was interested in knowing specially the personality differences in relation to sex and subject groups. He applied Cattell's 16 PF questionnaire and Torrance Tests of Creative Thinking as the tools. His sample consisted of 500 student teachers (200 male and 300 female) in the age range of 10 years to 47 years. He found that the personality differences between high and low creative student teachers were very slight because highly creative persons did not enter teacher-training colleges. Intelligence was found to be the most consistent personality correlate of creativity. Highly flexible student teachers were more guilt prone and less imaginative. Highly creative females were having more self-conflict, were moralistic, socially precise and bold. Higher intelligence, emotional stability and tough mindedness were common personality traits found in science and mathematics groups at higher and lower levels of creativity.

Lokesh Koul (1974) found that the attitude of school teachers towards teaching was positively related to factors A (Reserved Vs. Outgoing) and H (Shy *vs.* Venturesome). On the other hand attitude scores of school teachers were found to be related negatively to factors F (Sober *vs.* Happy-go-lucky), O (Placid *vs.* Apprehensive) and Q4 (Relaxed *vs.* Tense).

Sharma (1974) conducted an investigation into the relationship between personality factors and teaching effectiveness. The sample consisted of 175 B.Ed. students of both sexes. Cattell's 16 PF test was administered on the sample for the collection of data. The researcher found 6 factors out of 16, which were positively correlated with teaching effectiveness. These factors were intelligence, trusting, experimenting, self-sufficiency, happy-go-lucky nature and practical mindedness. Intelligence came out to be a very important factor for teaching effectiveness. Total personality of the teacher played an important role in teaching effectiveness. Prominent sex differences were also found in the teaching effectiveness.

Singh (1974) made a comparative study of the personality profiles of married and unmarried high school female teachers. He derived the personality profiles of these teachers with the help of Cattell's16 PF questionnaire. The investigator found that the unmarried female teachers differed significantly on factors A, F, L, O, Q1 and Q4 while the married teachers differed significantly on factors A, C, F, L from the general population. Low scores on factors O and Q4 were shown by the unmarried female teachers. Female teachers (married or unmarried) were found to be significantly higher on factors L and Q1. It means that they were more suspicious and self-opinionated. These were significant on factors A and F from general population. Thus, they are reserved, critical, cool, detached, rigid and aloof respectively.

The major objective of the study conducted by Singh (1974A) was to examine the relationship between some personality variables and teaching effectiveness. He found that the needs of superior, average and inferior teachers were clearly distinct from each other and superior teachers were clearly distinct from each other and superior teachers were distinct for the other two in the needs *viz.*, cognition, dominance autonomy and construction.

Srivastava (1974) used 16 PF Questionnaire (Cattell's Hindi Version) of 52 pupil teachers and 52 experienced teachers to know the impact of professional experience on the modification of personality traits. He found that experienced teachers differed on factors A, E, F, H, Q1, Q2, and Q3 from the pupil teachers.

Barbara Sherman, Robert and Blackburn (1975) analysed the personal characteristics and teacher effectiveness of college faculty. Students in a co-educational liberal art college rated faculty on two typical teaching instruments and on semantic differential form. Data were come from 1500 student judgements on 108 men and women faculty and found that there was significant relationship between personal characteristics and teacher effectiveness of college faculty.

Gupta (1975) applied Cattell's 16 PF test to predict teacher effectiveness through the use of a personality test. 300 male high school teachers having 5 – 6 years of teaching experience, 25 Principals and 350 students formed the sample. Other tools used were teacher's Rating Scale and Pupils' Rating Scale respectively. The researcher noticed that highly effective teachers were more effecto-thymic (A+), more intelligent (B+), having more ego- strength (C+), more surgent (F+), more self sentiment (Q3+) and were less guilt prone, less suspicious (O-) in comparison to the general adult population. Less effective teachers were less intelligent (B-) with lower self-concept control (Q3-) as compared to the general population. Highly effective teachers were significantly more intelligent (B+), emotionally stable (C+), assertive (E+), conscientious (G+), adventurous (H+), tenderminded (I+), with high self concept control (Q3+) and were more warm hearted (A+), in comparison to the less effective teachers. The average effective teachers were more outgoing (A+), surgent and happy-go-lucky (F+), controlled and socially precise in comparison to the less effective teachers.

Grewal (1976) reported that teacher effectiveness was significantly related to some personality traits of the teachers.

Gupta (1976) studied teacher effectiveness through personality tests. The teachers' personality was measured by using the Hindi Version by Kapoor of the Cattell's 16PF questionnaire. Major findings were as follows:

(i) The effective teachers differed significantly from the general population with respect to eight personality factors out of 16, they were A+, B+, C+, F+, O-, L, Q1- and Q3+;

(ii) In comparison to average effective teachers, high effective teachers were significantly more intelligent (B+), emotionally stable (C+), assertive (E+), conscientiousness (G+), adventurous (H+), tenderminded (I+) and had higher self concept control (Q3) and they were less suspicious (L-), less experimenting and radical (Q1-), less self-sufficient (Q2-) and less tense and frustrated (Q4-);

(iii) In comparison to low effective teachers, the high effective teachers were A+, B+, C+, F+, H+, Q3+, L-, M-, O-, Q1- and Q2-;

(iv) The average effective teachers, in comparison to low effective teachers were A+, F+, Q3 and M-.

Malhotra (1976) in his multistage randomized cluster design showed that poorly adjusted teachers were more direct in their classroom behavior than teachers who were well adjusted.

Mathew George (1976) concluded that:

(i) There was no significant relationship between creative personality and indirect/direct behaviour of teachers;

(ii) There was positive correlation between creative personality and 'teacher talk' and negative correlation between creative personality and other dimensions of teacher behaviour.

Singh (1976) found out the relationship of teacher's personality, success in teaching and impact on student's behaviour. He took a sample of 135 male and female teachers with minimum of 3 years experience and 2879 boys of class IX. The tools administered were Rating Scale, Information Schedule, Behaviour change Questionnaire, Interview Schedule, Critical Incidents Blanks, 16 PFQ, Incomplete sentences blank and Rorschach Inkblot tests. His study revealed that the theoretical and social values were positively related to teaching success but the economic and aesthetic values were negatively related. Highly successful teachers were controlled and emotionally stable and these teachers were better adjusted than the average and low teachers. Highly successful teachers possess better intellectual capacity and were able to induce learning, develop interest, etc.

Clapp (1977) listed out 10 qualities as the components of good teaching personality namely–address, personal appearance, optimism, reservedness, enthusiasm, fairness of mind, serenity, sympathy, vitality and scholarship.

Gupta (1977) conducted a study regarding the personality structure of primary and upper primary school teachers. 85 teachers constituted the sample—the age range was 23 years to 38 years. Cattell's 16 PF Test was used. Means, S.Ds were calculated for each factor in terms of stens and raw scores. The study showed that the primary school teachers were humble (E), sober (F-), tenderminded (H-), forth right (N-) and controlled (Q3+). Humbleness, tender-mindedness and forth righteousness are associated with submissiveness, daydreaming and feminity, simple and unsophisticated nature. They have control over emotions and general behaviour. In fact the primary school teachers who were facing the bare necessities of daily life cannot help but be submissive, day dreaming and unsophisticated in this materialistic age.

Gupta (1977A) performed a study on the personality characteristics, adjustment level, academic achievement and professional attitudes of successful teachers. The study intended to find out the personality traits of successful teachers and differentiate them from less successful teachers. It was found that teaching success was significantly related to the factors A, B, C, F, G, H, I, L, N, O, Q3 and Q4 of personality. The researcher also noticed that successful and less successful teachers were different in personality characteristics, adjustment and attitudes towards teaching. The personality factor as a group was better indicator of teaching success than individual factors.

Singh (1978) worked on the leadership behaviour of the heads of secondary schools Haryana. He compared the headmaster's leadership behaviour with that of some other professional leaders and noted the relationship of variables such as personality factors, sex, age, teaching and administrative experience with leadership. Five teachers from each of 100 schools of Haryana state were selected. Thus, 100 heads as known by their 500 teachers constituted the sample. 7 factory managers, 7 army officers, 7 college principals and 7 municipal committee presidents were included in the sample for the study of leadership. The study tools were the Leadership Behaviour Description questionnaire and Cattell's16 PF Inventory. It was found that the leadership behaviour was significantly related to the four personality factors *i.e.*, outgoingness, intelligence, emotional stability and assertiveness. Headmasters were on the 3rd portion in the leadership scale out of 5 professional leaders. The head's leadership behaviour was not related to his age (between 25 years to 62 years). Post-graduate heads' were significantly better than graduate heads but total leadership behaviour was neither related to academic qualification nor related to their teacher experience (between 6 years to 5 years).

Adaval (1979) observed that harmoniously developed and balanced personality was helpful for success in teaching.

Mishra (1979) conducted a study to know the personality traits of fluent teachers. He measured the fluency of teachers through Mehdi's Test of Verbal creativity. Subjects scoring more than 50 were labelled as HFT. The LFT had a score less than 34. These HFT and LFT groups were given Cattell's16 PF Test (Form A) to measure the 16 independent variables of personality. Differences at 0.05 level were observed on five personality dimensions *viz.*,

1. Affected by Feeling *vs.* Emotionally Stable
2. Sober *vs.* Happy-go-lucky
3. Shy *vs.* Venturesome
4. Tough Minded *vs.* Tender Minded
5. Conservative *vs.* Experimenting Respectively.

Sharma (1979) observed verbal classroom behaviour of high school science teachers of U.P. using Flanders Interaction Analysis Category system (FICAS). He found that structuring the learning had a significant positive relationship with some personality components like general activities, restraint, ascendance, emotional stability, objectivity, thoughtfulness and personal relations.

Thakur (1980) made a study on personality characteristics of teachers showing direct and verbal behaviour. He found that there was no significant difference in the teaching behaviour of the direct/indirect teachers due to the variables of age, sex and experience. Four personality factors namely C, O, Q3 and Q4 differentiated the direct and indirect teachers significantly.

Gupta (1981) made a comparative study of the scores of male and female teachers in the inventory of values, personality needs and moral judgement and scores of teachers belonging to different localities (rural and urban). The major findings were:

(i) Male and female teachers expressed high preference for the theoretical values and affiliation. The teachers of both sexes expressed keen moral sense;

(ii) Urban male teachers were more moral than rural;

(iii) Urban female teachers preferred economic and social values;

(iv) Teachers who were above 45 years preferred the needs of achievement, change and order. Teachers below 30 years had the need of affiliation;

(v) Achievement and moral judgement were the dominant factors in the personality of male and female teachers.

Suthar (1981) studied classroom behaviour of teacher trainees in the context of some personality variables. He reported that:

(i) There was no significant difference in the classroom behaviour of emotional and tough teacher trainees except in the case of i/d, which was found to be significant at 0.05 level in favour of emotional teacher trainees;

(ii) The difference in the mean i/d ratio of extrovert and introvert teacher-trainees was significant at 0.05 level and it was in favor of extrovert teacher-trainees;

(iii) Out of the 12 groups of teacher trainees, ten groups namely emotional, mature, sensitive, confident, insecure, experimenting, extrovert, introvert, submissive and dominating showed direct influence while the remaining two groups tough and conservative, showed direct influence.

Patnaik and Panda (1982) made a research on the personality and attitude patterns of good and poor teachers working in secondary schools. 35 good male and 25 good female, 35 poor male and 25 poor female teachers were selected as the sample. The instruments administered were 16P.F. scale Form-C and Teacher Attitude Inventory developed by Ahluwalia (1976). Males have more favorable attitude towards teaching professions, classroom teaching, child centered practices etc. Poor female teachers showed favourable attitude towards teaching profession than poor male teachers. Poor male teachers have significantly positive favourable attitude than the poor female teachers.

Kamala Chopra (1983) designed her study to identify the personality characteristics related to effective and ineffective teachers. 120 teachers were selected at random (49 effective, 19 average and 52 ineffective teachers) and measured with Teacher effective Scale used by Pramod Kumar and Mutta. 16 P.F.Q was also administered. The difference in personality traits of the teachers was significant in case of factors A, B, C, Q3 and Q4. However the difference was not statistically significant in case of factors F, G, I, L, O, Q2. Results showed that effective teachers were significantly more warm-hearted and good-natured. These results were in agreement with findings of Chhaya (1974) who observed that the effective teachers were emotionally stable than the ineffective teachers and Gupta (1976) who observed that the effective teachers differed significantly from the general population on nine personality characteristics.

Rama Mishra (1984) found that the relationship between professional attitude and personality adjustment (r = 0.49) of 200 secondary school teachers of Indore city was significant at 0.01 level. If a teacher had positive professional attitude hen his personality adjustment was also good.

Peters and William (1985) observed that teachers' intellectual disposition did not interact with complexity in the student's performance and that neither student intellectual disposition nor the individual teacher had an effect on student performance.

Dayakara Reddy, V (1987) studied on moral judgment in relation to intelligence, personality and other variables. He concluded that the factors A, B, D, G, H AND Q3 were significantly related to moral judgement scores of subjects.

Robinson and Michael (1987) investigated the Personality Traits of American Secondary teachers and administrators who work in the Association of American Schools of South America (AASSA). Subjects were divided into 3 groups *viz.*, 17 newly recruited teachers, 71 teachers already working in AASSA schools and 22 AASSA superintendents and principals. The 16PFQ and personal data form were administered. The investigation showed that newly recruited males and females differed from U.S. norms on nine and seven factors. Secondary teachers who apply for overseas teaching jobs were already different from U.S. norms.

Verma and Sushila Devi (1987) studied on personality traits and job satisfaction of 20 secondary school teachers by using 16 P.F. Cattell's Questionnaire and teacher job satisfaction Questionnaire. They found significant difference between more liked and disliked teachers in the 'Y' value of fourth personality factor *i.e.*, (Subdueness *vs.* Independence) most liked teachers appears to person the trait of independence.

Guyton, John William (1988) made a study on "Comparison of the Personality Traits of secondary school teachers in Mississippi Public Schools". The main purpose of the study was to identify the Personality differences between outstanding science teachers, regulated certified science teachers and provisional certified teachers of science. They found no significant difference existed in the personality traits of the 3 groups as measured by each important factor of cattell's 16 PFQ. The outstanding teachers group was more abstract in thinking, self-reliant, independent, resourceful, preferred thinking their own decisions, proper, moralistic, aggressive and preferred hard-working people. Discriminant analysis was used to identify six Personality factors that combined and differentiated the outstanding and regular groups on the factors B, G, H, I, O, Q2.

Sundararaja, Sakthivel and Ponnalagappan (1988) showed that the women B.Ed. student teachers had a more favourable attitude towards teaching than the men student teachers.

Parandhama, Amara (1992) studied on role expectations and role performance of science teachers in relation to certain personality factors. Results showed that role expectations of the science teachers are related to factors C, F, G, L, O, Q3. Secondly, role performance of the science teachers is related to factor C.

Values and beliefs and behaviors: A replication comparative study of catholic and public schools was undertaken by Vaugh, Kathryn (1998). The study enables the educators to examine possible differences in certain values, beliefs and behaviours:

(i) Between the catholic high school seniors in public schools;

(ii) Between the catholic high school senior males and catholic high school senior females; and

(iii) In relation to church attendance, Cronbach's coefficient alpha was used to confirm the factor structure of the instrument monitoring the future which was obtained from the institute of social research at the University of Michigan.

A group of 549 catholic high school seniors were randomly chosen from the national database of the institute for social research at the University of Michigan. Both descriptive and inferential statistics including Chi-square and analysis of variance were used to measure the four domains (concern for others, positive perception cigarette smoking, negative perception of the cigarette smoking and self-esteem). It appeared that the school type, gender or church attendance had no observable effect on concern for others, a positive or negative perception of cigarette smoking or self-esteem. In summary, there were no practical differences between the groups and therefore the findings were inconclusive. Moreover, catholic schools, as a functional community might not impact these certain values, beliefs or behaviors based on the similar findings. Catholic students in public schools and catholic schools indicated similar values, beliefs and behaviours.

Dunbar Edward (2000) made a study on Personality and social group value determinants of out-group bias. Findings showed that prejudice and tolerance significantly improved the prediction of out-group bias after in-group social values had been accounted for in the regression model.

Simic, Salvica and Soric, Izabela (2004) made an attempt to study personality factors and teacher attitude in relation to their evaluation methods. The examination of student knowledge, in the psychological sense, is a procedure whereby questions are directed toward the subject, causing reactions of knowledge. Evaluation entails value judgements of the students' answers using units of the school evaluation scale, thus directly measuring knowledge. However, a series of factors influences the situation of measuring student knowledge, causing a lack of objectivity in evaluating knowledge. One of the factors influencing the inadequate numeric value of grades, which depends on the teacher as the measuring instrument, is the teacher's personal education that is visible in the tendency to lower or raise evaluation criteria. Very little research has examined the personal equation of teachers. For this reason, it seemed interesting to examine the relationship of the teachers' personal equation and personality factors. We assumed that the role of the intermediary could be played by attitudes, feelings and expectations which teachers experience while grading knowledge. The investigation was carried out on a sample of 76 teachers, teaching individual subjects in Zadar primary schools. The teachers completed the following questionnaires: Goldberg's Inventory for measuring the five-factor personality model, the scale of external Locus of Control, The Self-actualization Scale and the Scale of Teacher Attitudes. The results have shown different combinations of predictor variables (sex, age, experience, self-actualization dimensions, extroversion, comfort, conscientiousness, emotional stability, intellect and locus of control) for a negative attitude toward knowledge, positive attitude toward knowledge and a positive attitude toward grading as well as insecurity in grading, High grading criteria and positive feelings while grading. Therefore, it seems that teacher attitudes toward knowledge and grading, as well as feeling while grading can be explained by personality factors. In view of the fact that tolerant, fair and strict teachers differ in their attitudes, it is possible to conclude that personality factors, through attitudes, influence the way teachers grade the knowledge of their students.

The above studies revealed that though there is lot of research on personality traits of teachers, the tools used, subjects selected for the study and the variables differed from one study to the other. The tool used in most of the studies is Cattell's 16 personalities Factor Questionnaire. Various studies showed that there is correlation between personality traits, values and effective teaching. This made the investigator to take up personality as one of the variables.

STUDIES THAT HAVE RELEVANCE FOR PRESENT STUDY

Aggarwall (1960) conducted a study on value system and dimension of university students of U.P. It was found that:

(i) The commonly liked ways of life are those having emphasis on self-restraint, moderation and integration of action, enjoyment and contemplation;

(ii) The conceived values of an individual largely take into account the cultural pattern of the requirements of the social system;

(iii) The value dimension isolated by the factor analysis are: To achieve the end or goal by any means, self-restraint, purity of thought, speech and action, Salvation through selfless actions;

(iv) In religious values and temporal change, much emphasis is placed on human effort and fate is also factor suggesting the dependence and adherence to this culture;

(v) In value preference the value items preferred were qualities of friendship, worthy aim and aspirations;

(vi) In case of social values subjection of parental authority is not very rigid and it seems to be based on rational ground, students are normally permissive towards sex and students have a congenial outlook towards the outer world;

(vii) In synthetic approach value of 'closeness' permeates in interpersonal relationship among Indian students.

Mitzel (1960) used the terms product criteria, process criteria and presage or predictive criteria. If one applies these terms to the body of accumulated literature it had been found that presage criteria have been the primary concern of researches. A presage criterion refers to teacher personality attributes, characteristics of the teacher training, teacher knowledge and achievement and in-service teacher status characteristics. Frequently pupils and other school personal were requested to rate the teacher on some checklist or rating scale.

Lueck and William (1965) identified several general and personality characteristics of teachers as intelligence, health, love of children, effective personality, broad interests, enthusiasm and sound philosophy.

Howie (1970) analysed the teachers' task in the world today. He pointed out that in today's restless world the teacher should nourish in young people the critical spirit and encourage the reappraisal ingrained and prejudiced attitude to the problems of humanity. According to him the distinguishing marks of a teacher is not simply that he is a store-house of information but that he must possess the ability constantly to adapt his own thinking to the new demands which changing circumstances of life make upon him and to encourage others to do the same. Teachers not only instruct but they also influence character.

Venukumar (1971) attempted to study "The Role of Teachers in Secondary Schools". The purpose of the study was to assess the tasks of teachers as perceived by the teachers themselves and the students. A Q was administered to 230 respondents including 100 teachers, 50 trainees and 80 students. The following were the major findings. The teacher develops character and loyalty among students. The teacher develops good habits and ideal personality. He also develops religious attitudes, cooperative spirit and patriotic feelings in the students.

Makhija (1973) did a study on 'values, interests and intelligence and its impact on scholastic achievement'. The main objective of the study was to enquire into interaction among values, interests, intelligence and scholastic achievement. The sample of the study was 130 first year students of arts, commerce and science groups. The tools used were: Ojha's Hindi Adaptation of Allport-Vernon-Lindzey study of values, Chatterji's Non-Language preference record and Jalota's Group Test of General Mental Ability. The collected data was analyzed by using ANOVA and 't' test. The findings revealed that:

(i) Students who valued power, competition, etc. in their life utilized mental abilities to excel in crafts and scientific studies;

(ii) Adolescent boys motivated by affection, friendship and love of people used their intelligence in household activities;

(iii) Those who cherished search of truth as the dominant ideal of life would not divert their capacities to mechanical computations;

(iv) None of the values had any significant influence on scholastic achievement.

Rokeach (1973) had selected 18 terminal and 18 instrumental values and asked respondents to put them in rank order. It was found that, the more stable one's terminal values system the more stable is the instrumental values system. It was more stable in the case of the younger students than the elder college students. Similarly those who aspire to moderate future incomes had significantly more stable instrumental value systems than those who aspire to relatively high or low future incomes. The correlation (rho) between the rank orders obtained on two separate occasions is useful not only as a measure of value stability but also of value system change. The rho between rank orderings obtained from any two persons is an index of the similarity between their value systems.

De (1974) made an attempt to study the values of high school boys and some schools in West Bengal. The main objective was to study the development of high school boys and their relation to their parents' and teachers' values. Findings of the study were:

(i) The mean scores of seven values of high school boys were round about 8 *i.e.*, 66.3 per cent of the maximum score, except in the case of sincerity;

(ii) There was no significant difference in values between boys of class V and VII were significantly higher than those of class IX except in the case of sincerity. As for sincerity, there were no difference among boys in class V, VII, and IX;

(iii) The pattern of development of different living areas, *viz.*, urban, rural and industrial were not alike. There was a difference of values between the areas at class V and IX levels but such difference was absent at class VII level;

(iv) There was no significant relation between the values of boys and those of their fathers and similarly between the values of boys and those of their mothers;

(v) There was no significant relation between the values of teachers and those of their pupils;

(vi) One and only one factor come out of the seven values through the process of factor analysis.

The purpose of Alexander's (1975) study was to find out the important teacher characteristics as perceived by B.Ed. trainees. A rating scale was prepared and administered to a sample of 720 trainees. Majority of the trainees gave more importance to personal and social qualities. The female trainees gave greater importance to social and personal qualities whereas the male trainees to professional qualities. It has been suggested that selection of candidate for the B.Ed. course be made giving due consideration to teacher characteristics.

Gaur (1975) conducted study on 'A study of values and perceptions of high school students of the state of Rajasthan and their relation to learning'. The major findings of the study were:

(i) On theoretical values, boys and girls of either rural or urban origin did not differ but urban differed from rural girls;

(ii) On economic values, rural boys and girls, rural and urban girls did not differ but urban boys were significantly higher than urban girls;

(iii) Rural boys and girls did not differ in aesthetic values, political and religious values;

(iv) Urban boys and girls did not differ significantly on perception of self-confidence;

(v) Rural boys and girls did not differ significantly on perception of self-confidence;

(vi) In case urban girls, learning was related positively to theoretical and social values but negatively to economic and religious values;

(vii) in case of rural girls, social and theoretical values was related to learning significantly;

(viii) In case of urban boys, theoretical values were related significantly.

A study of values and vocational preferences of the intermediate class students in U.P. was undertaken by Katiyar (1976). The major findings of the study were:

(i) The students were high in democratic, social and knowledge values medium on health, religious, family prestige and aesthetic values and low in power, hedonistic and economic values;

(ii) The value systems of the students of different courses were very much similar;

(iii) Hindu students were higher than Muslim and Christian students in health value and the Muslim students in social values;

(iv) The students of very high income of groups were higher than the very low, lower and middle income groups in Aesthetic, economic and knowledge values.

Pyari (1980) conducted a study on the relationship between feeling at security, insecurity family attachment and values on educational achievement. It was concluded that the relationship between security-insecurity scores and the educational achievement scores was negative and significant and the relationship between the security and insecurity scores, the family attachment and values were positive.

Manar (1981) compared the attitudes, values and self-concepts of the professional college students with non-professional college students. Hypothesis was that there would be significant difference in self-concepts of professional and non-professional college students. It was found that professional students perceived themselves as more confident and suffering from the feeling of emotional stability than the non-professional students.

Meintjes, Barend Jacobas Johannes (1981) investigated to find out fundamental pedagogical criteria for evaluating a teacher. The author believe that the teacher as an accompanying agent is the most influential factor in education and so attention is focused on the teacher's personality as a sufficient variable in the educational process. One of the interesting findings is that an efficient teacher is a mature adult who sets an example to his pupils in the way his life style measures up not only to those proposed pedagogical criteria but also to accepted ethics of the society.

Sinha (1981) attempted to study on valuational generation gap in the view of students and their parents on students unrest. The major findings of the study were:

(i) The generation gap was apparent in value patterns. Value-orientation on generation gap was not statistically significant;

(ii) There was growing dissatisfaction among students and their parents about the existing system of education in the country with reference to syllabi and teaching methods;

(iii) Students were treated apathetically by teachers, district authorities and social and political leaders;

(iv) The picture of an ideal education (from the students point of view) necessitated the need for developing a better and civilized person, the need for earning a livelihood, the need for strengthening of character, the need for promoting brotherhood and patriotic feeling;

(v) The role of parents, teachers, the principal of the college was helpful to the students whereas, the role of educational authorities and district authorities was neutral and just. But the role of political leader was not helpful to the educational setup resulting in more disturbances.

'An investigation into the changing social values and their educational implications was conducted by Diwedi (1983). The findings revealed that:

(i) The place of residence (rural/urban) had a closer relationship with values: religious, ethico-cultural, political and educational;

(ii) Age group of the respondents was significantly related with religious, societal, political, economic and educational values;

(iii) Women were more religious, ethical, cultural and keenly interested in social problems compared to men. Scores of men were higher on political values than those of women. The sex played an important role in the development of values;

(iv) The old values were not shared by the modern youth. Widow and inter-caste marriages, love marriages, casteless society, etc., were popular values of the student respondents;

(v) Devaluation in the personality, knowledge and character of the political leaders as well as the teachers of the day was revealed;

(vi) The traditional, caste-wise occupational structure was no longer liked by the students;

(vii) Students favored changes in the old curriculum of education as to them it was useless.

(viii) They like co-education and opposed traditional systems of education. They demanded students' participation in academic and administrative decision of educational institution.

Kundu and Sanyal (1984) found that a recognizable value pattern exists among the varied college student population. Besides, a common trend of highest preference for theoretical value has been observed among all groups of students. Lastly, sex and educational differences were found to be significant. It was seen that male and female students differ regarding their economic values, social values and aesthetic values. Regarding political values, it was observed that only that a few instances of significant differences on a variable with in the domain of religious value the medical students were found to differ from all other samples of the study.

McGowan, Patricia Mary (1984) studied the multi-dimensional representation of values and ethnic differences. The investigator had framed the following objectives:

(i) To understand how an individual perceives a value;

(ii) To examine if differences in the value structure occur due to cultural identity, specifically Anglo American and Asian American subculture.

The subjects for the study were 301 students, 68 education students and 54 Asian American students from Washington State University. The Rokeach value survey was used to collect the data. Multi dimensional scaling techniques, multi regression analysis and multiple correlations were used for data analysis. The major findings were:

(i) No significant difference was found between Anglo American and Asian Americans in their perception of instrumental values;

(ii) Some significance was found for the terminal values;

(iii) The Anglo American group placed greater importance on achievement oriented values than the American group;

(iv) A significant difference was also found on a dimension identified as having to do with aesthetic *vs.* political orientation.

Mathana Santiwat (1985) studied the college student values at Krungthep (Bakgok) University. The main objective was to investigate the type of students' value and to determine whether differences exist in students' values regarding sex, family, socio-economic status. 400 day-time freshmen were randomly selected from four major fields of study:

1. Accounting
2. Business Administration
3. Communication
4. Arts and Humanities.

Allport-Vernon-Lindzey study of values was employed to collect data, t-test and ANOVA were the major statistical procedures employed in the data analysis. Major findings were:

(i) The students were high only on economic values;

(ii) They were least interested in aesthetic values;

(iii) Significant difference was found between male and female students on aesthetic, social, political values;

(iv) Significant differences were found on economic, aesthetic, social values of the student perusing various major fields of study.

Robin, Musselman (1986) investigated the value patterns of freshmen entering temple university. The main objective was to measure the value patterns. 339 freshmen at Temple University were the sample of the study. Allport-Vernon-Lindzey study of values was used to collect the data. The main findings of the study were:

(i) Males score higher on the theoretical, economic and political scales and lower on the aesthetic, social and religious scale than the females;

(ii) Freshman aged 22 and above scored higher on the social scale than freshman aged 18-21;

(iii) Black non-Hispanic scored higher on the religious scale than white Non-Hispanic;

(iv) Non-urban freshman scored higher on the religious scale than urban freshmen.

Rathna Kumari (1987) conducted a study to identify different human values (and their interrelated) with a view to incorporate them in teaching programme. To develop a convenient tool for measurement of value judgments that are suited to Indian conditions, to identify specific association of the dependent variables like school efficiency and mass media with value orientation, the researcher included to study human values from a humanistic point of view and ethical values (with out religiously or supernatural contents) that are applicable for all human beings irrespective of their religion. The researchers identified 36 specific human values for excellence in all walks of life and to interrelate with these fellow beings. These values according to the researcher can be suitably built in the academic curriculum of the higher secondary school.

Arun Gupta and Renu Gangal (1989) studied the value emphasis as perceived by pupils of primary, middle and high school stage in different institutions. The major findings reveal that:

(i) The emphasis on values differs at different grade levels and in different institutions;

(ii) Teachers have been found to emphasize moral values, namely respect for others, honesty, love and sense of duty at the 5th and 8th grade levels while cooperation is emphasized more at the 10th grade level than at the 5th and 8th grade levels;

(iii) While values, namely mercy, cooperation, compassion and freedom are not being emphasized at the 5th grade level, the present results show that values, namely love, sacrifice, tolerance and freedom are nor being emphasized at the 8th grade level. At the 10th grade level, values namely social awareness, mercy, dignity of labour, determination and presence of mind, resourcefulness, courage, wisdom and reasoning are not emphasized by teachers;

(iv) In schools with western background (roman catholic) teachers have been found to give more stress on values namely mercy, honesty and love but in Laissez Faire (secular) and Eastern (Jain Hindu) schools, teachers have been found to emphasize sense of duty as a value in addition to the above. Presence of mind, resourcefulness, courage, wisdom and reasoning, social awareness and sense of duty are not being emphasized prominently by teachers in the western schools. Values namely sacrifice and cooperation are not being emphasized by teachers in Eastern and Laissez Faire schools;

(v) The structure of moral values being emphasized at the different schools at present has been found to be similar. Accordingly, the values being emphasized at present comprise truthfulness, good manners, discipline, respect for others, love, honesty, kindness, friendship, personal relationship, sense of duty and co-operation;

(vi) Pupils have been able to identify clearly several values which in their opinion are not being emphasized by their teachers. Values namely dignity of labour, social awareness, mercy, dynamism, determination, presence of mind, resourcefulness, courage, wisdom and reasoning, patriotism, endurance enterprise and comparison have been identified as those values which are not being prominently emphasized at school level at present;

(vii) The values which in the perception of students need to be prominently emphasized at the school level are being emphasized at present and values which are not being emphasized. Recommended values are presence of mind, resourcefulness, courage, wisdom and reasoning, kindness and truthfulness, honesty, good manners, love, sense of duty, sense of co-operation and social awareness.

Gupta, Ranjana (1989) in the present study made an attempt to study the values and moral judgement of adolescents of two representative centers of western and eastern Uttar Pradesh. The investigator has used a five point Value Clarification Scale (VCS) developed by Sanganwall and Singh to collect the data. There were 50 items in the scale. For Indian students, the split-half and test-retest reliability was established. All the students in the experimental group were from India and treated through Value Discussion model for 30 working days at the rate of one hour per day spread over three months. The two control groups (one from India and another from Canada) followed their routine activities and VCS was used twice before and after the treatment. The major finding of the study were:

(i) The mean sores of the Indian control group were significantly higher than the Canadian control group on choosing from alternatives, publicly affirming and acting dimensions of the VCS;

(ii) The mean scores of the Canadian control groups were higher than the Indian control group on prizing and cherishing and repeating dimensions of value clarification;

(iii) No significant difference was observed between the mean scores of the Indian and Canadian control groups on choosing freely, choosing after thoughtful consideration and clarification;

(iv) The t-values reveal that the Indian experimental group was significantly superior to the Indian control group with respect to overall VCS scores and all its dimensions;

(v) The Indian experimental and Canadian control groups were found to be par with respect to prizing, cherishing and repeating dimensions of the VCS, while on the other dimensions and overall VCS scores, the Indian experimental group was superior to Canadian group.

Macneil, Jeremiach Bernard (1991) studied the life roles and values of senior undergraduate education students. The findings indicated that education students tend to value areas of personal achievement and social orientation more than those that relate to working conditions as risk taking. The level of work important (Salience) was high across the total sample with role of home and family relates as the most important role for the majority of students. Community service was judged to be the least importance of the life roles measures. Generally, students were uncertain about their career in teaching less than half of the respondents indicated that they expected to seek a full time employment as a teacher and one third expected obtain a full time position different from teaching. The results of correlative analysis between values and life roles, career expectations and images of teaching revealed a number of statistically significant correlation coefficients at 0.05 level of the values which respondents will seek in future life role, leisure activities and work shared the greatest number of significant positive correlation. In results of the study suggested that the education students given importance to social orientation, personal development, home and family. They also approached their career with a degree of uncertainty. They were low risk takers and expressed interest into states of teacher education and profession.

Chhaganlal (1992) compared the teachers' children and non-teachers children in four selected variables. Objectives of the study were to study the value, adjustment, attitude towards the teaching profession and academic achievement factors of children in comparison with non-teachers children. To compare primary teachers children, secondary teachers children and college teachers children on the basis of the dependent variables. To construct a value scale in Gujarati language for the students of grade VIII to X and to construct a highest type attitude scale in Gujarati language for the students of Grade VIII to X, to study the attitude towards the teaching professions.

Stratified, Purposive sampling technique was followed in the study. 591 teachers' children and 591 non-teachers' children were taken. Findings revealed that non-teachers children were significantly better than teachers' children in social value, whereas teachers' children and non-teachers' children were found equal in power, religious, aesthetic, theoretical and economic values. Primary teachers' children were at a higher level than college teachers' children in power value and religious value whereas college teachers' children were at a higher level than the primary teachers' children in theoretical and social values.

Teacher's children were better adjusted than non-teachers children. Primary, secondary and college teachers' children did not differ significantly in adjustment. Teachers' children and non-teachers children did not differ significantly in their attitude towards teaching profession. Primary, teachers' children, secondary teachers' children and college teachers' children did not differ significantly in their attitude towards teaching profession. Non-teachers' children were at a higher level than teachers' children in academic achievement.

Padmanabhan (1992) attempted to assess the values of high school pupils to understand their value pattern in the present day social and educational environment and to offer a few suggestions for the improvement of values to schools in the light of the present findings. Findings of the study revealed that the value pattern of pupils studying IX was quite satisfactory. Though there was a rather wide disparity in different value scores, the rank order of mean scores for the different values showed the highest score in social value and the lowest score in political value. Boys and girls differed in respect of theoretical, economic, political, social and aesthetic values. There was an association between the pupil's most preferred value and their caste and religion. There was an association between the pupil's most preferred value and their parents' socio-economic status. There was an association between the pupils most preferred value and self-concept.

Arokiasamy (1993) attempted to study the value perception of the first-degree students in colleges affiliated to the Madhurai Kamraj University in relation to certain personality and environmental factors. The findings were:

(i) The value perception was dominant with loving, honest and ambitious as instrumental value was concerned;

(ii) As terminal value was concerned, students value perception was dominant with freedom, happiness and equality;

(iii) Male students were dominant with loving, ambitious, honest, freedom, happiness and equality;

(iv) Female students were dominant with honest, loving, helpful, happiness, freedom and world at peace;

(v) Arts students are dominant with loving, ambitious, honest, freedom, happiness and equality;

(vi) Science students are dominant with loving, ambitious, honest, freedom, happiness and equality;

(vii) Students of very low family income was dominant with loving, ambitious, helpful, freedom, happiness and a comfortable life;

(viii) Students of very high family income was dominant with loving, self-controlled, honest, happiness, wisdom and freedom.

Pandey (1994) a psycho linguistic study examines the democratic values such as liberty, justice, equality and fraternity of 100 monolinguals. 100 bilinguals and 100 trilingual were class V students. Balanced bilingual were founded to be higher on democratic values in comparison to monolinguals as well as non-balanced bilinguals.

Singh (1994) conducted study to compare academic achievement, social/ political/religious/ theoretical/ economic/ aesthetic values and self-disclosure of socially accepted, rejected and neglected students of senior secondary schools. Findings of the study revealed that there is a significant difference between socially rejected and neglected girls regarding their theoretical, aesthetic, social and economical values. But no differences were found in political and religious values. Scores for academic achievement of socially accepted girls were higher of socially rejected and neglected girls. Socially accepted girls significantly differences from other two groups on social values.

Vedprakash (1994) conducted the study to examine differences between science and arts students in their educational aspirations, school adjustment, values and school environment. Findings of the study revealed that the students belonging to rich school environment were significantly higher on social value than their counter parts from poor environment in all the three groups. The relationship between social values and social climate was positive and significant and it had inverse relationship.

Preston, Rondall Wayne (1995) conducted a descriptive study of values on educational programme in Texas public elementary schools. The purpose of the study was to provide descriptive information about values education programme in Texas elementary schools for policy makers, curriculum directors and educators. Insight into the contemporary issue is augmented by exploring:

(i) Commercially or locally developed value programmes that are in place in schools;

(ii) The relationship between student and a school district demographics and value education programmes;

(iii) The role that different interest groups have in the introduction of values programme;

(iv) The extent to which values education programmes are accepted by different groups.

A telephonic survey was administered to 310 elementary school principles in Texas to obtain descriptive data concerning values education programme in the state. The following generalizations were emerged from the study:

(i) Principals related that the values education programs in their schools are beneficial to students and are supported by parents, community, school boards and by the school administration;

(ii) School teachers and school administrators are the most influential groups for initiating existing values and education programmes;

(iii) The prominent vehicles for values instruction in schools is through the hidden curriculum.

Ninety-four per cent of the principals surveyed in this study reported using some type of approach with students to promote values in their schools. Finally, a longitudinal study to investigate the long-term benefits for value education programmes was recommended.

Verma, Dharmendra (1995) conducted a study on value pattern of arts, science and commerce students. The objectives of the study were:

(i) To find out correlation between values scores and that of sense of responsibility;

(ii) To study value patterns of students belonging to lower and higher income groups;

(iii) To study mean value scores of students of urban and rural areas when high and low groups of sense of responsibility are taken into account.

Findings of the study showed that social values were found highest among arts stream, theoretical values between science stream and commerce streams and aesthetic values the lowest in all the three streams. On economic values, the commerce and science students differed significantly. The socio-economic status did not affect the values of the students and so was the urban and rural locality. Students of lower income group were found to be more religious than the higher income group.

Ranu, Sarbjit Kaur (1995) studied the value dimensions as related to level of aspiration and intelligence of post graduate students of three universities. The findings revealed that there were minor deviations in the ranking order of the two most preferred values, while students at Punjab and Punjabi universities gave first preference to political and second to theoretical while GNDV students gave first preference to theoretical and second preference to political. Males were significantly higher on theoretical values but lower on the aesthetic and social values than the females. Art students were significantly higher on aesthetic, social and political values than the science students. In order of ranking, values for high level of aspiration and intelligence group were theoretical, political, economic, social, religious and aesthetic while for the low group were political, theoretical, aesthetic, economic, social and religious. High and low aspiration female groups were nearly homogeneous in their value patterns. Multiple correlation results indicate that level of aspiration and intelligence could be established in predicting theoretical, economic, aesthetic values in females.

Shukla, Shraddha (1996) conducted a study to investigate the difference between the values of literate and illiterate, working and non-working women. Findings of the study revealed that, there was no significant difference between literate and illiterate, working and non-working on their awareness of social, political and health values but on religious values they did differ. Literate working women had materialistic attitude than literate and non-working women. It was observed that illiterate and illiterate non-working women were much more conscious about their family reputation and women aware of adoption of new techniques in general than literate working women. Both working and non-working women had a positive attitude towards aesthetic values.

Verma (1996) conducted a study to examine the value pattern of college students with special reference to sense of responsibility. The major findings of this study reflected that social values were higher among arts students and theoretical values among science and commerce students. The socio-economic status did not affect the values of the students and the three streams did not differ significantly in their sense of responsibility.

Othman, Joharry (1997) studied the gender and ethnic relationship between values, attitudes and behaviour among selected Malaysian fourth and fifth form students. The purpose of the study was to investigate relationship among values, attitudes and behaviour for students from different cultures and different ethnic backgrounds. A stratified sample of 450 students in three urban schools in Malaysia was selected. The three main ethnic groups in Malaysia are Malay, Chinese and Indian. The sample is divided into equal gender and ethnic groups (*i.e.,* 225 per gender and 150 per ethnic groups). Four instruments were used to assess values, attitudes and behaviour in schools and behaviour out of schools. The data is analyzed by using ANOVA, correlation and tests of mean differences. It was found that means for all three constructs were different across gender and ethnicity. Members of different groups evidently understood and reacted differently to each construct. Females reported more positive values, attitudes and behaviour. Malay male students reported negative values, attitude and behaviour among the ethnic groups. The main findings from this study were:

(i) It was difficult to obtain a measure that was reliable and stable in a cross-cultural study of this nature;

(ii) The Malay group results neglect the current trend in Malaysian youth which is a concern to the relevant authorities.

Mohamood Ali (1998) examined the relationship among personal values career aspirations, socio-economic status, academic achievements and educational choice. Researcher conducted the study on sample 500 students (250 male 250 female). The findings of the study reveal that the academic achievement correlated significantly and positively with socio-economic status, knowledge value and occupational aspirations and negatively with power value. In the case of arts and science groups' academic achievement was correlated significantly with socio-economic status but in the case of commerce group these variables were found to be uncorrelated.

Christine Robert and Alex Pieterse (2004) observed that the cultural value differences among American undergraduate and graduate students were influenced by the participants' gender and racial identity status. Findings suggest that a strong preference for distinct cultural values orientations that reflect both traditional Asian and Europe American Cultural values. Results indicate that the participants in the study were endorsed orientations toward human nature, future time orientation and an activity orientation. The subjects of the study who actively reject white society and immersed themselves in their own cultural group had a preference for a past time value orientations.

Kulwanth Pathania, Anitha Pathania (2006) made an empirical analysis on teachers' opinions on certain selected values. As primary source of data, a questionnaire was prepared wherein the view of 50 colleges and university teachers from 10 different states were taken for analysis. The questions included in the questionnaire were based on socialization, imitation, conformity, interpersonal understanding, emotional education, physical education, spiritual education and autonomy. The analysis reveals that hundred per cent of the respondents (100%) felt that socialization and interpersonal understanding play a major role in development of values, whereas 91.3 per cent respondents emphasized the need of physical education. Regarding holistic approach of education, acting as a role model and spiritual education, 87 per cent, 85 per cent and 82.6 per cent teachers voted in favour of them respectively. Autonomy, conformity and emotional education were supported by 69 per cent, 65.2 per cent and 65 per cent respondents respectively.

AN OVERVIEW—RESEARCH REVIEWED

A close look at the studies reviewed clearly shows that the studies are reported on students' value patterns, teachers' value patterns and the value patterns of students and teachers and their attitudes and practices concerned to various values.

Number of studies were carried out on students' value patterns in India and abroad. Most of the studies had used the students of secondary and higher secondary levels as well as college levels, as the sample. Most of the foreign investigators has used Rokeach Value Survey as a tool for the collection of data (Bertera, Francis John, 1979). On the other hand, Indian investigators had, mostly used Allport-Vernon-Lindzey study of values (Makija, G.K., 1973) or its adopted version (Bajpai, Sunil, 1998 and Gaur, B.S., 1975). Many researches constructed their own tools depending on the context (Arun, K. Gupta and Prenu Gangal, 1989 and Diwedi, C.P., 1983). The Rokeach Value Survey does not seem to have been favoured much by Indian investigators though a few investigators have used the tool (Arokiasamy, S., 1993). Also many studies were conducted relating to the personality traits and values (Sombhi, 1982; Zamen, 1982; Aluja, Fabregat, 1996) personality traits and teachers (Bhagoliwal, 1962; Singh, 1974; Kamala Chopra 1983; Simic Salvica, 2004).

The variables covered have been sex, age, religion, socio-economic status, locality, family income, family background etc. The statistical procedures widely employed have been Mean, Standard Deviation, 't' test, chi-square test, ANOVA, Coefficient of correlation and product moment correlation. Factor analysis and regression have been used in a few cases.

When one look into the studies of values of students and teachers, very few studies are available (Rabindranatha Reddy, C., 2006, Barone, Thomas Nicholas, 1998; De, 1974; Murray Joseph Jr., 1995; Theodore, Alexander Philip, 1986; Sombhi 1982 and Varma, 1972) in India as well as in foreign countries. The review clearly delineates the need for research in India on the prevailing value system in students and teachers. The studies mentioned in this chapter clearly show that there is dearth of research in this area. In any educational system, one may be interested to know the values of teachers and values of students the relationship between teachers' values perceptions and students' value perceptions. Further, certain interesting things may come out if one tries to find out the influence of teachers' and students' personal variables on their value system and studies showing relationship between values and personality factors. Such studies, generally gives a comprehensive picture on their value system of students and teachers in relation to certain variables.

It may be seen from the brief review of the literature presented in the foregoing pages that a few studies have been carried out in the area of attitudes towards values and their practices. But by and large except on a few variables, the results obtained are not coinciding and hence warranting further exploration. Further, studies on the relative impact of each of the several independent variables that effect attitudes and practices of values are rare to find.

Selection of certain important demographic variables, sociological variables and psychological values is warranted by many other studies, even though; they are not exhaustive for obvious reasons.

Review of literature states that an extensive study of the attitudes towards values and value practices in relation to personality factors is very rare. The present study is an attempt to see the relationship between the attitudes towards values, practices of values and personality factors. The area under investigation is novel and unexplored one with respect to population of B.Ed. students and their nature of work.

THE PRESENT STUDY

In this chapter, the statement of the problem, need for the study, objectives, hypotheses, variables studied, definitions of certain terms and limitations of the study are presented.

STATEMENT OF THE PROBLEM

Accordingly, the topic chosen for the study is entitled as "A Study of Attitudes towards Values and Their Practices in relation to certain Personality factors among B.Ed. Students in Andhra Pradesh."

NEED FOR THE STUDY

Teachers have always played a crucial role in preparing communities and societies towards exploring new horizons and achieving higher levels of progress and development. They are prime agents of change. The significance of the emerging role of teachers has never been so critical as at this juncture, hence the need for the present study.

In the past, the learners through exemplary behaviour of teachers imbibed values. Ancient teachers had heightened emotional concern towards their pupils in order to inculcate desired virtues. In contrast, the behaviour of modern teachers, in general, is not exemplary in facilitating pupil to imbibe any quality that is virtually virtuous. Further, modern teacher in general had little emotional concern towards the pupils. The present day teacher is mostly concerned to transact the content and neglecting entirely the affective aspect of inculcating right attitudes and virtuous behaviour. Hence, at present it is desirable to know the attitudes towards values of B.Ed. Students (would be teachers). Also, the value practices of B.Ed. students require attention. Hence, it was felt appropriate from the viewpoint of the present investigation to answer the questions *viz.*,

- What are the attitudes towards various values of B.Ed. Students?
- To what extent the B.Ed. Students are practicing the values?
- Is there any relationship between personality factors and attitudes towards values and their practices? Which made the researcher to think about the present study.

Objectives of the Study

- To study the attitudes towards values among B.Ed Students.
- To know the practices of values among B.Ed. Students.
- To ascertain the influence of personal and demographic variables on attitudes towards values and value practices among B.Ed. Students.
- To assess the relationship between attitudes towards values and personality factors among B.Ed. students.
- To assess the relationship between value practices and personality factors among B.Ed. Students.
- To predict attitudes towards values and value practices of B.Ed. Students with the help of independent variables.

HYPOTHESES OF THE STUDY

To realize the above objectives the following hypotheses in null form are formulated for testing:

1. The attitudes towards various values to be formed by B.Ed. Students would not be different.
2. The practices of various values of B.Ed. Students would not be different
3. There is no gap between attitudes towards values and their practices for each of the values studied.
4. There is no significant difference between gender and attitudes towards values among B.Ed. Students.
5. There is no significant difference between gender and value practices among B.Ed. Students.
6. There is no significant difference between attitudes towards values and age of B.Ed. Students.
7. There is no significant difference between values practices and age of B.Ed. Students.
8. There is no significant difference between caste and attitudes towards values among B.Ed. Students.
9. There is no significant difference between caste and value practices among B.Ed. Students.

10. There is no significant difference between region and attitudes towards values among B.Ed. Students.
11. There is no significant difference between region and value practices among B.Ed. Students.
12. There is no significant difference between religion and attitudes towards values among B.Ed. Students.
13. There is no significant difference between religion and value practices among B.Ed. Students.
14. There is no significant difference between marital status and attitudes towards values among B.Ed. Students.
15. There is no significant difference between marital status and value practices among B.Ed. Students.
16. There is no significant difference between attitudes towards values of B.Ed. Students with qualification.
17. There is no significant difference between value practices of B.Ed. Students and qualification.
18. There is no significant difference among different Methodology students and attitudes towards values.
19. There is no significant difference among different Methodology students and practices on values.
20. There is no significant difference between locality and attitudes towards values among B.Ed. Students.
21. There is no significant difference between locality and value practices among B.Ed. Students.
22. There is no significant difference between father's occupation and attitudes towards values among B.Ed. Students.
23. There is no significant difference between father's occupation and value practices among B.Ed. Students.
24. There is no significant difference between mother's occupation and attitudes towards values among B.Ed. Students
25. There is no significant difference between mother's occupation and value practices among B.Ed. Students.
26. There is no significant relationship between personality factors and attitudes towards values among B.Ed. Students.
27. There is no significant relationship between personality factors and value practices among B.Ed. Students.

28. It would not be possible to predict significantly the major portion of attitudes towards value and practices of values of B.Ed. Students with the help of the independent variables included in the study.

VARIABLES STUDIED

The list of the variables is given below:

1. *Dependent Variables*

The two dependent variables in the study *viz.*,

(i) Attitudes towards Values

(ii) Practices of Values

2. *Independent Variables*

The independent Variables, which are considered in the study, are grouped under two categories as mentioned below:

(a) **Personal and Demographic Variables**

(i) Gender

(ii) Age

(iii) Caste

(iv) Region

(v) Religion

(vi) Marital Status

(vii) Educational Qualifications

(viii) Methodology

(ix) Locality

(x) Father's Occupation

(xi) Mother's Occupation

(b) **Personality Factors**

Cattell's 16 personality factors

DEFINITION OF CERTAIN TERMS

Value

It may be defined as "A set of principles or standards of behaviour".

Social Value

Social value refers to those values which are other oriented, they are concerning to society; which are cherished and practiced because of our association with others. The social values necessitate the interaction of two or more persons and they are always practiced in relation to our neighbours, community, society, nation and world. Social values may be defined in terms of charity, kindness, affiliation, love and sympathy for the people, efforts to serve God through the service of mankind, sacrificing personal comforts and gains to relieve the needy and the afflicted of their misery. One gets social values from friendship, love, family and participation in good activities.

Religious Value

Religious value is defined in terms of faith in God, attempt to understand Him, fear of divine wrath, act according to the ethical codes prescribed in the religious books. The outward acts of behavior expressive of this value are going on pilgrimage, living a simple life, having faith in the religious leaders, worshipping God and speaking the truth. If a person considers an object divine, it is said to have a religious value and its experience is called religious experience, which may be spiritual or divine.

Economic Value

It means that an object commands a money price and stands for the desire of money and material gains. A man with high economic value is guided by considerations of money and material gain in the choice of his jobs. His attitude towards the rich persons and the industrialists is favourable and he considers them helpful for the progress of the country.

Democratic Value

Democratic value is characterized by respect for individuality, absence of discrimination among persons on the bases of sex, language, religion, caste, colour, race and family status ensuring equal social, political and religious rights to all, impartiality and social justice and respect for the democratic institutions.

Knowledge Value

It stands for love of knowledge of theoretical principles of any activity and love of discovery of truth. A man with knowledge value considers knowledge of theoretical principles underlying a work essential for success in it. He values hard work in studies, only if it helps to develop the ability to find out new facts and relationships and aspires to be known as the seeker of knowledge, for him knowledge is virtue.

Power Value

Power value is defined as the conception of desirability of ruling over others and also of leading others. The characteristics are the person prefers a job where he gets opportunity to exercise authority over others, prefers to rule in a small place rather than serve in a big place, that the fear of law of the country rather than the fear of God deters him from having recourse to unapproved means for making money and that he is deeply status-conscious and can even tell a lie for maintaining the prestige of his position.

Hedonistic Value

Hedonistic value is defined as the conception of the desirability of loving pleasure and avoiding pain, for a hedonist present is more important than future. A man with hedonist value indulges more in pleasure of senses and avoids pain.

Aesthetic Value

One realizes aesthetic value when one perceives an object as a unified expression of meaningful feelings. The aesthetic experience is a special kind of experience and is an interaction between an object and a subject. The subject that is the person contributes sense organs and also depends on his past experiences for appreciation or dislike of objects. Generally, aesthetic value is characterized by appreciation of beauty, form, proportion, harmony and love for fine arts viz., drawing, painting, music, dance, sculpture, poetry and architecture, love for literature, love for decoration of the home and the surroundings, neatness and system in the arrangement of the things.

Health Value

Health value is the consideration for keeping the body in a fit state for carrying out one's normal duties and functions. It also implies the consideration for self-preservation. A man with high health value really feels sorry if through some act of negligence impairs his health, he considers good physical health essential for the development and use of his abilities.

Attitude

Attitude is a dispositional readiness to respond to certain situations, persons, and objects in a consistent manner, which has been learned and has become one's typical mode of response.

Attitude means the individual's prevailing tendency to respond favorably or unfavorably to an object (person or group of people, institutions or events). Attitudes can be positive (values) or negative (prejudice).

Practice

Practice is the behavioural manifestation of the knowledge of an individual in using a value. It is that which is customary, typical and habitual.

Practice is operationalized for the purpose of measuring various practices to inculcate different values considering different items relating to different values.

Personality

Personality is a word that signifies the personal traits and patterns of behavior that are unique to the individual. It is the sum total of all the biological innate dispositions, impulses, tendencies, aptitudes and instincts of the individual and the required dispositions and tendencies acquired by experiences.

According to Cattell (1950), 'Personality is that which permits a prediction of what a person will do in a given situation". According to Cattell, a trait of the only variety is a mental structure, which is relatively fixed characteristic of the individual functioning from time to time in behaviour.

Gender

Male and female B.Ed. Students were included in the study.

Age

B.Ed. Students who have just completed their Graduation and entered immediately into B.Ed. (age<=22) forms one group and students of age group above 22 years, forms the other.

Caste

For the purpose of study caste is divided into three categories namely Forward Caste, Backward caste (includes all the categories BC-A, BC-B, BC-C & BC-D) and Scheduled Caste (includes both SC and ST).

Region

Defined portion of the earth's surface known especially as distinguished by certain natural features, climate conditions, a special fauna or flora or the like, a separate part or division. In the present study, region refers to the Rayalaseema, Telengana and Coastal regions of Andhra Pradesh.

Religion

For the purpose of the study, three major religions namely Hinduism, Islam and Christianity were considered.

Marital Status

For the purpose of the study, the sample is divided into two groups namely married and unmarried.

Educational Qualifications

The qualification of the students may exert influence on attitudes and practices of values of B.Ed. students. The minimum qualification to enter into B.Ed. is completion of a degree at graduate level. So, graduation in the minimum subject is considered as the minimum degree, some have post graduation degree in their subject. The first group to have the minimum required qualification may be designated as suitably qualified, the other group of students are said to be over qualified. The variation in the level of qualification may bring about variation in their attitudes and practices of values. In this study the B.Ed. students are divided into two groups' *viz.*, graduates and postgraduates.

Methodology

Generally B.Ed. programme comprises of four methodologies viz., Mathematics, Physical Sciences, Biological Sciences and Social Studies. For the present study these four methodologies were considered.

Locality

A place considered with reference to some particular events or circumstances connected with it, a quarter in which certain things are done or which chosen for particular operations. Only Urban and rural localities were included. Places that have more than two lakhs population are considered as urban and the areas with around 10 to 20 thousand population are considered as rural.

Occupation

Here occupation is divided into three categories: unskilled/skilled/ professional:

(i) Unskilled: Those who are involved into the activities of cultivation, coolie or who do not work;

(ii) Skilled: Those who are involved in the skilled activities like carpentry, pottery, goldsmith, and factory worker;

(iii) Professional: Those who are belonging to professional activities *i.e.*, Doctors, Engineers, Teachers, Lawyers.

Personality Factors

Factor—A

(Low Score) Reserved, detached, critical, aloof and stiff Vs. (High Score) Warm-hearted, outgoing, easy-going and participating.

The person, who scores low on Factor—A, is in no sense abnormal, but has a temperamental inclination to be cautious in emotional expression, uncompromising and critical in outlook and awkwardly aloof in manner. He likes things or works (e.g., machinery, logic), working alone, hard headed, intellectual approaches and rejection of compromise.

The person, who scores high on Factor—A will have characteristic of easy goingness, accessible emotions, interest in people, attentive to people, soft-hearted, kindly, adoptable, etc. He likes occupations dealing with people and socially impressive situations. He is generally willing to 'go along' with expediency. He readily forms active groups. He is generous in personal relations, less afraid of criticism and better able to remember the names of the people.

Factor—B

(Low Score) Low intelligence, concrete-thinking *vs.* (High Score) More intelligence, abstract thinking.

The person, who scores low on Factor—B, tends to be slow to learn and grasp, dull, sluggish. His dullness may be simply a reflection of low intelligence

The person, who scores high on Factor—B, tends to be quick to grasp ideas, a fast learner, intelligent. There is some correlation with level of culture and some with alertness.

Factor—C

(Low Score) Affected by feelings, emotionally less stable, easily upset, changeable *vs.* (High Score) Emotionally stable, mature, faces reality, calm.

The person scoring low on Factor—C, is easily annoyed by things and people, is dissatisfied with the world situation, his family, the restriction of life and his own health and he feels unable to cope with life. He shows generalized neurotic responses in the form of phobias, psychosomatic disturbances, sleep disturbances and hysterical and obsessional behaviour.

The person scoring high on Factor—C, tends to be emotionally mature, stable, calm, realistic about life, unruffled, better able to maintain high group morale. He does not let emotional needs. Sometimes he may be a person making a resigned adjustment to unsolved emotional problems.

Factor—E

(Low Score) Obedient, mild, easily led, docile, accommodating, *i.e.*, submissiveness *vs.* (High Score) Assertive, aggressive, competitive, stubborn, *i.e.*, dominance or ascendance.

The person scoring low on Factor—E tends to be submissive, dependent, considerate, diplomatic, expressive, conventional, confirming, easily upset by authority and humble. This passivity is part of many neurotic syndromes.

The person scoring high on Factor—E tends to be assertive, independent minded, stern, hostile, unconventional, rebellious, tough-minded and authoritarian (managing others).

Factor—F

(Low Score) Sober, taciturn, serious *vs.* (High Score) Enthusiastic, headless, happy-go-lucky.

The person, who scores low on Factor—F, tends to be silent, introspective, full of cares, concerned, reflective, incommunicative, slow and cautious. He sticks to inner values.

The person, who scores high on Factor-F, tends to be quick, alert, cheerful, talkative, frank and expressive. He reflects the group.

Factor—G

(Low Score) Disregards rules, expedient *vs.* (High Score) Conscientious, persistent, moralistic.

The person, who scores low on Factor—G, tends to be self-indulgent, slack, indolent and undependable. He disregards obligations to people. He lacks acceptance of group moral standards.

The person, who scores high on Factor—G, tends to be responsible, emotionally disciplined, consistently ordered, determined, persevering and dominated by sense of duty. He is concerned about moral standards and rules.

Factor—H

(Low Score) Shy, timid, restrained, threat-sensitive *vs.* (High Score) Adventurous, "thick-skinned", socially bold.

The person, who scores low on Factor—H, reports himself to be intensely shy, tormented by an unreasonable sense of inferiority, slow and impeded in expressing himself, disliking occupations with personal contacts, preferring one or two close friends to large groups, and not able to keep in contact with all that is going on around him.

The person, who scores high on Factor-H, tends to be friendly, adventurous and impulsive. He shows little inhibition by environmental threat feels free to participate and makes more socio-emotional than task-oriented remarks. He has a history of being more frequently involved in organizing clubs or teams. The individual will have interest in opposite sex and is associated with more heart attacks.

Factor—I

(Low Score) Tough-minded, reject illusions *vs.* (High Score) Tender-minded, sensitive, dependent.

The person, who scores low on Factor—I, tends to be unsentimental, self-reliant and hard. He will have some sort of tough, masculine, practical, mature, group-solidarity generating and realistic temperamental dimensions. He holds responsibility, is unaffected by 'Fancies', acts on logical evidence and does not dwell on physical disabilities.

The person, who scores high on Factor—I, tends to be kindly, gentle and imaginative in inner life and in conversation. He seeks sympathy and help from others. He expects affection and attention from others. He acts on sensitive intuition. High score on Factor-I is associated primarily with an overprotected or atleast sheltering from urgent demands of life bringing.

Factor—L

(Low Score) Trusting, conciliatory, accepting conditions *vs.* (High Score) Suspecting, jealous, irritable.

The person, who scores low on Factor—L, is one of the easy going. He lacks ambition and striving, readily forgets difficulties and accepts personal unimportance. He tends to be adaptable, cheerful, uncompetitive, concerned about other people and a good team worker.

The person, who scores high on Factor—L, tends to be jealous, dogmatic, tyrannical and easily irritable. He is often involved in his own ego, is self-opinionated, is uninfluenced by the views of prominent people and declines to be generous.

Factor—M

(Low Score) Practical, conventional and careful *vs.* (High Score) Imaginative, absent-minded, unconventional.

The person, who scores low on Factor—M, tends to do the right things, alert to practical needs and conventional. He is dependable in practical judgement and earnest in thinking. He is concerned with immediate interests and issues. But sometimes, he is unimaginative.

The person, who scores high on Factor—M, inclines to be disregardful of practical matters. He has higher internal, spasmodic anxiety and conflict tensions. He walks and talks in his sleep. He tends to feel in group, unaccepted, but unconcerned. He participates and makes original leadership suggestions, which are not immediately ignored, though in the long run his suggestions turnout to be rejected. He expresses significantly more dissatisfaction with the group unity and the group's regard for rules of procedure.

Factor—N

(Low Score) Forthright, natural, unpretentious *vs.* (High Score) Polished, worldly, shrewd.

The person, who scores low on Factor—N, tends to be unsophisticated, sentimental and simple.He lacks self-insight. He contents with what comes. He has blind trust in human nature and has simple tastes. He gets warmly, emotionally involved. He has vague and injudicious mind.

The person, who scores high on Factor—N, tends to be polished, experienced worldly and shrewd. He has exact calculating mind. He is emotionally detached and disciplined, is ambitious and possibly insecure. He is insightful regarding self and others.

Factor—O

(Low Score) Self-assured, placid, secure, complacent *vs.* (High Score) Apprehensive, self-reproaching, insecure, worrying troubled.

The person, who scores low on Factor—O, tends to be self-confident, cheerful, placid and impenitent. He is expedient and insensitive to people's approval or disapproval. He is rude, vigorous and has no fears.

The person, who scores high on Factor—O, tends to be depressed, worried, troubled, insecure, anxious and lonely. He is easily touched and overcome by moods. He has strong sense of obligation. He is sensitive to people's approval and disapproval.

Factor—Q1

(Low Score) Conservative, respecting, established ideas, tolerant of traditional difficulties *vs.* (High Score) Experimenting, liberal, analytical, free thinking.

The person, who scores low on Factor—Q1, tends to be conservative. He is reluctant to any change, inclined to go along with traditions, and tends to be interested in analytical "intellectual" thought. He respects established ideas.

The person, who scores high on Factor—Q1, is more well-informed, more inclined to experiment with problem solutions, less inclined to moralize, less unquestioning about views generally, etc. In group dynamics he contributes significantly more remarks to discussion, a high percentage being of a critical nature.

Factor-Q2

(Low Score) Sociably group dependent, a "joiner" and sound follower *vs.* (High Score) Self-sufficient, resourceful, prefers own decisions.

The person, who scores low on Factor—Q2, goes with the group, definitely depends on social approval more and is conventional and fashionable. He is sound follower of the group.

The person, who scores high on Factor—Q2 is significantly more dissatisfied with the group integration, makes remarks, which are more frequently independent solutions than questions, and tends to be rejected.

Factor—Q3

(Low Score) Uncontrolled, lax, follows own urges, careless of social rules *vs.* (High Score) Controlled, exacting will power, socially precise, compulsive, following self-image.

The person, who scores low on Factor—Q3, does not bother about social rules. He follows his own urges. He is negligent. He may feel maladjusted and may show maladjustment.

The person, who scores high on Factor—Q3 shows socially, approved character responses, self-control, persistent, fore-right, considerateness of others, conscientiousness. He makes more remarks in committee than others, especially problem raising and solution-offering comments, receive fewer votes as hinderers, and fewer rejections at the end of the sessions.

Factor—Q4

(Low Score) Relaxed, tranquil, torpid, unfrustrated *vs.* (High Score) Tense, frustrated, driven overwrought, fretful.

The person, who scores low on Factor—Q4, tends to be relaxed, calm and satisfied (not frustrated). In some situations, his over satisfaction can lead to laziness and low performance.

The person, who scores high on Factor—Q4, rarely achieves leadership. Also, he takes a poor view of the degree of group unity, its orderliness, and the quality of the existing leadership. High Q4 is best interpreted as 'id' energy excited in excess of the ego strength capacity to discharge it, and which is therefore misdirected, converted into psychosomatic disturbances, anxiety, etc. and is generally disruptive of steady application and emotional balance.

LIMITATIONS OF THE STUDY

1. The study is limited to Andhra Pradesh, comprising three areas namely, Rayalaseema, Telengana and Coastal.
2. The study is limited to B.Ed. Students alone.
3. The study is limited to following personal and demographic variables.

(i) Gender

(ii) Age

(iii) Caste

(iv) Region

(v) Religion

(vi) Marital Status

(vii) Educational Qualifications

(viii) Methodology

(xi) Father's Occupation

(x) Mother's Occupation

4. There are number of values, but the study is limited to following 9 values.

(i) Social

(ii) Religious

(iii) Economic

(iv) Democratic

(v) Knowledge

(vi) Power

(vii) Hedonistic

(viii) Aesthetic

(ix) Health

METHODS OF INVESTIGATION

This chapter deals with research design, methods employed in the measurement of variables, selection of sample, collection of data, scoring the responses and analysis of data.

THE RESEARCH DESIGN

The research method adopted by the investigator was the descriptive survey method which is very often employed in educational and social sciences research. Tuckman (1978) expressed "a potentially useful technique in education, as it is in public opinion polling and the social sciences, the value of the survey as a means of gathering data is not to be denied."

Moulay (1964) also was of the same opinion that "no category of educational research is more widely used than the survey type. Educational Surveys are particularly versatile and practical in that they identify present conditions and point to present needs. Descriptive surveys are oriented towards the description of the present status of a given phenomenon."

MEASUREMENT OF VARIABLES

The variables investigated in the present study are 47 including both dependent and independent variables. Out of these 47 variables, 11 are personal and demographic variables, for which the information was gathered through a personal data sheet developed by the investigator and the remaining variables were measured with the following suitable instruments:

- Rating Scale to obtain data on attitudes towards values among B.Ed. Students.
- Practices Questionnaire to obtain data on Value Practices among B.Ed. Students.

- 16 Personality Factor Questionnaire to find out personality factors characteristic of B.Ed. Students

Method of Measuring Attitudes towards Values Among B.Ed. Students

The rating scale is most commonly used device. Moulay (1964) stated "the rating scale is best conceived as an instrument, which permits the quantification of observation through the assignment of numerical values to the ratings into a overall index of his status". While selecting the rating scales various rating methods *viz.*, numerical rating, cumulated points, multiple choice method, etc. were carefully examined. Keeping in view the level of the proposed sample the Likert type rating scale was used.

Construction of the Pilot Form

The Likert type rating scale was selected to measure the attitudes towards values. In the present study, the rating scale covered nine dimensions on values *viz.*, Social, Religious, Economic, Democratic, Knowledge, Power, Hedonistic, Aesthetic and Health. To select the items for the rating scale the information was collected from the following sources:

- Scrutiniztion of various instruments already developed in the field.
- Opinions of experienced persons in the field concerned.
- The investigators experience as a lecturer in college of Education.

From all the above resources a total of 81 items were collected which is called 'item pool'. Three experts in the field of educational research were requested to go through the item pool and recommend the items, which can be incorporated in the pilot form. Thus 63 statements were obtained in the pilot form.

The Pilot Study

The rating scale thus obtained of 63 statements belonging to the 9 dimensions of the values is as follows:

- Social value
- Religious value
- Economic value
- Democratic value
- Knowledge value
- Power value
- Hedonistic value
- Aesthetic value
- Health value

The pilot form of rating scale was self-explanatory as all the necessary instructions were clearly given in the beginning of the instrument and administered to 200 B.Ed. Students both male and female selected by random sampling procedure belonging to the urban and rural areas. The scale is self-explanatory and they were given assurance that the data would be used only for research work and would be kept confidential. For the purpose of scoring the numerical weights were assigned in the Table 4.1 to each of the five categories of responses.

Table 4.1 Numerical Weights Given to the Five Alternative Responses Given in Rating Scale

Statement	Strongly Agree	Agree	Undecided	Disagree	Strongly Disagree
Positive	5	4	3	2	1
Negative	1	2	3	4	5

Note: *a* Items 16,18,22,29,39,41,56,60,62 are negative and all the other items are positive (Preliminary/Pilot Form).

b Items 15,16,18,24,32,34,44 are negative and all the other items are positive (Final Form).

Item Analysis

After scoring the ratings of the B.Ed. students as mentioned earlier, item analysis was carried out by the method of internal consistency suggested by Likert (1932). The results thus obtained by this method of criterion of internal consistency agree very well with the results of the traditional method of item analysis, not only that, this method is far less laborious than the latter and is advocated by many investigators like Likert (1932), Murphy and Likert (1937) and Edwards (1969).

This method of item analysis consists of rank ordering the respondents with respect to their total scores on each one of the 9 dimensions and taking high (27%) and low (27%) group on the basis of the total score and calculated the internal consistency of each statement using the following formula:

Internal Consistency of any statement = the difference between the mean scores of the high and low groups on the statement.

The highest scoring 27 per cent and lowest scoring 27 per cent were taken to represent the criterion groups because with this tail proportions the coefficient is more sensitive (Kelly, 1939). The difference between the mean scores of high and low groups on each of the items has tested for significance by applying't' test. The results of item analysis are presented in Table 4. 2. The criterion "those items whose discriminative value or internal consistency was significant at 0.05 level of probability" was employed in selecting the items for the final form. Thus a total of 45 items were selected for the final form including 5 items under each dimension.

Reliability of Attitude Scale

Split-half method was used to find the Reliability of the scale. The scores on the odd and even numbered items were correlated using Pearson's formula for Product Moment Correlation. This gave the reliability of the half-test. The Reliability of the half-test is 0.76. This was corrected for full length of the test by Spearman-Brown Prophecy formula. The 'R' then obtained was 0.88 for the final instrument.

Table 4.2 Results of Item Analysis of the Rating Scale to Measure Attitudes towards Values of B.Ed. Students

Item No.	High Rating Group		Low Rating Group		Mean Difference	t-values
	Mean	SD^2	Mean	SD^2		
1.	4.34	0.51	4.01	0.58	0.33	3.16
2.	4.53	0.50	4.20	0.55	0.33	3.21
3.	4.30	0.65	3.67	1.43	0.63	4.36
4.	3.59	1.20	2.91	1.94	0.68	3.83
5.	4.25	1.05	3.41	2.09	0.84	4.74
6.	4.60	0.69	3.13	1.93	1.47	9.08
7.	4.93	1.22	4.08	1.96	0.81	4.76
8.	4.25	1.00	3.81	1.26	0.44	2.93
9.	3.15	2.20	2.30	1.64	0.85	4.87
10.	4.35	0.75	2.79	1.95	1.56	9.33
11.	4.59	1.04	3.95	1.84	0.64	3.76
12.	4.02	2.88	3.70	1.16	0.32	1.59 @
13.	4.89	0.50	4.38	0.90	0.51	4.28
14.	3.05	1.80	2.47	1.95	0.58	2.99
15.	4.55	0.60	3.36	2.33	1.19	6.95
16.	3.45	1.30	2.57	1.20	0.88	5.57
17.	3.44	1.72	3.24	1.60	0.20	1.12 @
18.	4.37	1.71	3.84	0.49	0.53	3.57
19.	5.00	0.37	4.30	1.31	0.70	5.40
20.	3.75	1.70	3.62	1.42	0.13	0.85 @
21.	2.25	1.60	2.11	1.64	0.14	1.78 @
22.	3.30	1.25	2.72	2.04	0.58	3.20
23.	4.25	0.60	3.89	0.95	0.36	2.92
24.	4.25	1.91	3.56	0.93	0.69	4.10

Contd...

Item No.	High Rating Group		Low Rating Group		Mean Difference	t-values
	Mean	SD^2	Mean	SD^2		
25.	3.01	1.95	2.76	1.85	0.25	1.28 @
26.	2.70	1.60	2.09	1.67	0.61	3.37
27.	2.90	2.00	2.49	1.56	0.41	2.96
28.	3.85	0.29	3.45	0.90	0.40	3.50
29.	4.80	0.82	4.47	0.42	0.33	2.97
30.	4.82	1.28	4.19	0.71	0.53	4.47
31.	4.75	0.75	4.23	1.45	0.52	4.28
32.	5.00	1.15	4.36	1.75	0.64	3.76
33.	2.20	1.50	2.06	1.74	0.14	0.77 @
34.	4.30	1.00	3.69	1.99	0.61	3.53
35.	4.33	0.75	2.77	1.95	1.56	9.49
36.	3.15	2.25	2.30	1.55	0.85	4.84
37.	2.01	1.50	1.76	2.30	0.25	1.28 @
38.	4.00	1.00	3.56	1.60	0.44	2.93
39.	3.95	1.30	3.10	1.88	0.85	4.76
40.	4.50	1.00	3.05	1.62	0.45	9.09
41.	3.85	1.45	3.18	1.97	0.67	3.59
42.	4.25	0.60	3.80	1.05	0.45	3.50
43.	4.20	1.10	3.35	2.04	0.85	4.75
44.	4.25	0.70	3.62	1.38	0.63	4.36
45.	3.57	1.20	2.89	1.94	0.68	3.83
46.	2.20	1.50	2.06	1.72	0.14	0.77 @
47.	3.56	1.65	3.41	1.47	0.15	0.85 @
48.	3.65	1.30	3.03	1.44	0.62	3.74
49.	3.05	1.86	2.80	1.94	0.25	1.28 @
50.	3.80	1.35	3.50	1.54	0.30	1.75 @
51.	4.46	0.50	3.90	1.10	0.56	4.42
52.	3.64	1.69	3.15	2.14	0.49	2.51
53.	3.84	1.49	3.17	1.19	0.67	3.59
54.	4.00	1.95	3.74	1.85	0.26	1.28 @
55.	3.25	1.33	2.63	1.41	0.62	3.74
56.	4.53	0.96	3.59	2.12	0.94	5.36

Contd...

57.	3.80	1.46	3.13	2.02	0.67	3.58
58.	4.00	1.00	3.70	1.92	0.30	1.76 @
59.	4.75	0.44	4.56	0.74	0.19	1.76 @
60.	3.25	2.16	3.18	1.68	0.07	0.35 @
61.	3.44	1.70	3.24	1.60	0.44	1.10 @
62.	1.69	1.13	1.50	0.71	0.19	1.39 @
63.	2.16	1.53	2.12	1.00	0.04	0.25 @

Note: @ indicates an item for which 't' is not significant at 0.05 level. Items thus marked @ were eliminated and remaining 45 items were taken for final study.

Validity of Attitude Scale

The validity refers to the accuracy of the measures provided by the test. According to Garrett (1967) "The validity of a test or any measuring instrument depends upon the fidelity with which it measures what it purports to measure". The following types of validity were established for the rating scale developed for B.Ed. students' attitudes towards values on different dimensions viz., Social, Religious, Economic, Democratic, Knowledge, Power, Hedonistic, Aesthetic and Health.

Content Validity: The content Validity is determined by finding out how well the test content represents the subject matter and situations upon which the test is supposed to be based. In this study, equal consideration was given to all the dimensions of the values while selecting the items for the rating scale. In order to cover all the possible characteristics, the items were collected from large number of B.Ed. students. To the relevant items thus collected, the investigator conceived to be essential added a few more.

Thus the list (content/the items of the test) prepared was submitted to a group of subject matter experts, *viz.*, educationists, psychologists etc. for the selection of most important items for the finalization of the list. After obtaining the comments of the judges and on the basis of their ratings, necessary modifications were made by removing some ambiguous items and replacement of appropriate meaningful words, etc. also done accordingly. So, good care was taken in wording the statements and avoiding the duplication and overlapping. Thus it can be reasonably arranged that the rating scale have content validity.

Intrinsic Validity: Guilford (1954) defined intrinsic validity as 'the degree to which a test measures what it measures'. This also be stated in terms of how well the obtained scores measure the test's true score component. This validity is given by the square root of the proportion of true variance, i.e., square root of its reliability. The intrinsic validity of the rating scale in the present study is therefore $\sqrt{0.88} = 0.94$.

Method of Measuring Value Practices Among B.Ed. Students

To measure value practices a Questionnaire was prepared. Questionnaire is a general device and it can be used for collecting all kinds of information. It is used generally when factual information is desired. Questionnaire can be of closed form type or open form type. Questionnaires that call for short, check mark responses are the restricted or closed type. The open form also called unrestricted questionnaire. Keeping view the proposed sample the closed type of questionnaire was used.

Construction of the Pilot Form

A Questionnaire schedule of 'Yes or No' was selected to measure the Value Practices. In the present study, the Questionnaire Schedule covered nine dimensions on values *viz.*, Social, Religious, Economic, Democratic, Knowledge, Power, Hedonistic, Aesthetic and Health. To select the items for the Questionnaire Schedule the information was collected from the following sources

- Scrutinization of various instruments already developed in the field.
- Opinions of experienced persons in the field concerned.
- The investigators experience as a lecturer in college of Education.

From all the above resources a total of 81 items were collected which is called 'item pool'. Three experts in the field of educational research were requested to go through the item pool and recommend the items, which can be incorporated in the pilot form. Thus 63 statements were obtained in the pilot form.

The Pilot Study

The questionnaire schedule thus obtained of 63 questions belonging to the 9 dimensions of the values is as follows:

- Social value
- Religious value
- Economic value
- Democratic value
- Knowledge value
- Power value
- Hedonistic value
- Aesthetic value
- Health value

The pilot form of Questionnaire Schedule was self-explanatory as all the necessary instructions were clearly given in the beginning of the instrument and administered to 200 B.Ed. Students both male and female selected by random sampling procedure belonging to the urban and rural areas. The scale is self-explanatory and they were given assurance that the data would be used only for research work and would be kept confidential. For the purpose of scoring the numerical weights were assigned in the Table 4.3 for the two categories of responses.

Table 4.3 Numerical Weights Given to the Two Alternative Responses Given in the Questionnaire Schedule

Statement	Yes	No
Positive	2	1
Negative	1	2

Note: *a* Items 2, 21, 29, 40, 49, 57 are negative and all the other items are positive (Preliminary/Pilot Form).

b Items 2, 24, 33, 45 are negative and all the other items are positive (Final Form).

Item Analysis

It is carried out to establish the item validity. The two common values associated with the process of item analysis are the discrimination value and difficulty value. These values are calculated by considering criterion groups *viz.,* top 27 per cent scorers and bottom 27 per cent scorers. Discrimination refers how well a particular item discriminate between students who do well on the overall test and those who do poorly. One procedure to determine discrimination is to divide the subjects into high scorers (top 27%) and low scorers (bottom 27%) on the test Then the number of students in the high and low groups answered a particular item is found out. An item is judged to have good discrimination if more students from the high score group answered correctly than the students from the low score group. If the reverse happens, the item is said to be of poor discrimination value. Thus, discrimination index (D.I.) of the instrument was established.

Item Difficulty is the average percentage of subjects correctly answered the item among both top and bottom groups. Of course, this is applicable only to achievement and ability tests.

The results of the discrimination index are presented in Table 4.4. Items whose discrimination value is 0.1 and above were found appropriate to be included in the final form. Thus, a total of 45 items were retained for the final form including 5 items under each dimension.

Table 4.4 Discrimination Values of Different Items in the Pilot Form

Item No.	Mean (Top Group)	Mean (Bottom Group)	Discrimination Index	Remarks
1.	1.97	1.87	0.10	Retained
2.	2.00	1.90	0.10	Retained
3.	1.93	1.70	0.23	Retained
4.	1.97	1.80	0.17	Retained
5.	1.96	1.80	0.16	Retained
6.	1.97	1.67	0.30	Retained
7.	1.78	1.60	0.18	Retained
8.	1.96	1.16	0.80	Retained
9.	1.97	1.20	0.77	Retained
10.	1.97	1.40	0.57	Retained
11.	1.67	1.50	0.17	Retained
12.	2.00	1.96	0.04	Deleted
13.	2.00	1.87	0.13	Retained
14.	1.93	1.57	0.36	Retained
15.	1.67	1.57	0.10	Retained
16.	1.78	1.53	0.25	Retained
17.	1.56	1.60	-0.04	Deleted
18.	2.00	1.80	0.20	Retained
19.	2.00	1.83	0.17	Retained
20.	2.00	1.93	0.07	Deleted
21.	1.96	1.96	0.00	Deleted
22.	1.87	1.73	0.14	Retained
23.	1.90	1.50	0.40	Retained
24.	1.96	1.60	0.36	Retained
25.	1.66	1.62	0.04	Deleted
26.	1.96	1.63	0.33	Retained
27.	1.73	1.47	0.26	Retained
28.	1.80	1.56	0.24	Retained
29.	1.73	1.46	0.27	Retained
30.	1.74	1.47	0.27	Retained

Contd...

Item No.	Mean (Top Group)	Mean (Bottom Group)	Discrimination Index	Remarks
31.	1.80	1.67	0.13	Retained
32.	1.93	1.67	0.26	Retained
33.	1.47	1.63	-0.24	Deleted
34.	1.76	1.66	0.10	Retained
35.	1.77	1.67	0.10	Retained
36.	1.96	1.76	0.20	Retained
37.	1.97	1.93	0.04	Deleted
38.	2.00	1.60	0.40	Retained
39.	2.00	1.70	0.30	Retained
40.	1.87	1.70	0.17	Retained
41.	1.83	1.70	0.13	Retained
42.	1.97	1.70	0.27	Retained
43.	1.97	1.50	0.47	Retained
44.	1.80	1.50	0.30	Retained
45.	2.00	1.90	0.10	Retained
46.	1.96	1.93	0.03	Deleted
47.	1.73	1.90	-0.17	Deleted
48.	2.00	1.74	0.26	Retained
49.	1.97	1.97	0.00	Deleted
50.	2.00	1.93	0.07	Deleted
51.	1.83	1.73	0.10	Retained
52.	1.77	1.67	0.10	Retained
53.	1.76	1.60	0.16	Retained
54.	2.00	1.99	0.01	Deleted
55.	1.80	1.33	0.47	Retained
56.	1.53	1.36	0.17	Retained
57.	1.93	1.83	0.10	Retained
58.	1.89	1.80	0.09	Deleted
59.	1.80	1.78	0.02	Deleted
60.	1.80	1.90	-0.10	Deleted
61.	1.90	1.91	-0.01	Deleted
62.	1.20	1.30	-0.10	Deleted
63.	1.50	1.60	-0.10	Deleted

Reliability of Questionnaire

Split-half method was used to find the Reliability of the Questionnaire. The scores on the odd and even numbered items were correlated using Pearson's formula for Product Moment Coefficient of Correlation between the odd items and even items was 0.925. It was significant at 0.01 level of probability.

Validity of Questionnaire

The validity refers to the accuracy of the measures provide by the test. According to Garrett (1967) "The validity of a test or any measuring instrument depends upon the fidelity with which it measures what it purports to measure". The following types of validity were established for the rating scale developed for B.Ed. students' attitudes towards values on different dimensions *viz.*, Social, Religious, Economic, Democratic, Knowledge, Power, Hedonistic, Aesthetic and Health.

Content Validity: The Validity of the test was constructed by the experts' judgements. The content (on the items of the test) was submitted to a group of subject matter experts, *viz.*, educationists, psychologists etc. These experts were requested to judge whether the items represent the area in which the investigation is being done or not. They were also asked to add any relevant items and delete the irrelevant. After obtaining the comments of the judges and on the basis of their ratings, necessary modifications were made by removing some ambiguous items and replacement of appropriate meaningful words, etc. also done accordingly. Therefore it may be reasonably assumed that the instrument has content validity.

Intrinsic Validity: It can be stated in terms of how well the obtained scores measure the test's true score component. This validity is given by the square root of the proportion of true variance, *i.e.*, square root of its reliability. The intrinsic validity of the rating scale in the present study is therefore $\sqrt{0.925} = 0.962$ (reveals that the instrument is valid).

Sixteen Personality Factor Questionnaire

According to Cattell (1950), "Personality is that which permits a prediction of what a person will do in a given situation". His theory is based on personality sphere concept (Cattell, 1946, 1957, 1964) — a design to ensure initial item coverage for all the behaviour that commonly enters rating. It focuses heavily on 'source traits'. Cattell defines source trait as the spring of human behaviour. Much is becoming known about the nature of these dimensions through studies with ratings, with laboratory measures and with life situations.

According to Cattell, a trait of any variety is a mental structure, which is relatively fixed characteristic of the individual functioning from time to time in behaviour.

Selection of Tool and Its Uses

Research regarding personality studies was done by number of people in India and also abroad. The tool used by most of them was Cattell's 16 Personality Factor test and the study of the same was supported by Stern (1921), Allport (1937) and Vernon (1963).

Stern observes, "We have the right and obligation to develop a concept of trait as definite doctrine, for in all activities of the person, there is besides a variable portion, likewise, a constant purposive portion and this later we isolate as the concept of trait".

Allport's contention was equally forceful. He asserts "Traits are discovered not by deductive reasoning, not by faith, not by naming and are themselves never directly observed. They are discovered only through an inference made necessary by the demonstrable consistency of the separate observable acts of behaviour".

Vernon says that "a person's behaviour in any situation depends, of course on specific features of that situation and on his temporary feelings or state of mind, but it depends also on his more enduring characteristics—abilities/habits/and more general dispositions which be called traits".

Cattell (1962) says that the source traits, as measured by the 16 P F test are the spring of human behaviour. His definition of personality as given earlier is consistent and in the view of Mary and Hillex (1973) that "the theory of Personality is really identical with general theory of behaviour" for Cattell definition would fit the theories of behaviour.

In view of the above theoretical as well as practical consideration Cattell's16 P F Q was selected and it is objectively acceptable test devised by basic research in Psychology to give the most complete coverage of personality possible in a brief time. Coverage of Personality is ensured by the 16 functionally individual and psychologically meaningful dimensions isolated by over 20 years of factor analytical research on normal and clinical groups. Therefore, having a certain position on one factor does not prevent the person having some other position, whatever on any other.

The experience with the 16 P F Q in clinical, educational and industrial psychology shows that the use of 16 traits gives actual prediction. In view of the above theoretical as well as practical considerations and as Cattell's 16 P F Q was a cultural fair test, this tool was selected to be used in the study.

Adoption of the Instrument

16 Personality Factor Questionnaire (PFQ) Form C was adopted for the present investigation. The Telugu version was adopted for the present study prepared by C. Manchala, Department of Education, S.V. University, Tirupati. The 16 P. F. Q, as its name implies provides a multidimensional measurement of personality through normative scores on 16 bipolar factors.

Reliability and Validity of 16PF Form—C

The Measures of Reliability Coefficients and Validity for the 16 P.F. were as follows:

Factor	Reliability	Validity	Factor	Reliability	Validity
A	0.675	0.822	L	0.596	0.772
B	0.709	0.842	M	0.679	0.824
C	0.593	0.770	N	0.718	0.847
E	0.713	0.844	O	0.693	0.832
F	0.792	0.890	Q1	0.636	0.797
G	0.677	0.823	Q2	0.591	0.769
H	0.721	0.849	Q3	0.739	0.860
I	0.734	0.857	Q4	0.699	0.836

PERSONAL DATA SHEET

The personal data sheet was carefully designed and the information regarding personal and demographic variables included in the study was obtained.

SELECTION OF THE SAMPLE

The state of Andhra Pradesh consists of 3 regions namely Rayalaseema, Telengana and Coastal Regions. All the three regions were included in the study. Out of the different B.Ed. Colleges existing in the regions, a sample of three colleges was randomly chosen. All the B.Ed. students studying in the respective colleges were included in the sample. Thus, the sample of the study consisted of 960 B.Ed. Students.

COLLECTION OF DATA

The instruments *viz.,* Rating Scale to measure B.Ed. Student's Attitudes towards Values, Questionnaire to measure Value Practices of B.Ed. Students, 16 P.F.Q. and the personal data sheet were administered to the 960 B.Ed. Students individually after establishing proper rapport with them. The B.Ed. students were explained, the purpose and significance of the study and the method in which they had to answer the different items under different instruments or tools used in the study. Sufficient time was given to them to respond to the items. Sufficient care was taken to see that the respondents answered all the items in all the data gathering tools.

SCORING

The rating scale to measure the B.Ed. students' attitudes towards values (which was on 5-point scale) in nine dimensions of values was scored by assigning numerical weights to each of the responses as explained earlier. The total scores of each dimension and the grand total on the instrument were obtained by simple addition.

The 2-point questionnaire to measure B.Ed. students value practices in nine dimensions of values were scored by assigning numerical weights to each response as explained earlier. The total scores of each dimension and the grand total on the instrument were obtained by simple addition.

Cattell's 16 P.F. Questionnaire was scored as per the weight ages provided by Cattell and others. The factor totals were obtained by adding the scores on the items in each factor. The data against personal and demographic variables were also coded suitable to computer analysis.

ANALYSIS OF THE DATA

The data collected thus was analyzed by using relevant statistical techniques like descriptive statistical measures, 't'-test, ANOVA (F-ratio) to find out whether differences in the independent variables accounted for significant differences in the dependent variables. Multiple correlation coefficient 'R' was calculated by carrying out Multiple Regression Analysis to find out whether it was possible to predict the two dependent variables viz., Attitudes towards Values and Value Practices with the help of the independent variables. The usual levels of significance *viz.*, 0.05 and 0.01 were employed to test the significance of the values obtained. The obtained results were also represented graphically wherever necessary. The results obtained are discussed in the following chapter.

ANALYSIS AND INTERPRETATION OF THE DATA

The data collected were analyzed and the findings obtained were interpreted to realize the objectives and answer the questions raised through testing the hypothesis. The analysis of the study is presented under the following headings:

- Deals with description of dependent variables *viz.,* Attitudes towards Values and Practices of Values and comparison between the Attitudes and Practices scores of different values of B.Ed. Students.
- Discloses relationship between personal and demographic variables and different values in B.Ed. Students.
- Explain the personality factors of the sample population and the relation between the Personality factors and Attitudes towards values and Practices of values of B.Ed. Students.
- Illustrates the prediction of Attitudes towards values and Practices of values of B.Ed. Students through Multiple Regression Analysis.

SECTION — I

DESCRIPTION OF DEPENDENT VARIABLES

The two variables considered as dependent variables in investigation are:

1. Attitudes towards values; and
2. Practices of values of B.Ed. Students.

Description of the Distribution of Scores of Attitudes Towards Values

As explained earlier there were 9 different values and in each value there were 5 items for which the scoring pattern ranges from 1 to 5 for alternative responses. The total scores on the entire scale of each subject and for each value are computed. All the descriptive statistics viz., Mean, Median, Mode, Quartile Deviation (Q.D.), Standard Deviation (S.D.), Skewness and Kurtosis were calculated for each value and as well as for the total attitudes towards values.

The frequency distribution of total scores regarding the attitudes towards values along with the descriptive statistics is presented in the table 5.1.

Table 5.1 The Distribution of Scores of Overall Attitudes Towards Values of B.Ed. Students

Class Interval	Mid Values	Frequency	Cumulative Frequency
286-300	293.50	4	4
301-315	308.50	7	11
316-330	323.50	21	32
331-345	338.50	59	91
346-360	353.50	147	238
361-375	368.50	188	426
376-390	383.50	248	674
391-405	398.50	175	849
406-420	413.50	88	937
421-435	428.50	19	956
436-450	443.50	4	960

Mean = 377.279
Median = 380.000
Mode = 388.000
Range = 152.000

Quartile Deviation (Q.D.) = 16.000
Standard Deviation (S.D.) = 23.960
Skewness = -0.370
Kurtosis = 0.232

In general it is evident that the B.Ed. Students have high attitudes about different values they possess. The overall mean scores of attitudes towards values was 377 (the lowest and highest possible scores on the scale being 288 and 440 respectively) and by looking at the mean and standard deviation score it is evident that the scores were stable and consistent.

Even by the observation at the other measures of central tendency, it was clear that the B.Ed. Students possess positive and high attitudes about various values and the distribution of the scores of total attitudes towards values was slightly deviated from the symmetry.

With regard to the nature of the distribution of overall attitudes towards values it can be said that the distribution was negatively skewed to a little extent and there exists a little bit of kurtosis too. By verifying the empirical relationship between Standard Deviation and Quartile Deviation (Q.D. = 2/3

S.D.) it was evident that the distribution of overall attitude scores was slightly divergent from the normal distribution.

An observation into the frequencies disclosed that the distribution followed normality with little divergences. The frequency polygon shown in Figure 5.1 indicates that the distribution was negatively skewed to a little extent.

Even though there was slight divergency in the distribution of overall attitude scores, they can be assumed as normal and employed all parametric statistical techniques for further statistical analysis.

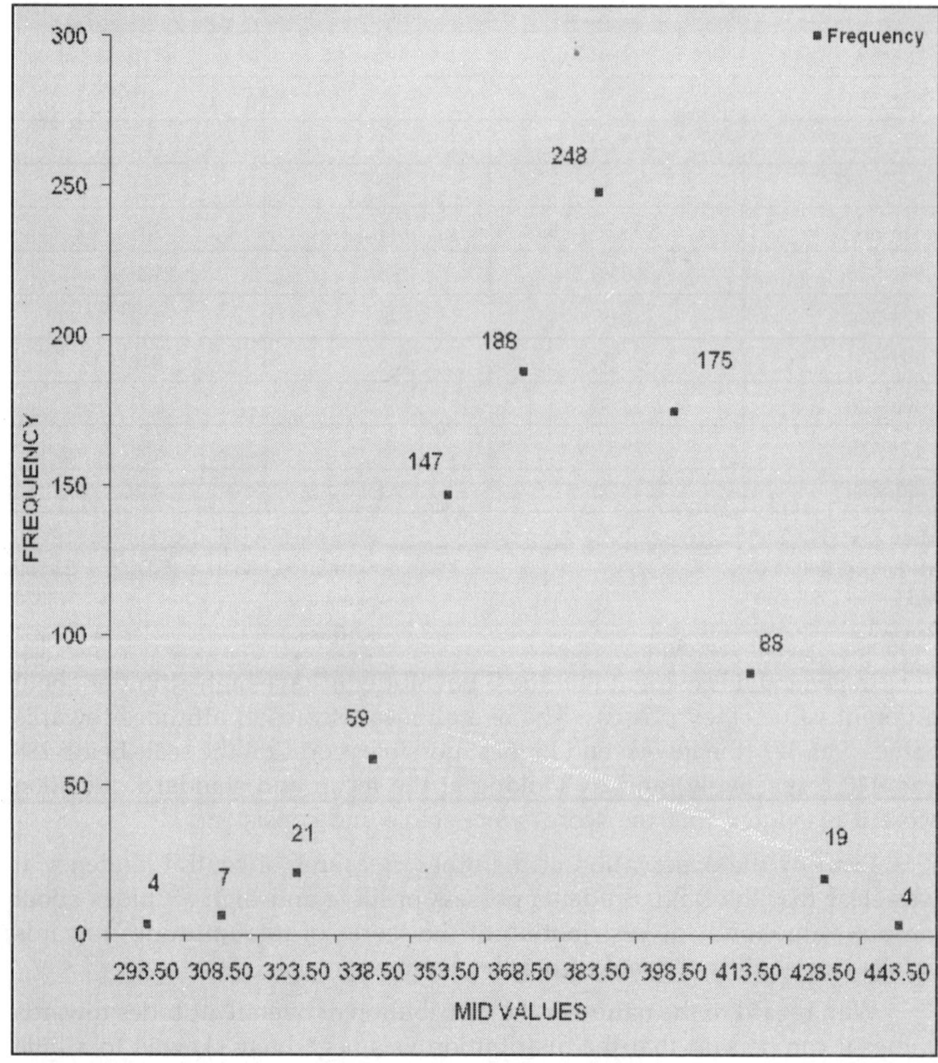

Figure 5.1 **Frequency Polygon Showing the Distribution of Scores of Overall Attitudes Towards Values of B.Ed. Students**

It would be interesting to observe various descriptive statistics for each value to see whether the B.Ed. Students attitudes about various values would be different. Table 5.6 shows the descriptive statistics of the nine values.

Table 5.2 The Mean, Median, Mode, Q.D., S.D., Skewness and Kurtosis of the Distribution of Scores of Different Attitudes Towards Values of The B.Ed. Students

Sl. No.	Values	Mean	Median	Mode	Q.D.	S.D.	Skewness	Kurtosis
1.	Social	43.250	42.000	42.000	3.250	4.595	-0.531	0.327
2.	Religious	34.575	34.000	34.000	5.000	7.038	-0.352	-0.075
3.	Economic	39.085	40.000	40.000	5.000	6.469	-0.562	0.197
4.	Democratic	44.283	44.000	50.000	3.000	5.049	-0.814	0.731
5.	Knowledge	44.088	44.000	50.000	4.000	4.696	-0.567	-0.182
6.	Power	38.969	40.000	42.000	5.000	6.998	-0.822	0.800
7.	Hedonistic	44.027	44.000	46.000	3.000	4.696	-0.714	0.032
8.	Aesthetic	42.275	44.000	46.000	3.000	5.507	-1.089	1.488
9.	Health	46.727	48.000	48.000	3.000	4.303	-1.506	2.080
10.	**Total Attitudes towards Value**	**377.254**	**380.000**	**388.000**	**16.000**	**23.960**	**-0.370**	**0.232**

It would be interesting to observe various descriptive statistics for each value to see whether the B.Ed. Students attitudes about various values would be different. Table 5.2 shows the descriptive statistics of the nine values.

An observation into the table reveals that, in general, the attitudes of B.Ed. Students were very high on all the values, although there were variations. The three measures of central tendency, Q.D., S.D., Skewness and Kurtosis disclosed that there were slight divergences from the normality in these distributions too.

The first and foremost important value as perceived by the B.Ed. Students where the attitudes were high was the Health value. The next three values Democratic Value, Knowledge Value and Hedonistic Value were more or less equally perceived. The fifth place is for Social Value and the next place goes to Aesthetic Value. The last but one place goes to Power Value and the last place regarding the forming of attitudes is the Religious value. So it can be said that the attitudes towards values of B.Ed. Students towards different values would be different. Hence the hypotheses "the attitudes towards various values to be formed by B.Ed. Students would not be different was not accepted."

Description of the Distribution of Scores of Value Practices

As is the case of attitudes towards values, the same nine values with same number of items (5) having two alternative responses were taken for the study and total scores on the entire scale of each subject and for each value were computed. All the descriptive statistics were calculated for each value as well as for the total value practices as in the case of attitudes towards values. The frequency distribution for total value practice scores along with the descriptive statistics was presented in Table 5.3.

Table 5.3 The Distribution of Overall Scores of Value Practices of the B.Ed. Students

Class Interval	Mid Values	Frequency	Cumulative Freuency
281 – 295	286.50	7	7
296 – 310	303.50	23	30
311 – 325	318.50	79	109
326 – 340	333.50	129	238
341 – 355	348.50	151	389
356 – 370	363.50	185	574
371 – 385	378.50	170	744
386 – 400	393.50	123	867
401 – 415	408.50	70	937
416 – 430	423.50	17	954
431 – 445	438.50	6	960

Mean = 364.547
Median = 365.000
Mode = 360.000
Range = 155.000

Quartile Deviation (Q.D.) = 20.000
Standard Deviation (S.D.) = 29.245
Skewness = - 0.058
Kurtosis = -0.587

It is quite natural that even though the B.Ed. Students have high attitudes regarding different values, they may not practice as per their attitudes. Table 5.3 in comparison with the Table 5.3 shows lower practice of B.Ed. students regarding values. It is evident form the fact that practices mean score was 364.547 and from the observation of other measures of central tendency it was clear that the practice of various values of the B.Ed. Students was high but not as high when compared to the scores of the attitudes of B.Ed. students.

The distribution of the total practice scores was also slightly disturbed from the symmetry. It can also be said that the distribution was negatively skewed to a little extent and there exists a little of kurtosis too. It was a little bit platykurtic. An examination into the empirical relationship between S.D. and Q.D. (2/3S.D. = Q.D. or P.E.) it was evident that the distribution was more divergent from the normal distribution in comparison with the attitudes of B.Ed. Students.

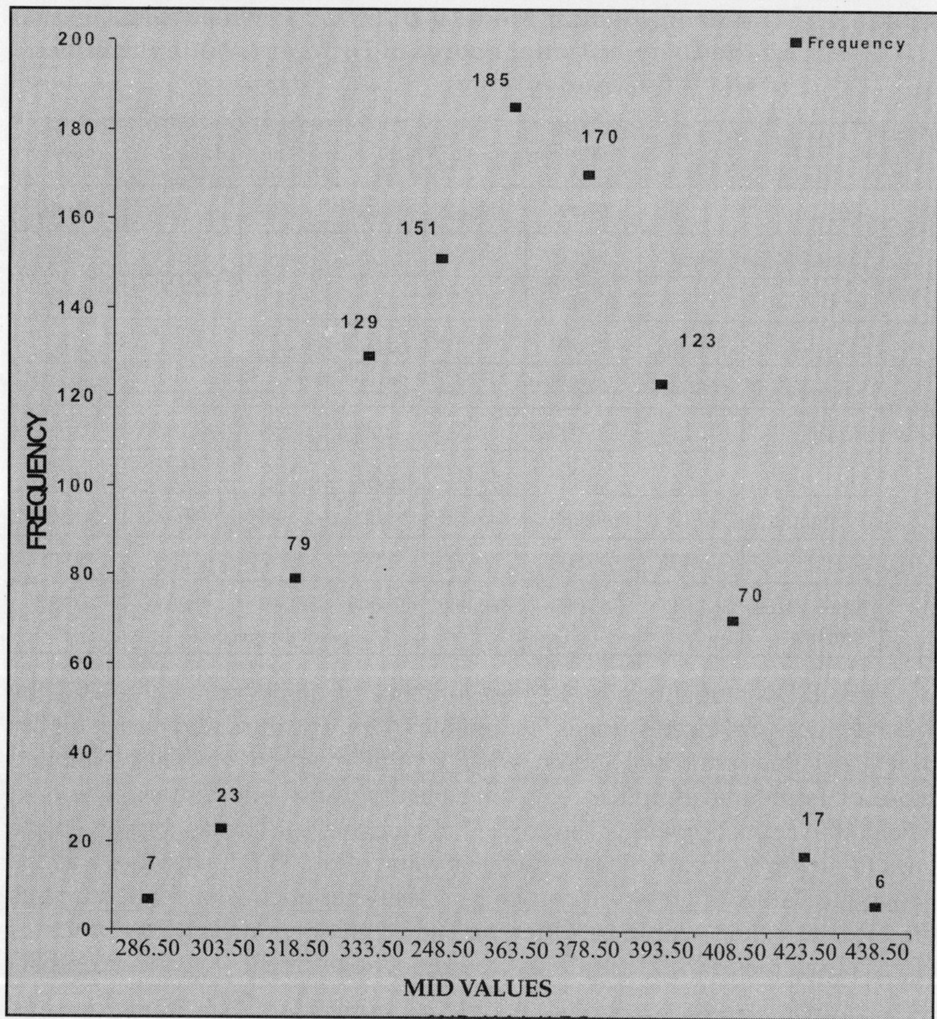

Figure 5.2 **Frequency Polygon Showing the Distribution of Scores of Overall Value Practices of B.Ed. Students**

An observation into the frequency disclosed that the distribution followed normally with little divergences. The frequency polygon shows in Figure 5.2 also indicated that the distribution was negatively skewed to a little extent.

Inspite of the slight divergency in the distribution of overall value practices scores, they can be assumed as normal and employed all parametric statistical techniques for further statistical analysis and presented in the Table 5.4.

Table 5.4 reveals that the Practices of B.Eds regarding various values was less than attitudes although there were variations. The scores of Mean, Median, Mode and the scores of Q.D., S.D., Skewness and Kurtosis disclosed that there were slight divergences from the normality in these distributions too.

Table 5.4 The Mean, Median, Mode, Q.D., S.D., Skewness and Kurtosis of the Distributionof Scores of Different Value Practices of the B.Ed. Students

Sl. No.	Values	Mean	Median	Mode	Q.D	S.D	Skewness	Kurtosis
1.	Social	42.498	45.000	45.000	5.000	6.996	-0.830	0.046
2.	Religious	39.641	40.000	40.000	5.000	6.344	-0.285	-0.529
3.	Economic	35.578	35.000	35.000	5.000	6.115	0.272	-0.529
4.	Democratic	44.026	45.000	50.000	5.000	6.250	-0.973	0.200
5.	Knowledge	41.651	45.000	45.000	5.000	7.282	-0.675	-0.491
6.	Power	37.135	35.000	35.000	5.000	6.856	-0.107	-0.585
7.	Hedonistic	43.177	45.000	45.000	2.500	5.673	-0.784	0.212
8.	Aesthetic	40.135	40.000	45.000	5.000	6.876	-0.522	-0.546
9.	Health	40.495	40.000	50.000	5.000	7.367	-0.228	-1.101
10.	**Total Value Practices**	**364.547**	**365.000**	**360.000**	**20.000**	**29.245**	**-0.058**	**-0.587**

The B.Ed. students possess high practice of democratic value and the second highly practiced value is Hedonistic value. The third and fourth highly practiced values are Social and knowledge values respectively. They exhibited more or less equal practice regarding Health, Aesthetic Values. The next level in their practice was given to the Religious value. The last but one place goes to Power value, the least practiced value by the B.Ed. students was the Economic Value. Therefore it can be said that the practice of B.Ed. students on different values would be different. Hence, the hypothesis "The practices of various values of B.Ed. Students would not be different was not accepted".

Comparison Between Attitudes Towards Values and Value Practice Scores of Different Values of B.Ed. Students

The table 5.5 and 5.7 revealed that there was a gap between the overall Attitudes towards Values and Practices of Values of the B.Ed. Students. It was also proved in the case of different attitudes towards values and their practices by an observation into tables 5.2 and 5.4. To test the significance of this statement the 't'-test was employed and presented in the table 5.5.

The mean scores and standard deviation scores of the Table 5.9 shows that there was much difference between the attitudes towards values and the practices of values. The 't'-values also revealed that the gap was significant even at 0.01 level of probability. Therefore, the hypothesis "There is no gap between the attitudes towards values and value practices of B.Ed. Students for each of the values studied is not accepted".

Table 5.5 Means and S.D.s of the Total Individual Attitudes Towards Values and Value Practices by the B.Ed. Students and the 'T'-values

Values	Attitude Scores		Practice Scores		'T'-test
	Mean	S.D.	Mean	S.D.	
Social Value	43.250	4.595	42.498	6.996	2.785 **
Religious Value	34.575	7.038	39.641	6.344	16.502 **
Economic Value	39.085	6.469	35.578	6.115	12.177 **
Democratic Value	44.283	5.049	44.026	6.250	0.985 @
Knowledge Value	44.088	4.696	41.651	7.282	8.735 **
Power Value	38.969	6.998	37.135	6.856	5.767 **
Hedonistic Value	44.027	4.696	43.177	5.673	3.557 **
Aesthetic Value	42.275	5.507	40.135	6.876	7.509 **
Health Value	46.727	4.303	40.495	7.367	22.580 **
Total	**377.279**	**23.960**	**364.547**	**29.245**	**10.436 ****

@ not significant at 0.05 level
* significant at 0.05 level
** significant at 0.01 level

The comparison between the individual mean scores and standard deviations of different attitudes towards values and value practices exhibited that even though there is a gap between B.Ed. Students attitudes towards values and value practices their order of high attitudes towards values and their practices regarding various values was different. But it is found from the above table 5.5 that t-test values show that there is significant difference between attitudes and practices of all values, except for Democratic Value.

The t-test indicate that for all the values *viz.*, Social (2.785), Religious (16.502), Economic (12.177), Knowledge (8.735), Power (5.767), Hedonistic (3.557), Aesthetic (7.509) and Health (22.580) there is significant difference between attitudes and practices of values at 0.01 level.

Also the total score (10.436) indicates that there is significant difference between attitudes and practices of values at 0.01 level. The t-test indicates that for democratic value there is no significant difference between attitudes and practices even at 0.05 level.

The value, which has highest attitude (46.727), is the health value and it is placed fifth regarding practice (40.495). The second higher value regarding attitude (44.283) is democratic value and that is the most practiced (44.026) value. The third value regarding attitude (44.088) is knowledge, but it is placed fourth regarding the practice (41.651).

The fourth and fifth place goes to Hedonistic (44.027) and Social (43.250) values regarding attitudes and they are placed second (43.177) and third (42.498) respectively regarding practice. The sixth place goes to Aesthetic value regarding both attitudes (42.275) and practices (40.135).

The next successive value, which has high attitude (39.085) is the Economic value but this is the least practiced (35.578) value. The eighth place goes to Power value regarding attitudes (38.969) and practices (37.135). The value, which has lowest attitude (34.575), is the Religious value and it is placed seventh regarding practice (39.641).

The means of individual attitudes towards values and value practices of B.Ed. Students are diagrammatically shown in Figure 5.3.

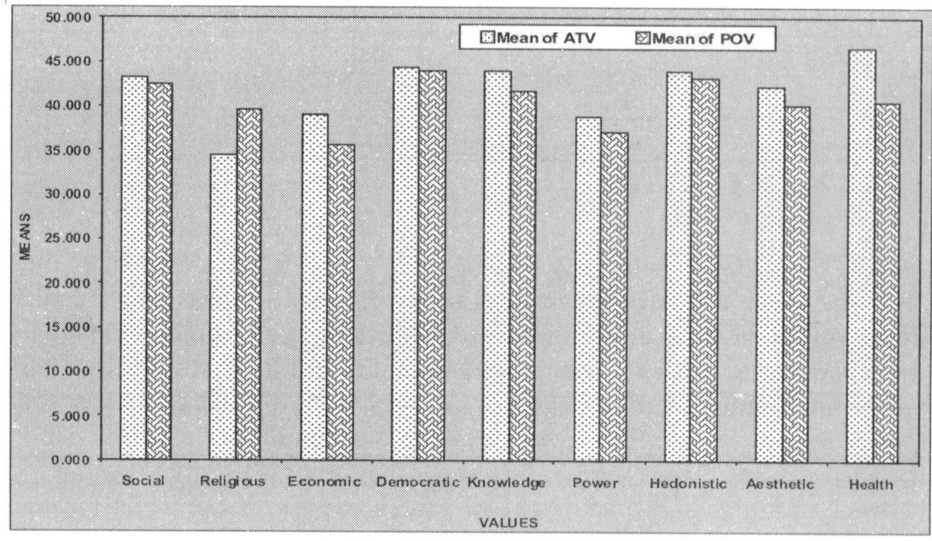

Figure 5.3 **Histogram Showing the Means of Overall Attitudes towardsValues and Values Practices of B.Ed. Students**

The total mean attitude score is 377.28 greater than mean practice score, 364.55 which indicates that the B.Ed. students possess high attitudes towards values but low in practicing the values. The diagrammatic representation is shown in Figure 5.4.

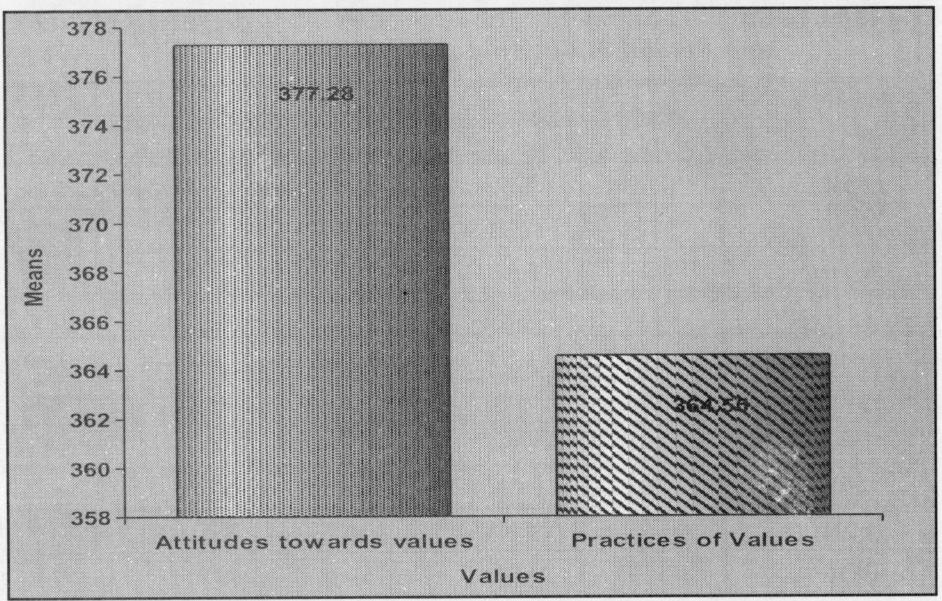

Figure 5.4 **Histogram Showing the Individual Attitudes Towards Values and Value Practices of B.Ed Students**

SECTION – II

THE RELATIONSHIP BETWEEN PERSONAL AND DEMOGRAPHIC VARIABLES AND DIFFERENT VALUES OF B.ED. STUDENTS

As explained earlier the personal and demographic variables included in the study *viz.*, gender, age, caste, region religion, marital status, methodology, educational qualifications nativity, father's occupation, mother's occupation were considered for analyzing how these variables could bring variations in attitudes and practices of various values of B.Ed. Students.

1. Gender

A sample of 510 male and 450 female B.Ed. students were taken in the present study. The mean scores on attitude towards values and value practices of male and female B.Ed. Students on each value separately were calculated and t-test was employed to test the mean differences between the two sub-groups. The results are presented in the following Tables 5.6 and 5.7 respectively.

It is evident from Table 5.6 that the female B.Ed. Students (Mean = 378.098) have higher attitudes towards values than male B.Ed. Students (Mean = 376.557), Vide Figure 5.5 Also, it is clear that none of the t-values except the Religious (2.180*) and Aesthetic values (3.769**) could bring variation in the attitudes among B.Ed. students. Hence the hypothesis "There is no significant difference between gender and attitudes towards values among B.Ed. Students" was accepted.

Table 5.6 Means and S.Ds of the Attitudes towards Values of Male and Female B.Ed. Students and the 't'-Values

Values	Male (N=510)		Female (N=450)		't'-value
	Mean	S.D.	Mean	S.D.	
Social	43.498	4.577	42.969	4.605	1.781 @
Religious	34.110	6.979	35.102	7.074	2.180 *
Economic	39.231	6.657	38.920	6.254	0.746 @
Democratic	44.377	4.805	44.178	5.315	0.605 @
Knowledge	44.110	4.778	44.062	4.606	0.158 @
Power	38.930	7.068	39.013	6.925	0.183 @
Hedonistic	43.824	4.917	44.258	4.426	1.437 @
Aesthetic	41.655	5.814	42.978	5.052	3.769 **
Health	46.824	4.108	46.618	4.515	0.738 @
Total	**376.557**	**24.530**	**378.098**	**23.298**	**0.997 @**

@ not significant at 0.05 level
* significant at 0.05 level
** significant at 0.01 level

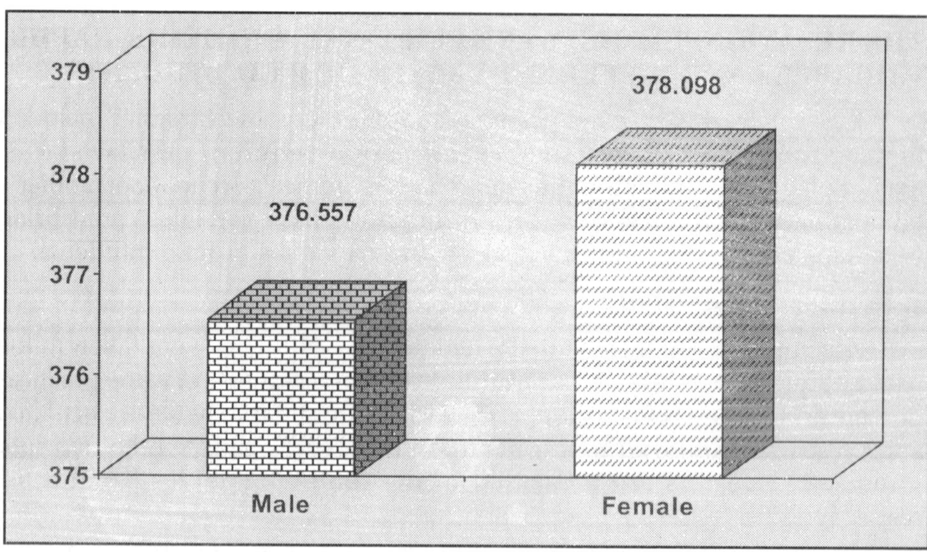

Figure 5.5 Histogram Showing the Means of Overall Attitudes Towards Values of Male and Female B.Ed. Students

It could be seen from the Table 5.7 that the overall mean practice scores of male (Mean = 364.029) and female (Mean = 365.133) B.Ed. students did not show significant difference, vide Figure 5.6 However, t-test was employed to see whether the variation in the practice of both the sexes was significant or not. The t-values of male and female B.Ed. students indicate that the mean difference was significant for Social (2.841**), Religious (3.341**), Knowledge (3.918**), Aesthetic (7.269**) and Health (3.681**) and not significant for economic, democratic, power, and hedonistic values. So the hypothesis "There is no significant difference between gender and value practices among B.Ed. Students" was accepted.

Table 5.7 Means and S.Ds of the Value Practives of Male and Female B.Ed. Students and the 't'-values

Values	Male (N=510)		Female (N=450)		't'-value
	Mean	S.D.	Mean	S.D.	
Social	43.275	5.725	42.067	7.262	2.842 **
Religious	40.284	6.010	38.911	6.635	3.341 **
Economic	35.441	5.968	35.733	6.280	0.734 @
Democratic	43.961	6.142	44.100	6.377	0.343 @
Knowledge	42.520	6.580	40.667	7.897	3.918 **
Power	36.843	6.487	37.467	7.244	1.396 @
Hedonistic	43.363	5.582	42.967	5.773	1.080 @
Aesthetic	38.667	6.944	41.800	6.400	7.269 **
Health	39.677	7.239	41.422	7.408	3.681 **
Total	**364.029**	**25.949**	**365.133**	**32.600**	**0.575 @**

@ not significant at 0.05 level
* significant at 0.05 level
** significant at 0.01 level

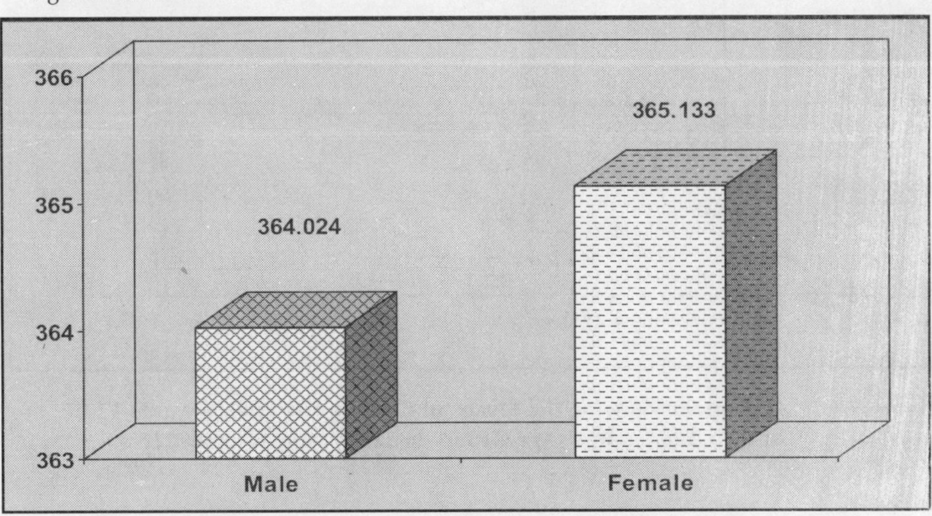

Figure 5.6 Histogram Showing the Means of Overall Value Practives of Male and Female B.Ed. Student

2. Age

The age may bring changes in different dimensions of the personality of the individual. So it may bring variation among the attitudes and practices on different values of B.Ed. Students. In the present study the whole group was divided into two, *viz.*, 455 Students of age group below and equal to 22 years (students age<=22years) 505 Students of age group above 22 years (students age> 22years). The mean scores on attitude towards values and value practices of above mentioned two age groups B.Ed. Students on each value separately were calculated and t-test was employed to test the mean differences between the two sub-groups. The results are presented in the following Tables 5.8 and 5.9 respectively.

It is evident from the Table 5.8 that the total mean attitude scores show that there was no significant difference among the attitudes of B.Ed. Students of two age groups *viz.*, age group<=22 years (Mean =377.662) and age group>22 years (Mean = 376.935), Vide Figure 7 Also, it is clear that the mean difference was significant for the values Knowledge (3.776**), Power (2.431*), Aesthetic (3.412*) and Health (2.421*) and not significant for Social, Religious, Economic, Democratic, Hedonistic. So, the hypothesis that "There is no significant difference between attitudes towards values and age of B.Ed. Students" was accepted.

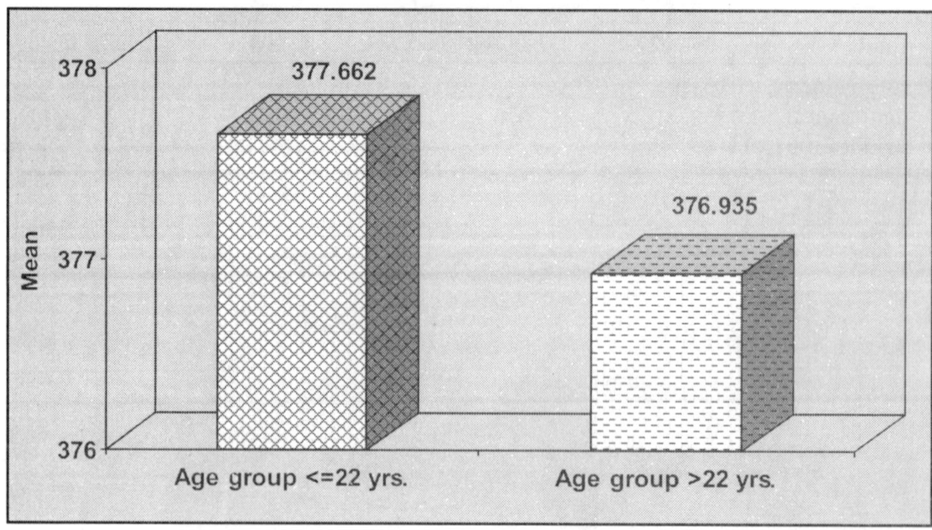

Figure 5.7 **Histogram Showing the Means of Overall Attitudes Towards Values of of Two Age Groups (Age Group <= 22 yrs., Age Group> 22yrs.)**

Table 5.8 Means and S.Ds of the Attitudes Towards Values of B.Ed. Students of Different Age Groups and the 't'-values

Values	Age Group <=22years (N=455)		Age Group> 22years (N=505)		't'-value
	Mean	S.D.	Mean	S.D.	
Social	43.037	4.881	43.442	4.318	1.359 @
Religious	34.431	7.079	34.705	7.005	0.602 @
Economic	39.222	6.584	38.962	6.368	0.622 @
Democratic	44.048	5.176	44.495	4.927	1.367 @
Knowledge	43.486	4.853	44.630	4.485	3.776 **
Power	39.547	7.151	38.448	6.822	2.431 *
Hedonistic	43.952	4.613	44.095	4.773	0.472 @
Aesthetic	42.857	4.934	41.751	5.932	3.142 **
Health	47.081	4.284	46.408	4.298	2.421 *
Total	**377.662**	**24.516**	**376.935**	**23.468**	**0.468 @**

@ not significant at 0.05 level
* significant at 0.05 level
** significant at 0.01 level

It was clear from the Table 5.9 (*See on next page*) that there was no significant difference between total mean practice scores of two age groups *viz.,* age group <=22 years (Mean =363.802) and age group>22 years (Mean = 365.218), *See vide Figure 5.8 on next page* However, t-test was employed to see whether the variation in the practice of both the age groups was significant or not. The t-values of both the age groups of B.Ed. students indicate that the mean difference was significant for the values Social (2.062*), Religious (2.221*), Hedonistic (2.853*) and Aesthetic (2.309*). But, the mean difference was not significant for Economic, Democratic, Knowledge, Power and Health values. So the hypothesis that, "There is no significant difference between values practices and age of B.Ed. Students" was accepted.

3. Caste

The whole sample was divided into three groups *viz.,* Forward Caste (305), Backward Caste (363) and Scheduled Caste (292). The mean scores on attitude towards values and value practices of B.Ed. Students belonging to different castes were calculated and F-test was employed to test the mean differences between the three groups. The results are presented in the following Tables 5.10 *(See page 113)* and 5. 11 (*See page 114*) respectively.

It is evident from Table 5.10 that there is no significant difference among the total mean attitude scores of B.Ed. students belonging to different castes

Table 5.9 Means and S.D. of the Value Practies of B.Ed. Student of Different Age Groups and the 'T'-values

Values	Age Group <=22years (N=455)		Age Group> 22years (N=505)		'T'-value
	Mean	S.D.	Mean	S.D.	
Social	42.253	6.343	43.119	6.646	2.062 *
Religious	39.165	5.980	40.069	6.633	2.221 *
Economic	35.198	5.887	35.921	6.299	1.835 @
Democratic	44.374	5.543	43.713	6.816	1.653 @
Knowledge	41.352	7.015	41.921	7.512	1.213 @
Power	37.495	7.000	36.812	6.714	1.538 @
Hedonistic	42.626	5.971	43.673	5.347	2.853 **
Aesthetic	40.670	6.344	39.654	7.287	2.309 *
Health	40.670	7.197	40.337	7.519	0.701 @
Total	**363.802**	**28.456**	**365.218**	**29.951**	**0.751 @**

@ not significant at 0.05 level
* significant at 0.05 level
** significant at 0.01 level

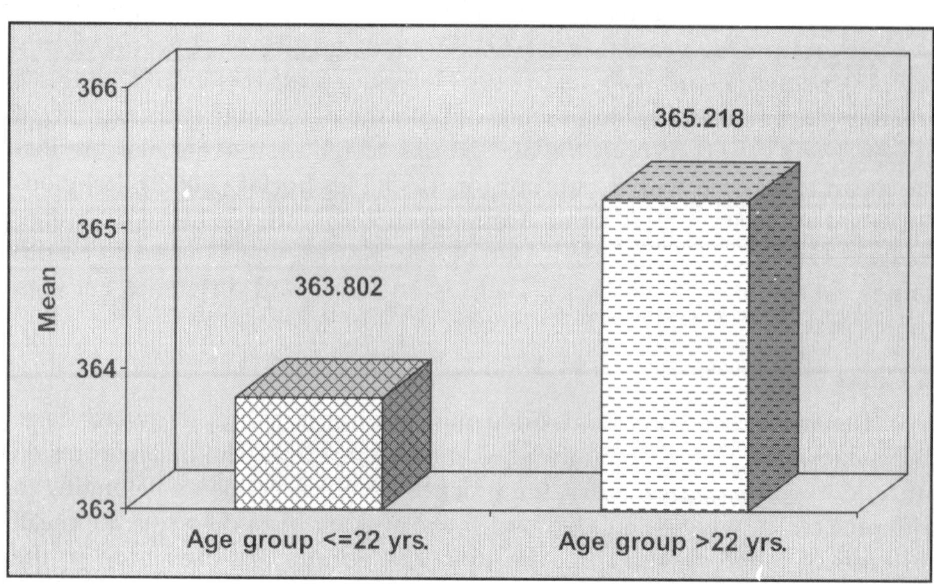

Figure 5.8 **Histogram Showing the Means of Overall Value Practives of Two Age Groups (Age group<= 22 yrs., Age group> 22 yrs.)**

viz., Forward Castes (Mean = 375.502), Backward Castes (Mean = 376.975) and Scheduled Castes (Mean = 379.514), Vide Figure 9 Also results of the F-Ratio reveal that there was no significant difference in the individual means on different values, except for the Social Value (3.619*). Hence the hypothesis "There is no significant difference between caste and attitudes towards values among B.Ed. Students" was accepted.

Table 5.10 Means and S.Ds of the Attitudes Towards Values of B.Ed. Student of Different Castes and the 'F'-values

Values	Forward Caste (N=305)		Backward Caste (N=363)		Scheduled Caste (N=292)		F-value
	Mean	S.D.	Mean	S.D.	Mean	S.D.	
Social	42.708	5.016	43.344	4.587	43.699	4.077	3.619 *
Religious	34.531	6.996	34.270	6.983	35.000	7.152	0.880 @
Economic	38.990	6.546	39.030	6.616	39.253	6.220	0.143 @
Democratic	44.190	4.998	44.391	4.972	44.247	5.209	0.157 @
Knowledge	44.072	4.775	43.851	4.744	44.397	4.548	1.112 @
Power	38.597	7.244	38.716	7.186	39.671	6.450	2.149 @
Hedonistic	43.869	4.652	44.077	4.724	44.130	4.719	0.249 @
Aesthetic	42.125	5.551	42.320	5.315	42.377	5.706	0.181 @
Health	46.420	4.691	46.975	4.045	46.740	4.182	1.378 @
Total	**375.502**	**25.214**	**376.975**	**23.246**	**379.514**	**23.391**	**2.143 @**

@ not significant at 0.05 level
* significant at 0.05 level
** significant at 0.01 level

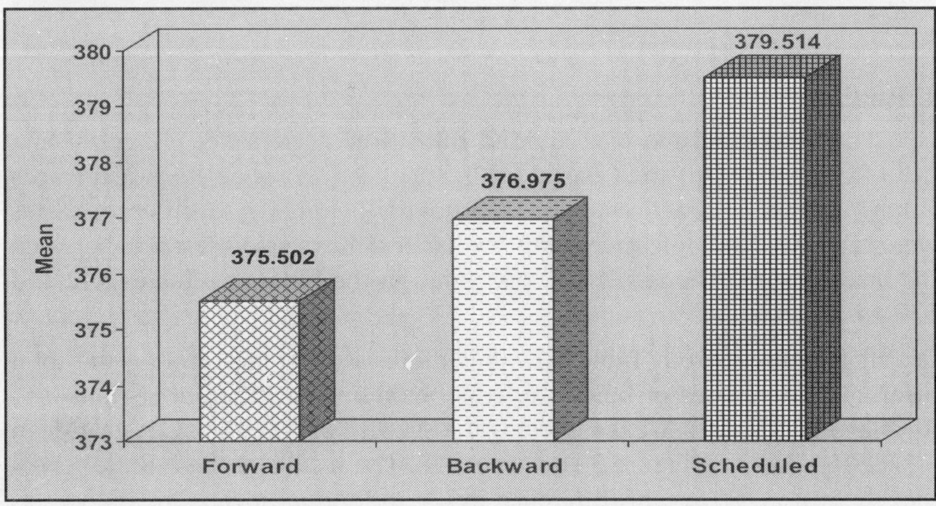

Figure 5.9 Histogram Showing the Means of Attitudes Towards Values of Different Castes (Forward/Backward/Schedule Castes)

It is evident from Table 5.15 that there is difference among the total mean practice scores of B.Ed. students belonging to different castes *viz.*, Forward Castes (Mean = 363.393), Backward Castes (Mean = 366.667) and Scheduled Castes (Mean = 363.116), Vide See Figure 5.10. *(on next page)* Also results of the F-Ratio reveal that there was no significant difference in the individual means on different values, except for the Health Value (7.849**). Hence the hypothesis "There is no significant difference between caste and value practices among B.Ed. Students" was accepted.

Table 5.11 Means and S.Ds of the Value Practices of B.Ed. Student of Different Castes and the 'F'-values

Values	Forward Caste (N=305)		Backward Caste (N=363)		Scheduled Caste (N=292)		F-value
	Mean	S.D.	Mean	S.D.	Mean	S.D.	
Social	42.787	6.471	43.044	6.418	42.209	6.671	1.367 @
Religious	39.672	6.235	39.601	6.245	39.658	6.597	0.012 @
Economic	36.098	6.152	35.551	6.150	35.069	6.007	2.118 @
Democratic	43.853	6.539	44.353	5.882	43.801	6.390	0.806 @
Knowledge	41.328	7.563	42.052	6.882	41.490	7.468	0.924 @
Power	37.295	6.952	36.584	6.472	37.654	7.184	2.101 @
Hedonistic	42.721	5.875	43.43	5.463	43.339	5.705	1.478 @
Aesthetic	40.115	6.607	40.386	6.730	39.846	7.314	0.497 @
Health	39.525	7.335	41.667	7.191	40.051	7.444	7.879 **
Total	**363.393**	**29.257**	**366.667**	**29.243**	**363.116**	**29.182**	**1.542 @**

@ not significant at 0.05 level
* significant at 0.05 level
** significant at 0.01 level

4. Region

The whole sample was divided into three regions *viz.*, Rayalaseema (320), Telengana (320) and Coastal (320). The mean scores on attitude towards values and value practices of B.Ed. Students belonging to different castes were calculated and F-test was employed to test the mean differences between the three groups. The results are presented in the following Tables 5.12 and 5.13 respectively

It is evident from Table 5.12 that there is difference among the total mean attitude scores of B.Ed. students belonging to different regions *viz.*, Rayalaseema (Mean = 375.056), Telangana (Mean = 377.969) and Coastal (Mean = 378.813), See vide Figure 5.11 *on page 116*. The results of the F-Ratio reveal that there was significant difference in the individual means for the values Religious (5.430**), Economic (22.179**) and Aesthetic (49.717**). Moreover,

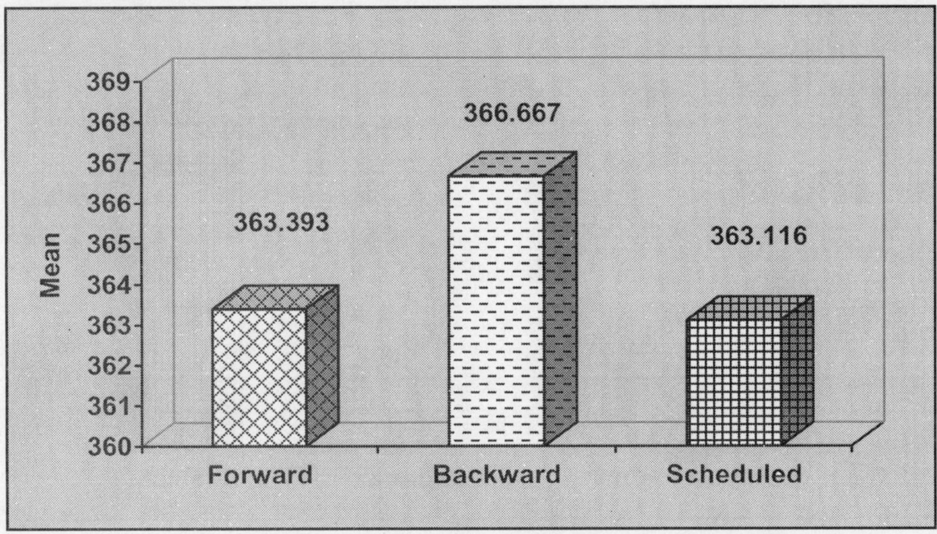

Figure 5.10 Histogram Showing the Means of Value Practices of Different Castes (Forward/ Backward/Schedule Castes)

Table 5.12 Means and S.Ds of the Attitudes Towards Values of B.Ed. Students of Different Regions and the 'F'-values

Values	Rayalaseema (N=320)		Telangana (N=320)		Coastal (N=320)		F-value
	Mean	S.D.	Mean	S.D.	Mean	S.D.	
Social	43.406	4.643	43.306	4.466	43.038	4.682	0.568 @
Religious	33.538	6.716	35.250	7.106	34.938	7.186	5.430 **
Economic	37.825	6.539	40.975	6.152	38.456	6.297	22.179 **
Democratic	43.944	5.215	44.319	4.986	44.588	4.935	1.335 @
Knowledge	44.038	4.684	44.406	4.798	43.819	4.599	1.316 @
Power	38.200	7.218	39.369	6.774	39.338	6.953	2.922 @
Hedonistic	44.244	4.653	43.675	4.785	44.163	4.644	1.362 @
Aesthetic	43.119	4.572	39.919	6.559	43.788	4.320	49.717 **
Health	46.744	4.400	46.750	4.164	46.688	4.357	0.027 @
Total	**375.056**	**25.047**	**377.969**	**23.871**	**378.813**	**22.824**	**2.170 @**

@ not significant at 0.05 level
* significant at 0.05 level
** significant at 0.01 level

the F-ratio was not significant for Social, Democratic, Knowledge, Power, Hedonistic and Health values. Hence the hypothesis "There is no significant difference between region and attitudes towards values among B.Ed. Students" was accepted.

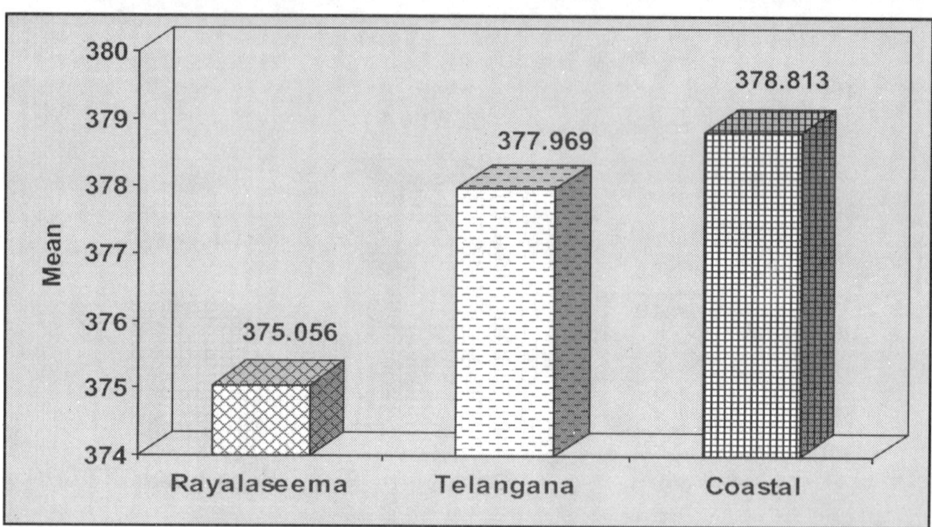

Figure 5. 11 Histogram Showing the Mean of Attitudes towards Values of Different Regions (Rayalaseems/Telangana/Coastal)

Table 5.13 Means and S.D.s of the Value Practices of B.Ed. Students of Different Regions and the 'F'-Values

Values	Rayalaseema (N=320)		Telangana (N=320)		Coastal (N=320)		F-value
	Mean	S.D.	Mean	S.D.	Mean	S.D.	
Social	46.328	4.118	39.500	5.646	42.297	7.425	108.810 **
Religious	42.188	5.107	36.938	5.859	39.797	6.837	61.891 **
Economic	34.344	5.741	37.906	6.334	34.484	5.582	37.490 **
Democratic	46.875	4.124	38.672	6.472	46.531	3.919	278.251 **
Knowledge	45.484	4.531	36.547	6.460	42.922	7.395	173.893 **
Power	36.156	5.784	40.797	6.101	34.453	7.000	86.480 **
Hedonistic	45.531	4.080	38.688	5.370	45.312	4.572	218.753 **
Aesthetic	43.750	4.018	37.891	6.197	38.766	8.207	78.676**
Health	45.656	4.837	37.188	6.022	38.641	7.895	161.384 **
Total	**386.313**	**19.049**	**344.125**	**19.93**	**363.203**	**30.262**	**255.660 ****

@ not significant at 0.05 level
* significant at 0.05 level
** significant at 0.01 level

It is evident from Table 5.13 that there is difference among the total mean practice scores of B.Ed. students belonging to different regions *viz.*, Rayalaseema (Mean = 386.313), Telangana (Mean = 344.125) and Coastal (Mean=363.203), See vide Figure 5. 12. (*on next page*) The results of the F-

Ratio also reveal that there was significant difference in the all the individual mean scores at 0.01 level of different values. Hence the hypothesis "There is no significant difference between region and value practices among B.Ed. Students" was not accepted.

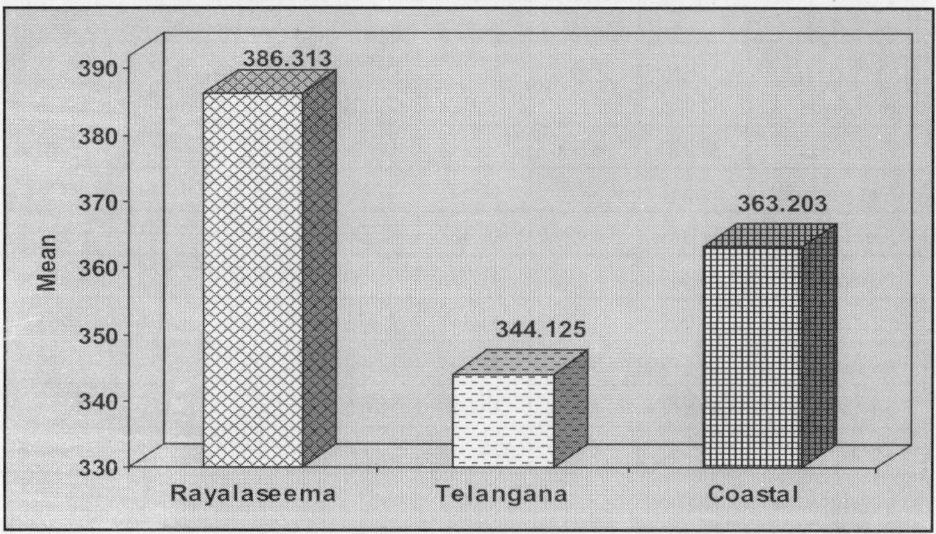

Figure 5. 12 Histogram Showing the Means of Value Practices of Different Regions (Rayalaseema/Telangana/Coastal)

5. Religion

The whole sample was divided into three religions *viz.*, Hinduism (505), Islam (229) and Christianity (226). The mean scores on attitude towards values and value practices of B.Ed. Students belonging to different religions were calculated and F-test was employed to test the mean differences between the three groups. The results are presented in the following Tables 5.14 and 5.15 respectively.

It is evident from Table 5.14 that there is no significant difference among the total mean attitude scores of B.Ed. students belonging to different religions *viz.*, Hinduism (Mean = 376.487), Islam (Mean = 379.022) and Christianity (Mean = 377.283), See vide Figure 5.14 *(on next page)*. Also results of the F-Ratio reveal that there was no significant difference in the individual means on different values, except for the Religious value (4.433*). Hence the hypothesis "There is no significant difference between religion and attitudes towards values among B.Ed. Students" was accepted.

It is evident from Table 5. 15 that there is difference among the total mean practice scores of B.Ed. students belonging to different religions *viz.*, Hinduism (Mean = 372.436), Islam (Mean = 357.205) and Christianity (Mean = 354.358), See vide Figure 5.14 *(on page 119)*. The results of the F-Ratio also

Table 5.14 Means and S.D.s of the Attitudes towards Values of B.Ed. Students of Different Religions and the 'F'-values

Values	Hindus (N=505)		Muslims (N=229)		Christians (N=226)		F-value
	Mean	S.D.	Mean	S.D.	Mean	S.D.	
Social	43.097	4.861	43.563	4.395	43.274	4.166	0.828 @
Religious	33.936	7.012	35.328	7.326	35.239	6.682	4.433 *
Economic	38.959	6.500	39.284	6.375	39.168	6.517	0.227 @
Democratic	44.222	5.167	44.533	4.766	44.168	5.073	0.372 @
Knowledge	44.044	4.727	44.507	4.556	43.761	4.755	1.498 @
Power	38.863	7.150	38.786	7.170	39.389	6.469	0.541 @
Hedonistic	44.004	4.732	44.341	4.414	43.761	4.891	0.884 @
Aesthetic	42.519	5.095	41.991	6.060	42.018	5.797	0.010 @
Health	46.844	4.358	46.690	4.316	46.504	4.171	0.486 @
Total	**376.487**	**24.669**	**379.022**	**23.569**	**377.283**	**22.724**	**0.881 @**

@ not significant at 0.05 level
* significant at 0.05 level
** significant at 0.01 level

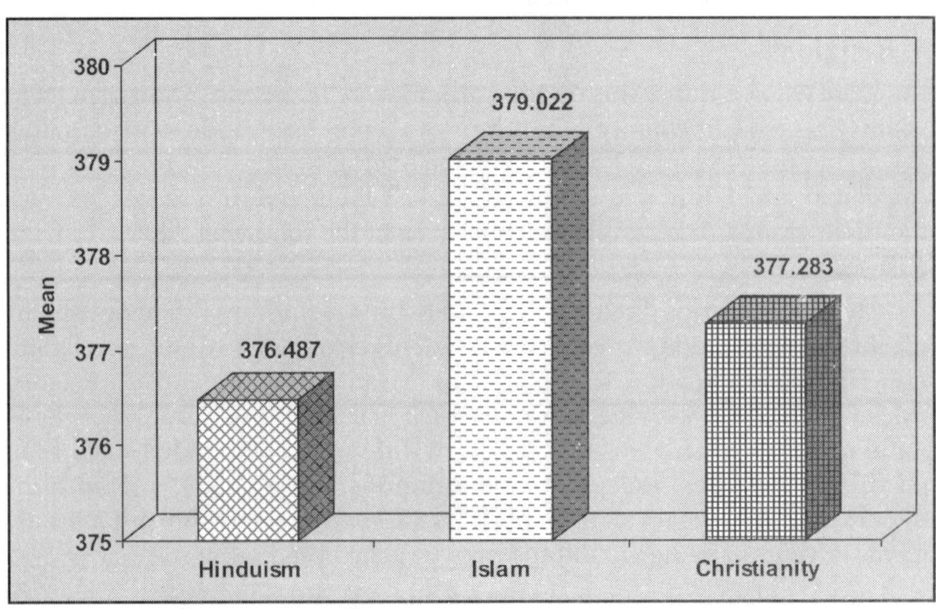

Figure 5. 13 Histogram Showing the Means of Attitudes towards Values of Different Religions (Hinduism/Islam/Christianity)

Table 5.15 Means and S.D.s of the Value Practices of Different Religions and the 'F'-values

Values	Hindus (N=505)		Muslims (N=229)		Christians (N=226)		F-Value
	Mean	S.D.	Mean	S.D.	Mean	S.D.	
Social	44.079	5.984	41.376	6.719	40.996	6.783	24.958 **
Religious	40.396	6.037	39.323	6.563	38.274	6.558	9.262 **
Economic	35.436	6.253	35.939	5.951	35.531	5.976	0.548 @
Democratic	44.951	5.955	43.428	6.347	42.566	6.468	13.042 **
Knowledge	42.960	6.614	40.284	7.796	40.111	7.637	17.870 **
Power	36.842	6.468	37.576	7.413	37.345	7.105	1.043 @
Hedonistic	44.040	5.263	42.249	5.780	42.190	6.143	12.620 **
Aesthetic	41.406	6.181	38.908	7.218	38.540	7.429	19.064 **
Health	42.327	6.921	38.122	7.328	38.805	7.311	35.870 **
Total	**372.436**	**27.707**	**357.205**	**28.448**	**354.358**	**28.408**	**42.723 ****

@ not significant at 0.05 level
* significant at 0.05 level
** significant at 0.01 level

reveal that there was significant difference in the all individual mean scores at 0.01 level on different values, except for Economic and Power values. Hence the hypothesis "There is no significant difference between religion and value practices among B.Ed. Students" was not accepted.

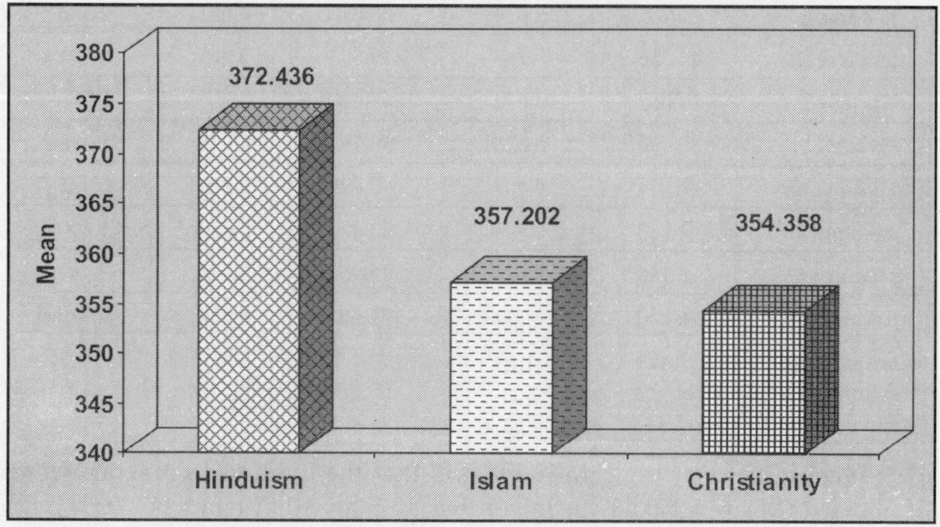

Figure 5.14 Histogram Showing the Means of Value Practices of Different Religions (Hinduism/Islam/Christianity

6. Marital Status

To find out whether marital Status of an individual may bring change in attitudes towards values and their practices of an individual a sample of 270 married and 690 unmarried B.Ed. students were taken in the present study. The mean scores on attitude towards values and value practices of married and unmarried B.Ed. Students on each value separately were calculated and t-test was employed to test the mean differences between the two sub-groups. The results are presented in the following Tables 5.16 and 5.17 respectively.

It is evident from Table 5.16 that the unmarried B.Ed. Students (Mean = 377.481) have higher attitudes towards values than married B.Ed. Students (Mean = 376.763), See the vide Figure 5.15 *(on next page)*. Also results of the t-test reveal that there was no significant difference in the individual means on different values, except for the Economic (2.206*) and Health (2.461*) values. Hence the hypothesis "There is no significant difference between marital status and attitudes towards values among B.Ed. Students" was accepted.

Table 5.20 Means and S.Ds of the Attitudes Towards Values of Married and Unmarried B.E.d. Students and the 't'-values

Values	Married (N=270)		Unmarried (N=690)		'T'-value
	Mean	S.D.	Mean	S.D.	
Social	43.096	4.354	43.310	4.688	0.671 @
Religious	35.030	7.228	34.397	6.959	1.232 @
Economic	39.785	5.934	38.812	6.651	2.206 *
Democratic	44.356	5.267	44.256	4.964	0.271 @
Knowledge	44.067	4.692	44.096	4.700	0.086 @
Power	38.400	6.828	39.191	7.055	1.598 @
Hedonistic	44.104	4.409	43.997	4.806	0.328 @
Aesthetic	41.770	5.976	42.473	5.303	1.690 @
Health	46.156	4.620	46.951	4.154	2.461 *
Total	**376.763**	**23.224**	**377.481**	**24.256**	**0.425 @**

@ not significant at 0.05 level
* significant at 0.05 level
** significant at 0.01 level

It could be seen from the Table 5.17 that the total mean practice scores of married (Mean = 355.889) is lower than unmarried (Mean = 367.935) B.Ed. students, See vide Figure 516. (*on the page 123*) However, t-test was employed to see whether the difference in the value practices of both the groups was

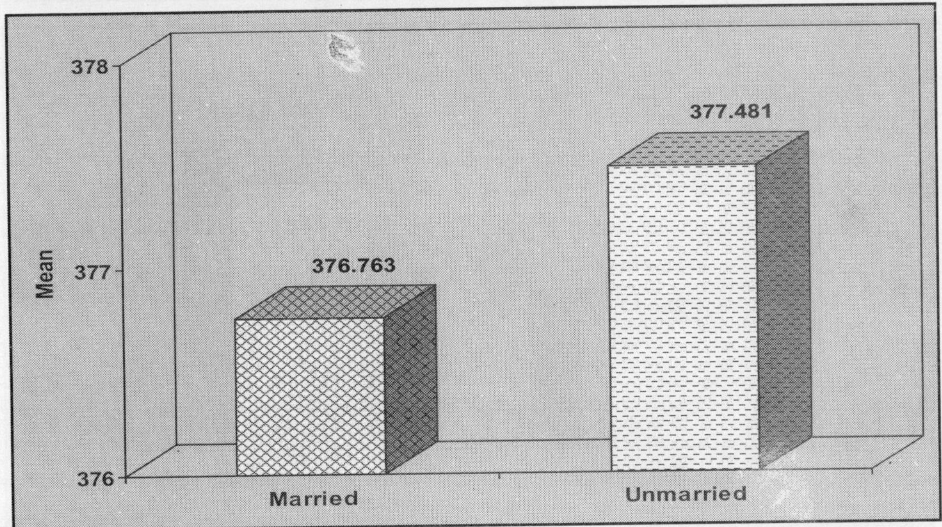

Figure 5.15 **Histogram Showing the Means of Overall Attitude Towards Values Married and Unmarried B.Ed. Students**

significant or not. The t-values of married and unmarried B.Ed. students indicate that the mean difference was significant with regard to all values except for Power and Aesthetic values. So the hypothesis "There is no significant difference between marital status and value practices among B.Ed. Students" was not accepted.

Table 5.21 Means and S.Ds of the Value Practices of Married and Unmarried B.Ed. Students and the 't'-values

Values	Married (N=270)		Unmarried (N=690)		'T'-value
	Mean	S.D.	Mean	S.D.	
Social	41.389	7.368	43.225	6.078	3.636 **
Religious	38.185	6.737	40.210	6.095	4.299 **
Economic	36.796	6.219	35.102	6.011	3.835 **
Democratic	42.222	7.193	44.732	5.692	5.133 **
Knowledge	39.926	8.088	42.326	6.830	4.317 **
Power	36.685	7.306	37.311	6.668	1.225 @
Hedonistic	42.574	5.583	43.413	5.694	2.082 *
Aesthetic	39.463	7.663	40.399	6.523	1.769 @
Health	38.648	7.400	41.217	7.231	4.866 **
Total	**355.889**	**28.978**	**367.935**	**28.666**	**5.808 ****

@ not significant at 0.05 level
* significant at 0.05 level
** significant at 0.01 level

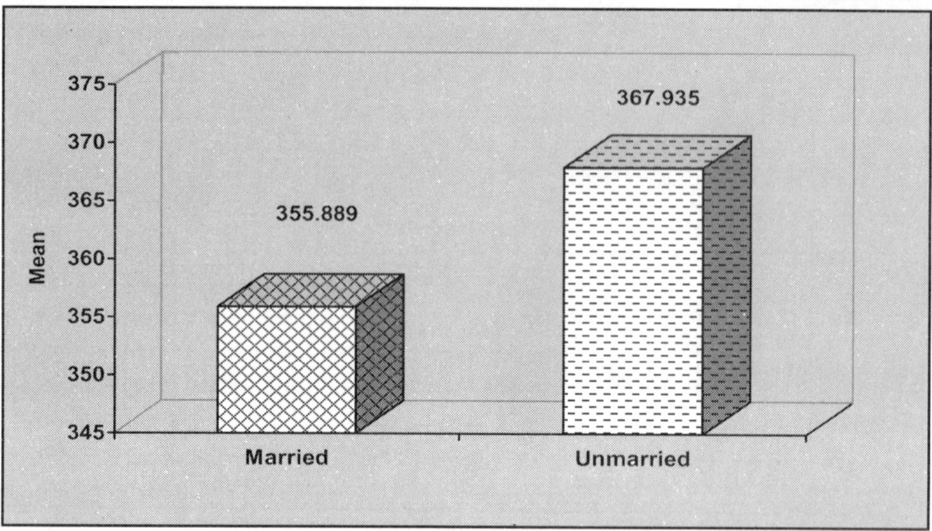

Figure 5.16 Histrogram Showing the Means of Overall Value Practices of Married and Unmarried B.Ed. Students

7. Educational Qualifications

Based on the educational qualifications there may be difference in the attitudes and practices of values of the individuals. Hence depending on educational qualifications the whole sample was divided into two groups viz., graduates and postgraduates. The mean scores on attitude towards values and value practices of graduate (553) and postgraduate (407) B.Ed. Students on each value separately were calculated and t-test was employed to test the mean differences between the two sub-groups. The results are presented in the following Tables 5.18 and 5.19 respectively.

It is evident from Table 5.18 that the graduate B.Ed. Students (Mean = 377.989) has higher attitudes towards values than postgraduate B.Ed. Students (Mean = 376.314), See vide Figure 5.17. (*on next page*) Also results of the t-test reveal that there was no significant difference in the individual means on different values, except for the Aesthetic value (2.419*). Hence the hypothesis "There is no significant difference between educational qualifications and attitudes towards values among B.Ed. Students" was accepted.

It could be seen from the Table 5.19 that the total mean practice scores of graduate (Mean = 367.676) and postgraduate (Mean = 360.295) B.Ed. students showed difference, See vide Figure 5.18. (*on page 124*) However, t-test was employed to see whether the difference in the value practices of both the groups was significant or not. The t-values of graduate and postgraduate B.Ed. students indicate that the mean difference was not significant for the values Religious, Economic, Knowledge, Power and Hedonistic and the mean difference was significant for the values Social (3.147**), Democratic (2.432*), Aesthetic (4.333**)

Table 5.18 Means and S.Ds of the Attitudes towards Values of Graducate and Post-Graduate B.Ed. Students and the 'T'-values

Values	Graduates (N=553)		Postgraduates (N=407)		'T'-value
	Mean	S.D.	Mean	S.D.	
Social	43.224	4.566	43.288	4.640	0.219 @
Religious	34.391	7.267	34.826	6.715	0.956 @
Economic	39.172	6.404	38.968	6.563	0.481 @
Democratic	44.380	5.159	44.152	4.898	0.697 @
Knowledge	43.870	4.704	44.383	4.674	0.717 @
Power	39.175	6.881	38.688	7.152	1.059 @
Hedonistic	44.213	4.638	43.774	4.767	1.425 @
Aesthetic	42.647	5.303	41.769	5.740	2.419 *
Health	46.919	4.244	46.467	4.373	1.597 @
Total	**377.989**	**23.678**	**376.314**	**24.334**	**1.066** @

@ not significant at 0.05 level
* significant at 0.05 level
** significant at 0.01 level

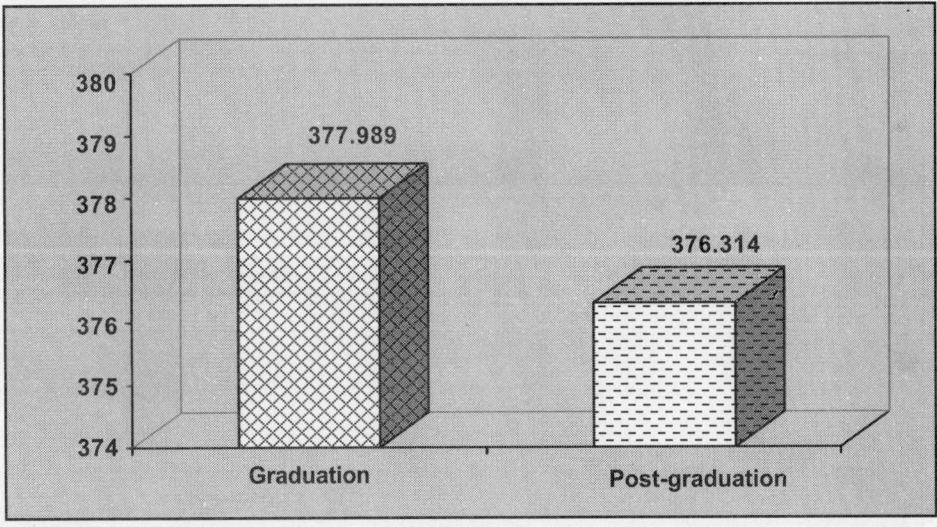

Figure 5. 17 Histogram Showing the Means of Overall Attitude Towards Values of Graduate and Post-graduate B.Ed. Students

and Health (3.330**). So the hypothesis "There is no significant difference between educational qualifications and value practices among B.Ed. Students" was not accepted.

Table 5.19 Means and S.Ds of the Value Practices of Graduate and Post-graduate B.Ed. Students and 'T'-values

Values	Graduates (N=553)		Postgraduates (N=407)		'T'-value
	Mean	S.D.	Mean	S.D.	
Social	43.282	6.215	41.929	6.834	3.147 **
Religious	39.919	6.208	39.263	6.514	1.573 @
Economic	35.497	5.965	35.688	6.318	0.474 @
Democratic	44.449	6.117	43.452	6.389	2.432 *
Knowledge	42.034	6.999	41.130	7.629	1.876 @
Power	36.962	6.810	37.371	6.919	0.909 @
Hedonistic	43.400	5.543	42.875	5.838	1.404 @
Aesthetic	40.959	6.661	39.017	7.002	4.333 **
Health	41.175	7.234	39.570	7.453	3.330 **
Total	**367.676**	**28.961**	**360.295**	**29.128**	**3.889 ****

@ not significant at 0.05 level
* significant at 0.05 level
** significant at 0.01 level

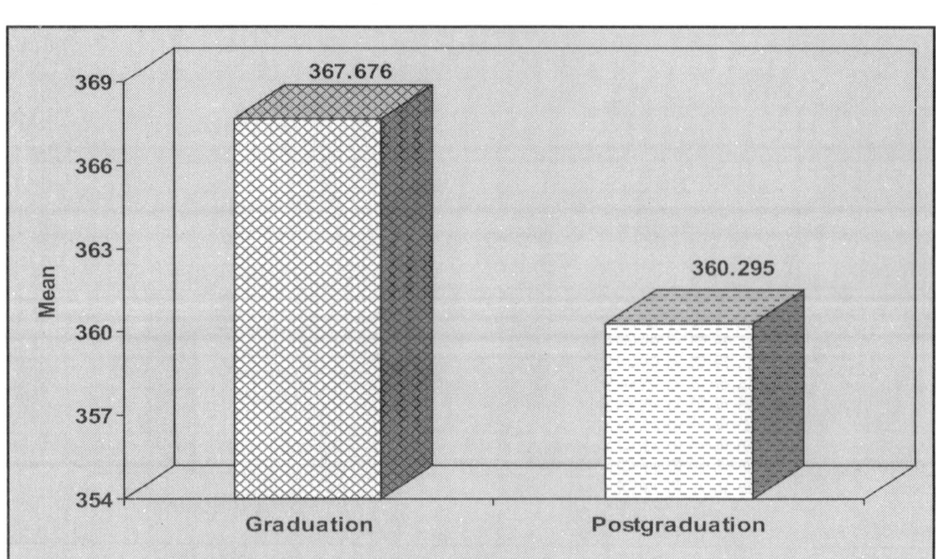

Figure 5. 18 Histogram Showing the Means of Overall Value Practices of Graduate and Post-graduate B.Ed. Student

8. Methodolgogies

The sample was divided into four groups *viz.*, Mathematics (240), Physical Sciences (240), Biological Sciences (240) and Social Studies (240). The mean scores on attitude towards values and value practices of B.Ed. Students belonging to different methodologies were calculated and F-test was employed to test the mean differences between the three groups. The results are presented in the following Tables 5.20 and 5.21 respectively.

It is evident from Table 5.20 that there is significant difference among the total mean attitude scores of B.Ed. students belonging to different methodologies *viz.*, Mathematics (Mean = 373.767), Physical Sciences (Mean = 374.767), Biological Sciences (Mean = 381.042) and Social Studies (Mean =379.542), See vide Figure 5.19. Also results of the F-test reveal that there was no significant mean difference for the values Social, Religious, Aesthetic, Health and there was significant mean difference for the values Economic (4.321**), Democratic (2.934*), Knowledge (5.961**), Power (2.924*), Hedonistic (2.644*). Hence the hypothesis "There is no significant difference between methodologies and attitudes towards values among B.Ed. Students" was not accepted.

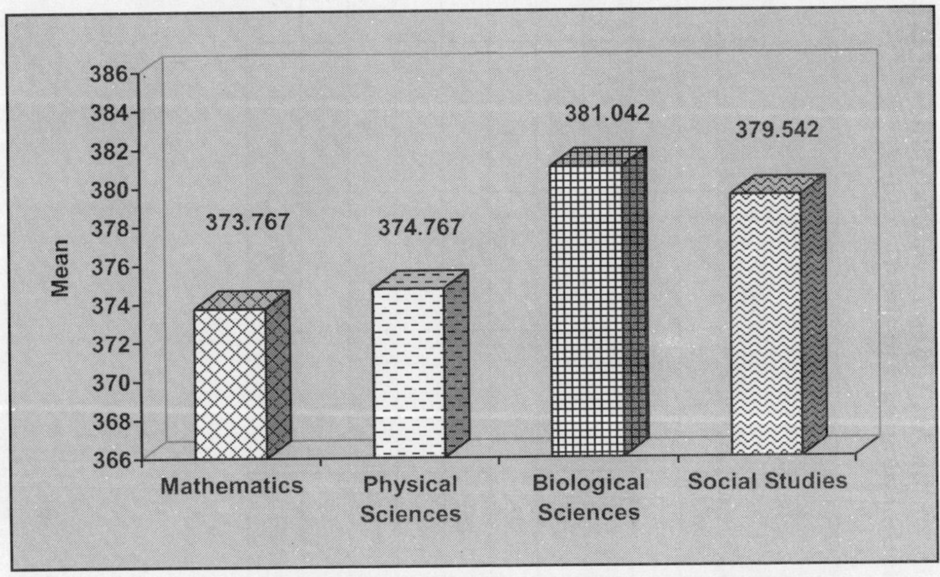

Figure 5. 19 **Histogram Showing the Means of Overall Attitude Towards Values of B.Ed. Students of Different Methodologies (Mathematics/ Physical Sciences/Biological Sciences / Social Studies)**

It is evident from Table 5.21 that there is no significant difference among the total mean practice scores of B.Ed. students belonging to different methodologies *viz.*, Mathematics (Mean = 365.646), Physical Sciences (Mean = 365.854), Biological Sciences (Mean = 364.396) and Social Studies (Mean = 363.292), See vide Figure 5.20. (*on page 127*) Also, the results of the F-Ratio reveal that there was no significant difference in the individual mean practice

Table 5. 20 Means and S.Ds of the Attitudes Towards Values of B.Ed Students of Different Methodologies and the 'f'-values

Values	Mathematics (N=240)		Physical Sciences (N=240)		Biological Sciences (N=240)		Social Studies (N=240)		F-value
	Mean	S.D.	Mean	S.D.	Mean	S.D.	Mean	S.D.	
Social	43.625	4.680	43.400	4.299	42.950	4.802	43.025	4.581	1.153 @
Religious	34.733	6.553	33.692	7.253	34.733	7.325	35.142	6.956	1.869 @
Economic	38.167	6.304	38.550	5.800	39.967	6.868	39.658	6.72	4.321 **
Democratic	44.117	5.247	43.658	5.390	44.992	4.806	44.367	4.654	2.934 *
Knowledge	43.500	4.648	43.508	4.705	44.367	4.854	44.975	4.429	5.691 **
Power	38.275	7.473	38.450	6.432	39.958	7.146	39.192	6.814	2.924 *
Hedonistic	43.325	4.668	44.208	4.651	44.467	4.709	44.108	4.708	2.644 *
Aesthetic	41.700	5.310	42.408	4.992	42.900	5.635	42.092	6.002	2.040 @
Health	46.325	4.608	46.892	3.965	46.708	4.565	46.983	4.029	1.099 @
Total	**373.767**	**24.39**	**374.767**	**22.676**	**381.042**	**24.938**	**379.542**	**23.12**	**5.357 ****

@ not significant at 0.05 level
* significant at 0.05 level
** significant at 0.01 level

scores on different values, except for Democratic (3.526*) and Power (3.264*) values. Hence the hypothesis "There is no significant difference between methodologies and value practices among B.Ed. Students" was accepted.

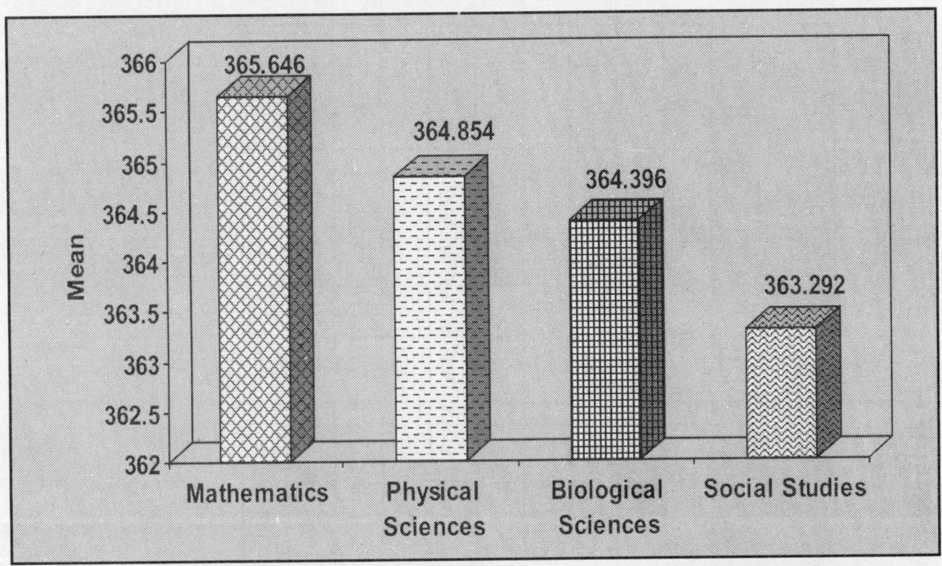

Figure 5. 20 Histogram Showing the Means of Overall Value Practices of B.Ed. Students of Different Methodologies (Mathematics / Physical Sciences / Biological Sciences / Social Studies)

9. Locality

Locality may bring difference in the attitudes and practices on values of the individuals. Hence depending on locality the whole sample was divided into two groups *viz.,* urban (463) and rural (497) localities. The mean scores on attitude towards values and value practices of urban and rural locality B.Ed. Students on each value separately were calculated and t-test was employed to test the mean differences between the two sub-groups. The results are presented in the following Tables 5.22 and 5.23 respectively.

It is evident from Table 5.22 that the urban B.Ed. Students (Mean = 377.585) has higher attitudes towards values than rural B.Ed. Students (Mean = 376.994), See vide Figure 5. 21. (*on page 129*) The t-test of urban and rural B.Ed. students indicates that the mean difference was not significant for any of the values. Hence the hypothesis "There is no significant difference between locality and attitudes towards values among B.Ed. Students" was accepted.

Table 5.21 Means and S.Ds of the Value Practices of B.Ed Students of Different Methodologies and the 'F'-values

Values	Mathematics (N=240)		Physical Sciences (N=240)		Biological Sciences (N=240)		Social Studies (N=240)		F-value
	Mean	S.D.	Mean	S.D.	Mean	S.D.	Mean	S.D.	
Social	43.312	5.978	42.354	6.451	42.958	6.861	42.208	6.716	1.510 @
Religious	39.604	5.763	39.583	6.241	39.729	6.74	39.646	6.627	0.025 @
Economic	34.833	5.674	35.667	5.599	36.021	6.313	35.792	6.769	1.725 @
Democratic	45.042	5.031	44.063	6.326	43.750	6.792	43.250	6.601	3.526 *
Knowledge	42.313	6.530	41.750	7.337	41.042	7.705	41.500	7.491	1.271 @
Power	36.000	6.710	37.188	6.621	37.792	6.976	37.563	7.011	3.264 *
Hedonistic	43.813	5.129	43.458	5.939	42.958	5.981	42.479	5.546	2.540 @
Aesthetic	40.229	6.773	39.979	6.884	40.000	6.404	40.333	7.424	0.148 @
Health	40.500	7.215	40.813	7.002	40.146	7.659	40.521	7.602	0.331 @
Total	**365.646**	**24.231**	**364.854**	**30.365**	**364.396**	**33.071**	**363.292**	**28.743**	**0.310 @**

@ not significant at 0.05 level
* significant at 0.05 level
** significant at 0.01 level

Table 5.22 Means and S.Ds of the Attitudes Towards Values of Urban and Rural B.Ed. Students and the 'T'-value

Values	Urban (N=463)		Rural (N=497)		'T'-value
	Mean	S.D	Mean	S.D	
Social	43.231	4.508	43.268	4.680	0.125 @
Religious	34.501	7.269	34.644	6.822	0.314 @
Economic	39.296	6.057	38.889	6.831	0.978 @
Democratic	44.350	4.999	44.221	5.098	0.396 @
Knowledge	43.991	4.639	44.177	4.750	0.614 @
Power	39.037	6.698	38.905	7.272	0.293 @
Hedonistic	43.948	4.733	44.101	4.664	0.505 @
Aesthetic	42.436	5.005	42.125	5.937	0.879 @
Health	46.795	4.087	46.664	4.498	0.471 @
Total	**377.585**	**22.558**	**376.994**	**25.216**	**0.383 @**

@ not significant at 0.05 level
* significant at 0.05 level
** significant at 0.01 level

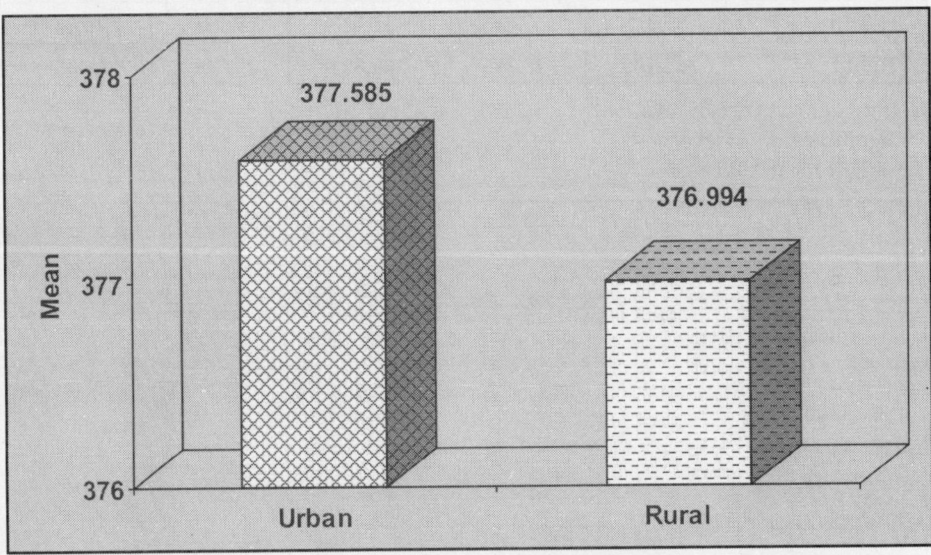

Figure 5.21 Histogram Showing the Means of Overall Attitude Towards Values of Urban and Rural B.Ed. Students

It could be seen from the Table 5.23 that the total mean practice scores of urban (Mean = 362.106) B.Ed. Students is lower than rural (Mean = 366.821) B.Ed. Students, See vide Figure 5.22. (*on next page*) However, t-test was employed to see whether the variation in the practice of both the groups was significant or not. The t-values of graduate and postgraduate B.Ed. students indicate that the mean difference was significant. But t-values are not significant with regard to all values except for Aesthetic (2.851**) and Health (2.766*) values. So the hypothesis "There is no significant difference between locality and value practices among B.Ed. Students" was not accepted.

Table 5.23 Means and S.Ds of the Value Practices of Urban and Rural B.Ed. Students and the 'T'-values

Values	Urban (N=463)		Rural (N=497)		'T'-value
	Mean	S.D	Mean	S.D	
Social	42.408	6.764	42.988	6.268	1.371 @
Religious	39.492	6.226	39.779	6.456	0.700 @
Economic	35.572	5.815	35.584	6.387	0.031 @
Democratic	43.931	6.012	44.115	6.470	0.457 @
Knowledge	41.177	7.398	42.093	7.152	1.941 @
Power	37.117	6.913	37.153	6.809	0.081 @
Hedonistic	43.110	5.768	43.293	5.587	0.352 @
Aesthetic	39.482	6.826	40.745	6.865	2.851 **
Health	39.816	7.496	41.127	7.194	2.766 **
Total	**362.106**	**28.795**	**366.821**	**29.506**	**2.505 ***

@ not significant at 0.05 level
* significant at 0.05 level
** significant at 0.01 level

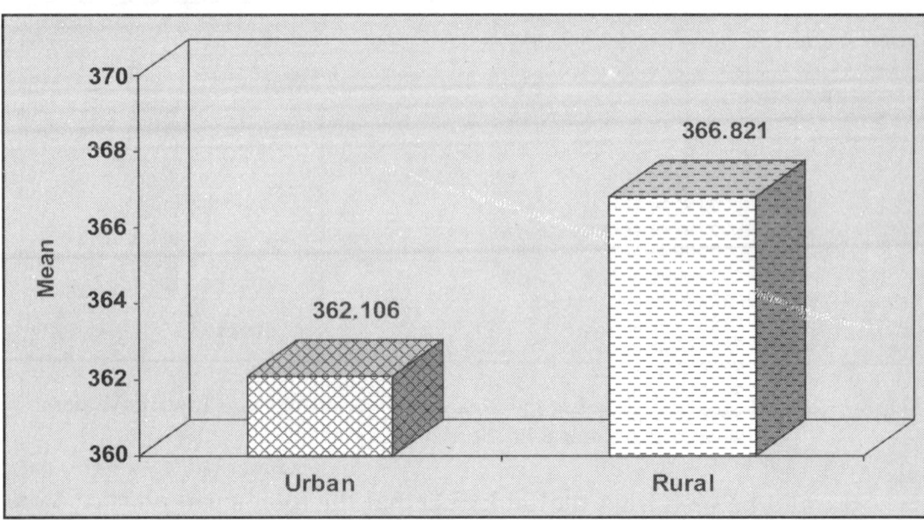

Figure 5.22 Histogram Showing the Means of Overall Value Practices of Urban and Rural B.Ed. Students

10. Father Occupation

Depending on Father's Occupation whole sample was divided into three categories *viz.*, Professional (225), Skilled (613) and Unskilled (122). The mean scores on attitude towards values and value practices of B.Ed. Students belonging to different above-mentioned categories were calculated and F-test was employed to test the mean differences between the three groups. The results are presented in the following Tables 5.24 and 5.25 respectively.

It is evident from Table 5.24 that there is difference among the total mean attitude scores of B.Ed. students depending on their father's occupation viz., Professional (Mean = 377.493), Skilled (Mean = 376.711), and Unskilled (Mean =379.738) See vide Figure 5.23. (*on next page*) Also, it is clear that none of the F-values could bring difference in the attitudes towards values of the B.Ed. Students. Hence the hypothesis "There is no significant difference between Father's Occupation and attitudes towards values among B.Ed. Students" was accepted.

Table 5.24 Means and S.Ds of the Attitudes towards Values of B.Ed Students Representing their Father's Occupation and the 'F'-values

Values	Professional (N=225)		Skilled (N=613)		Unskilled (N=122)		F-values
	Mean	S.D.	Mean	S.D.	Mean	S.D.	
Social	42.880	4.898	43.354	4.520	43.410	4.391	0.971 @
Religious	34.782	7.198	34.558	6.873	34.279	7.586	0.222 @
Economic	39.440	6.298	38.891	6.460	39.410	6.831	0.776 @
Democratic	44.293	4.833	44.199	5.126	44.689	5.063	0.470 @
Knowledge	44.187	4.542	43.984	4.632	44.426	5.277	0.521 @
Power	39.173	6.828	38.777	7.025	39.557	7.184	0.766 @
Hedonistic	43.733	4.762	43.984	4.734	44.787	4.322	2.068 @
Aesthetic	42.258	4.824	42.349	5.536	41.934	6.489	0.296 @
Health	46.747	3.929	46.617	4.489	47.246	3.986	1.054 @
Total	**377.493**	**23.361**	**376.711**	**23.842**	**379.738**	**25.629**	**0.823 @**

@ not significant at 0.05 level
* significant at 0.05 level
** significant at 0.01 level

It is evident from Table 5.24 that there is significant difference among the total mean practice scores of B.Ed. students depending on their father's occupation *viz.*, Professional (Mean = 357.022), Skilled (Mean = 367.896), and Unskilled (Mean =361.598), See vide Figure 5. 24. (*on page 133*) Also, the results of the F-Ratio reveal that there was no significant variation in mean differences

Religious, Economic and Power values but, there is significant mean difference for the values Social (11.717**), Democratic (5.739**), Knowledge (5.539**), Hedonistic (10.571**), Aesthetic (3.288*) and Health (8.478**). Hence the hypothesis "There is no significant difference between father's occupation and value practices among B.Ed. Students" was not accepted.

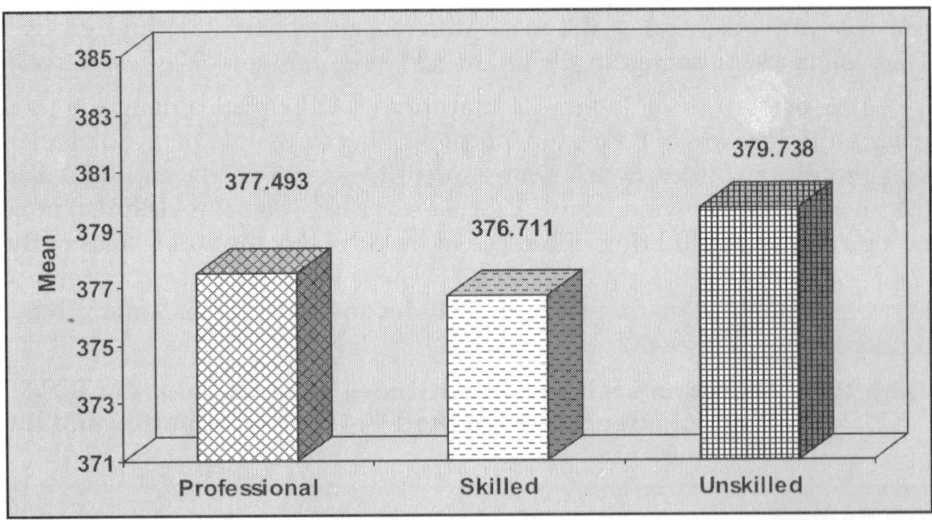

Figure 5. 23 Histogram Showing the Means of Overall Attitdues towards Values of B.Ed., Students Representing their Father's Occupation (Professional/ Skilled / Unskilled)

Table 5.25 Means and S.Ds of the Value Practices of B.Ed. Student Preprenenting their Father's Occupation and 'F'-values

Values	Professional (N=225)		Skille (N=613)		Unskille (N=122)		F-value
	Mean	S.D.	Mean	S.D.	Mean	S.D.	
Social	41.022	6.670	43.418	6.290	42.254	6.776	11.717 **
Religious	38.800	6.188	39.959	6.433	39.590	6.084	2.768 @
Economic	35.711	6.008	35.424	6.049	36.107	6.634	0.695 @
Democratic	43.311	6.253	44.527	6.052	42.828	6.953	5.739 **
Knowledge	40.333	7.691	42.194	7.149	41.352	6.895	5.539 **
Power	37.378	7.228	36.803	6.720	38.361	6.725	2.819 @
Hedonistic	42.178	5.951	43.801	5.445	41.885	5.833	10.571 **
Aesthetic	39.267	6.897	40.555	6.686	39.631	7.583	3.288 *
Health	39.022	7.391	41.215	7.345	39.590	6.971	8.478 **
Total	**357.022**	**28.297**	**367.896**	**29.227**	**361.598**	**28.374**	**12.373 ****

@ not significant at 0.05 level
* significant at 0.05 level
** significant at 0.01 level

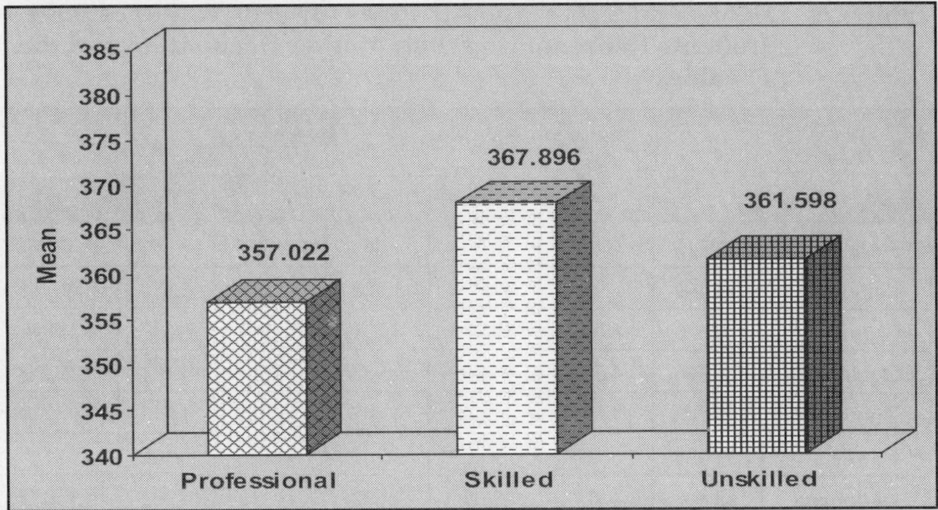

Figure 5. 24 Histogram Showing the Means of Overall Value Practices of B.Ed., Student Representing ehri Father's Occupation (Professional / Skilled /Unskilled)

11. Mother's Occupation

Depending on Mother's Occupation whole sample was divided into three categories *viz.*, Professional (91), Skilled (364) and Unskilled (505). The mean scores on attitude towards values and value practices of B.Ed. Students belonging to different above-mentioned categories were calculated and F-test was employed to test the mean differences between the three groups. The results are presented in the Tables 5.26 and 5.27 respectively.

It is evident from Table 5.26 that there is difference among the total mean attitude scores of B.Ed. students depending on their mother's occupation *viz.*, Professional (Mean = 379.099), Skilled (Mean = 378.082), and Unskilled (Mean =376.372), See vide Figure 5.25. *(on next page)* The F-values indicate that the mean difference was not significant for any of the values. Hence the hypothesis "There is no significant difference between Mother's Occupation and attitudes towards values among B.Ed. Students" was accepted.

It is evident from Table 5.27 that there is difference among the total mean practice scores of B.Ed. students depending on their mother's occupation *viz.*, Professional (Mean = 356.099), Skilled (Mean = 362.253), and Unskilled (Mean =367.723), See vide Figure 5.26. (*on page 135*) Also, the results of the F-Ratio reveal that there was no significant variation in the individual mean differences for the values religious, economic, democratic, aesthetic and there is significant difference for the values Social (6.228**), Knowledge (7.628**), Power (3.099*), Hedonistic (11.284**), Health (7.139**). Hence the hypothesis "There is no significant difference between mother's occupation and value practices among B.Ed. Students" was not accepted.

Table 5.26 Means and S.Ds of the Attitudes towards Values of B.Ed Students Reprenenting their Mother Occupation and the 'F'-values

Values	Professional (N=91)		Skilled (N=364)		Unskilled (N=505)		F-value
	Mean	S.D.	Mean	S.D.	Mean	S.D.	
Social	42.813	4.422	43.335	4.565	43.267	4.652	0.473 @
Religious	34.462	7.978	34.676	6.928	34.523	6.950	0.061 @
Economic	39.670	6.039	39.330	6.331	38.804	6.639	1.111 @
Democratic	44.066	4.575	44.462	4.982	44.194	5.181	0.392 @
Knowledge	44.703	4.386	44.148	4.707	43.933	4.740	1.089 @
Power	39.934	6.905	39.203	6.762	38.626	7.169	1.677 @
Hedonistic	43.890	4.727	43.945	4.692	44.111	4.701	0.158 @
Aesthetic	42.835	4.826	42.319	5.347	42.143	5.733	0.610 @
Health	46.725	3.718	46.665	4.275	46.772	4.425	0.054 @
Total	**379.099**	**21.914**	**378.082**	**23.730**	**376.372**	**24.478**	**0.829 @**

@ not significant at 0.05 level
* significant at 0.05 level
** significant at 0.01 level

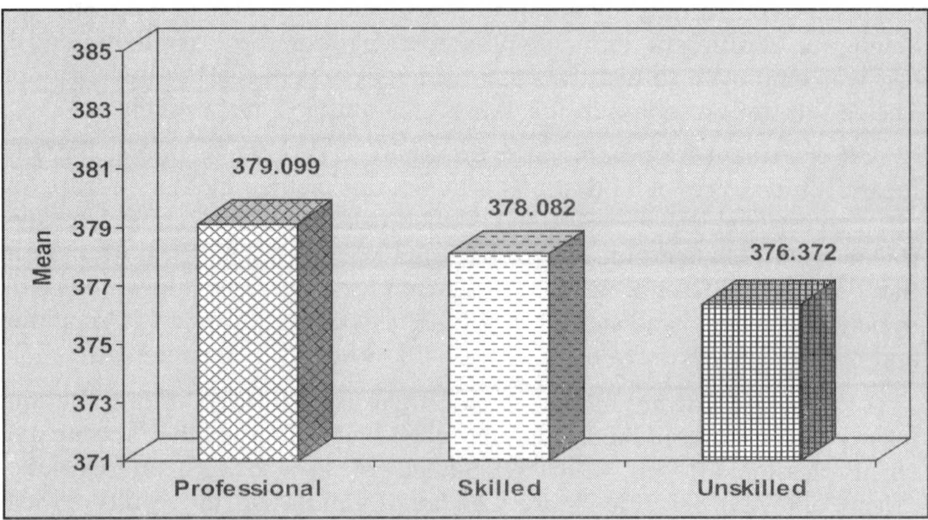

Figure 5.25 Histogram Showing the Means of Overall Attitude towards Values of B.Ed., Students Representing their Mother's Occupation (Professional / Skilled / Unskilled)

It is evident from Table 5.27 that there is difference among the total mean practice scores of B.Ed. students depending on their mother's occupation *viz.*, Professional (Mean = 356.099), Skilled (Mean = 362.253), and Unskilled (Mean =367.723), See vide Figure 5.26. Also, the results of the F-Ratio reveal that there was no significant variation in the individual mean differences for the values religious, economic, democratic, aesthetic and there is significant difference for the values Social (6.228**), Knowledge (7.628**), Power (3.099*), Hedonistic (11.284**), Health (7.139**). Hence the hypothesis "There is no significant difference between mother's occupation and value practices among B.Ed. Students" was not accepted.

Table 5.27 Means and S.Ds of the Value Practices of B.Ed. Students Representing their Mother's Occupation and the 'F'-values

Values	Professional (N=91)		Skilled (N=364)		Unskilled (N=505)		F-value
	Mean	S.D.	Mean	S.D.	Mean	S.D	
Social	40.769	6.909	42.431	6.508	43.257	6.380	6.228 **
Religious	39.066	6.451	39.313	6.048	39.980	6.524	1.580 @
Economic	35.879	6.774	35.742	6.064	35.406	6.033	0.427 @
Democratic	43.901	5.313	43.668	6.445	44.307	6.261	1.127 @
Knowledge	39.780	7.990	41.003	7.198	42.455	7.114	7.628 **
Power	37.692	7.122	37.720	6.733	36.614	6.866	3.099 *
Hedonistic	41.703	6.246	42.445	5.779	43.970	5.366	11.284 **
Aesthetic	38.736	6.691	40.027	6.953	40.465	6.823	2.507 @
Health	38.571	7.160	39.904	7.315	41.267	7.352	7.139 **
Total	**356.099**	**27.283**	**362.253**	**28.758**	**367.723**	**29.531**	**8.010 ****

@ not significant at 0.05 level
* significant at 0.05 level
** significant at 0.01 level

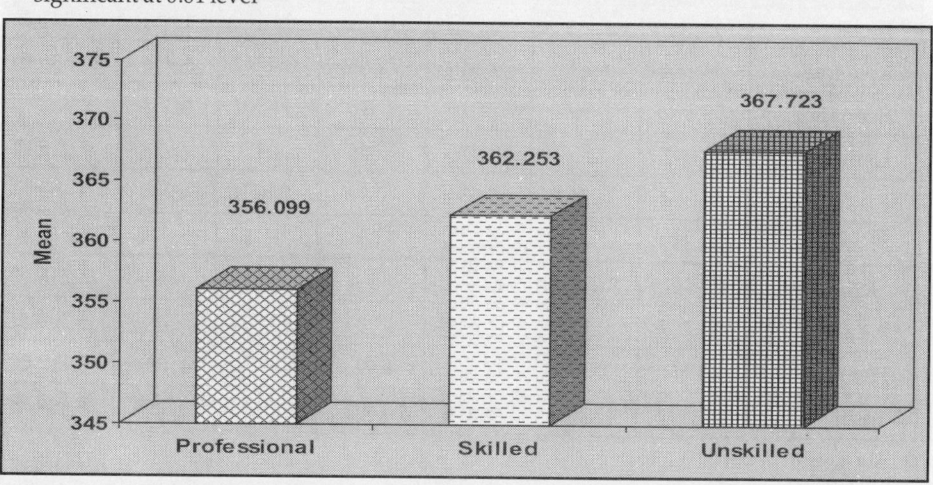

Figure 5. 26 Histogram Showing the Means of Overall Value Practices of B.Ed., Students Representing Their Mother's Occupation (Professional/Skilled/Unskilled)

Section—III

RELATIONSHIP BETWEEN PERSONALITY FACTORS AND ATTITUDES TOWARDS VALUES AND VALUE PRACTICES OF B.ED. STUDENTS

The relationship between the 16 personality factors and attitudes towards various values and value practices of B.Ed. Students was analyzed by calculating means, standard deviations and analysis of variance. The F-values show whether the personality factors could bring any significant variation in the attitudes and practices of different values of B.Ed. Students.

1. Factor—A

An observation into Table 5.32 reveals that there was significant variation among the total mean attitude scores of three personality groups *viz.*, Low scorers (Mean =373.532), Moderate scorers (Mean = 373.828) and High scorers (Mean = 379.520), Vide Figure 27. The results of F-Ratio reveal that three groups do not significantly differ for the values Social, Religious, Democratic, Knowledge, Health but they significantly differ for the values Economic (4.027*), Power (3.211*), Hedonistic (5.215**) and Aesthetic (3.364*). Also, it could be seen that the relationship between overall attitudes towards values and Factor—A was significant. Hence it is clear that the more outgoing B.Ed. Students have better attitudes towards values than reserved B.Ed. Students.

Table 5.28 Relationship Between Attitudes towards Values of B.Ed. Students and Factor—A

Values	Low Scorers (A) (171)		Moderate Scorers (A) (198)		High Scorers (A+) (591)		F-value (2,957 d.f)
	Mean	S.D.	Mean	S.D.	Mean	S.D.	
Social	43.088	4.778	42.707	4.589	43.479	4.534	2.231 @
Religious	34.164	6.896	34.343	7.286	34.772	6.998	0.636 @
Economic	38.877	6.598	38.020	6.610	39.503	6.351	4.027 *
Democratic	44.047	4.951	43.930	5.345	44.470	4.973	1.079 @
Knowledge	44.374	4.865	43.950	4.522	44.051	4.708	0.453 @
Power	38.339	7.201	38.172	7.390	39.418	6.774	3.211 *
Hedonistic	43.146	5.260	43.717	4.582	44.386	4.525	5.215 **
Aesthetic	41.287	6.256	42.445	4.904	42.504	5.444	3.364 *
Health	46.211	4.514	46.546	4.395	46.937	4.199	2.112 @
Total	**373.532**	**24.701**	**373.828**	**24.308**	**379.52**	**23.387**	**6.809 ****

@ not significant at 0.05 level

* significant at 0.05 level

** significant at 0.01 level

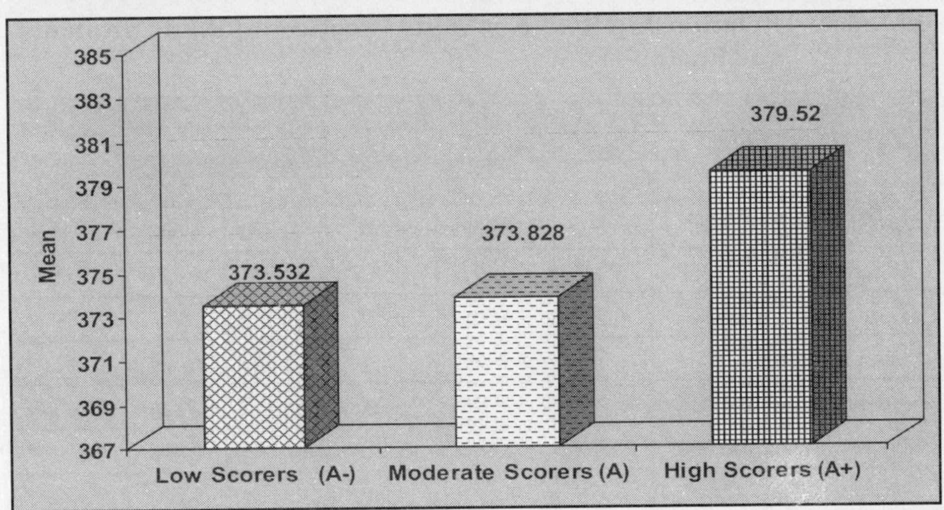

Figure 5. 27 Histogram Showing the Relationship Between Overall Attitudes Towards Values of B.Ed. Students and Factor—A

It is evident from Table 5.29 that the total mean practice scores differ significantly for three personality groups *viz.*, Low scorers (Mean =354.503), Moderate scorers (Mean = 367.273) and High scorers (Mean = 366.540), See vide Figure 5.28. (*on next page*) The results of F-Ratio reveal that three groups do not significantly differ for the values Social, Religious, Knowledge but they significantly differ for the values Economic (5.399**), Democratic (10.001**), Power (6.390**), Hedonistic (9.956**), Aesthetic (30.088**), Health (21.162**). The A+ group was significantly at higher level in their value practices than others. Also, it could be seen that the relationship between overall value practice and Factor—A was significant. Hence it is clear that the more outgoing B.Ed. Students practice values at better than reserved B.Ed. Students.

From the results of Tables 5.28 and 5.29, it is evident that in general, the outgoing B.Ed. Students have high attitudes towards values and they also practice well than the reserved B.Ed. Students.

2. Factor—B

An observation into Table 5.30 reveals that there was no significant variation among the total mean attitude scores of three personality groups *viz.*, Low scorers (Mean =376.274), Moderate scorers (Mean = 376.766) and High scorers (Mean = 381.154), See vide Figure 5.29. (*on page 139*) The results of F-Ratio reveal that three groups significantly differ for the values Social (4.508*), Knowledge, (4.615*), Health (4.434*) but they do not significantly differ for the values Religious, Economic, Democratic, Power, Hedonistic, Aesthetic. Also, it could be seen that the relationship between overall attitudes towards values and Factor—B was not significant. So it is clear that attitudes towards values of B.Ed. students were not affected by their intelligence.

Table 5.29 Relationship Between Value Practices of B.Ed., Students and Factor—A

Values	Low Scorers (A-) (171)		Moderate Scorers (A) (198)		High Scorers (A+) (591)		F-value (2,957 d.f.)
	Mean	S.D.	Mean	S.D.	Mean	S.D.	
Social	41.784	6.292	43.232	6.244	42.800	6.650	2.434 @
Religious	39.357	6.053	39.697	6.265	39.704	6.460	0.211 @
Economic	36.842	6.392	34.798	6.084	35.474	5.997	5.399 **
Democratic	42.485	6.561	45.379	5.111	44.019	6.409	10.001 **
Knowledge	41.316	7.247	42.525	6.866	41.455	7.416	1.823 @
Power	36.960	7.502	35.682	6.790	37.673	6.616	6.390 **
Hedonistic	41.930	6.190	44.520	4.661	43.088	5.740	9.956 **
Aesthetic	36.579	7.306	40.480	7.028	41.049	6.351	30.088 **
Health	37.252	6.624	40.960	7.376	41.278	7.325	21.162 **
Total	**354.503**	**24.535**	**367.273**	**28.617**	**366.540**	**30.127**	**12.615 ****

@ not significant at 0.05 level
* significant at 0.05 level
** significant at 0.01 level

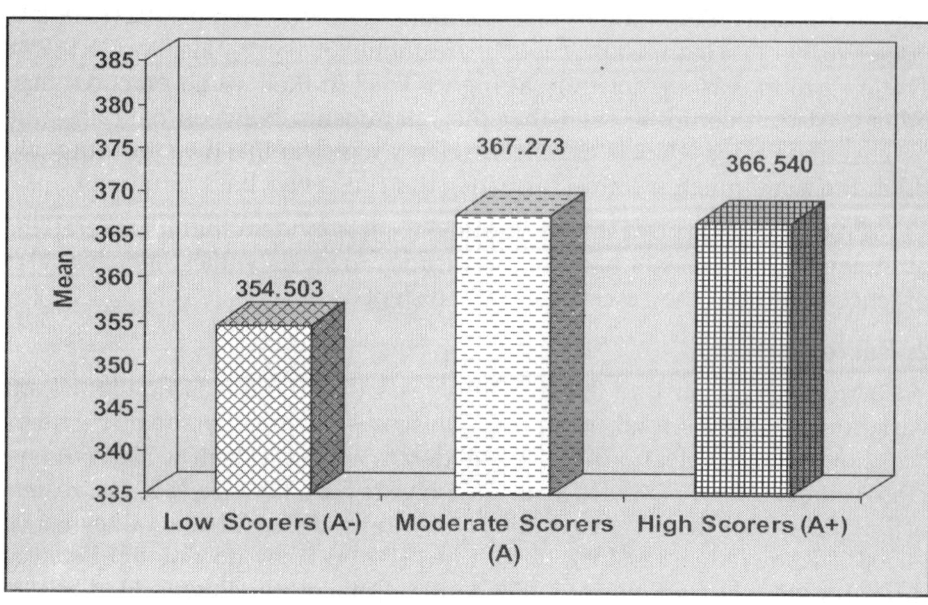

Figure 5. 28 **Histogram Showing the Relationship Between Overall Value Practices of B.Ed., Students and Factor—A**

Table 5.30 Relationship Between Attitudes towards Values of B.Ed. Students and Factor—B

Values	Low Scorers (B-) (328)		Moderate Scorers (B) (483)		High Scorers (B+) (149)		F-value (2,957 d.f.)
	Mean	S.D.	Mean	S.D.	Mean	S.D.	
Social	42.756	4.870	43.325	4.441	44.094	4.352	4.508 *
Religious	34.817	7.237	34.563	6.987	34.081	6.774	0.565 @
Economic	39.061	6.282	39.015	6.639	39.369	6.355	0.764 @
Democratic	44.061	5.302	44.414	4.912	44.349	4.931	0.490 @
Knowledge	43.921	4.753	43.872	4.664	45.154	4.557	4.615 *
Power	38.902	7.269	38.986	7.024	39.060	6.314	0.031 @
Hedonistic	43.939	4.679	43.917	4.578	44.577	5.090	1.202 @
Aesthetic	42.384	5.467	42.037	5.616	42.805	5.219	1.204 @
Health	46.433	4.684	46.638	4.191	47.664	3.627	4.434 *
Total	**376.274**	**25.043**	**376.766**	**23.811**	**381.154**	**21.671**	**2.355 @**

@ not significant at 0.05 level
* significant at 0.05 level
** significant at 0.01 level

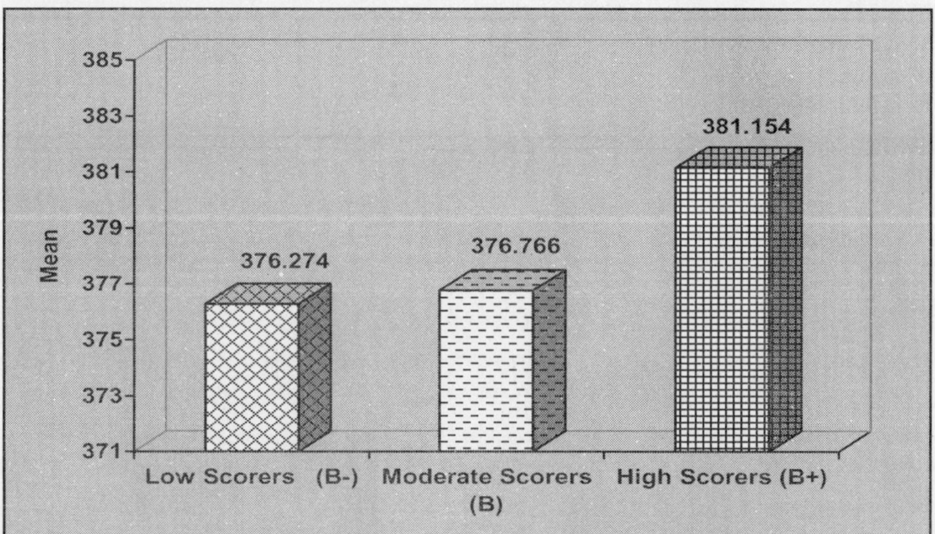

Figure 5. 29 Histogram Showing the Relationship Between Overall Attitudes Towards Values of B.Ed Students and Factor—B

It is evident from Table 5.31 that the total mean practice scores do not differ significantly for three personality groups *viz.*, Low scorers (Mean =364.482), Moderate scorers (Mean = 364.534) and High scorers (Mean =

364.732), See vide Figure 5.30. Moreover, the F-ratios also prove that there was no significant variation in the practice of values on Factor—B. It indicates that the intelligence do not have any relationship with value practice of the B.Ed. Students.

Table 5.31 Relationship Between Value Practices of B.Ed., Students of Factor—B

Values	Low Scorers (B-) (328)		Moderate Scorers (B) (483)		High Scorers (B+) (149)		F-value (2,957 d.f.)
	Mean	S.D.	Mean	S.D.	Mean	S.D.	
Social	42.698	6.410	42.743	6.708	42.618	6.140	0.024 @
Religious	39.558	6.344	39.700	6.300	39.631	6.527	0.050 @
Economic	35.366	6.282	35.518	6.029	36.242	6.010	1.097 @
Democratic	44.207	6.082	44.079	6.037	43.456	7.234	0.768 @
Knowledge	41.753	7.298	41.760	7.274	41.074	7.296	0.556 @
Power	37.119	7.082	37.008	6.848	37.584	6.383	0.404 @
Hedonistic	43.171	5.558	43.282	5.712	42.852	5.820	0.325 @
Aesthetic	40.290	6.829	40.000	6.915	40.235	6.861	0.190 @
Health	40.320	7.261	40.445	7.235	41.040	8.018	0.516 @
Total	**364.482**	**28.581**	**364.534**	**29.384**	**364.732**	**30.418**	**0.004 @**

@ not significant at 0.05 level
* significant at 0.05 level
** significant at 0.01 level

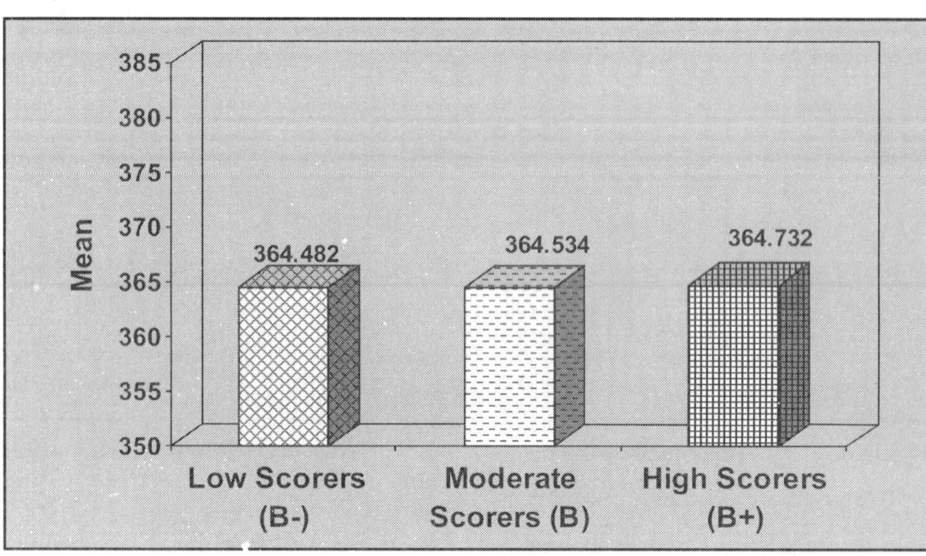

Figure 5.30 Histogram Showing the Relationship Between Overall Value Practices of B.Ed., Students and Factor—B

From the Tables 5. 30 and 5.31 it is evident that the Factor—B could not bring any variation either in the attitudes or in the practices of values of B.Ed. Students.

3. Factor—C

An observation into Table 5.32 reveals that there was no significant variation among the total mean attitude scores of three personality groups *viz.*, Low scorers (Mean =375.387), Moderate scorers (Mean = 376.953) and High scorers (Mean = 378.461), See vide Figure 5.31. (*on next page*) It is evident from the F-ratios that only on the Aesthetic value (6.454**) the C+ group was significantly at higher level in their attitudes towards values than others. Also, it could be seen that the relationship between overall attitudes towards values and Factor—C was not significant. It indicates that the emotional stability do not have any relationship with attitudes towards value of the B.Ed. Students.

Table 5.32 Relationship Between Attitudes Towards Values of B.Ed. Students and Factor—C

Values	Low Scorers (C-) (222)		Moderate Scorers (C) (300)		High Scorers (C+) (438)		F-value (2,957 d.f.)
	Mean	S.D.	Mean	S.D.	Mean	S.D.	
Social	43.063	4.428	43.113	4.891	43.438	4.472	0.686 @
Religious	34.306	7.482	34.813	7.138	34.548	6.742	0.353 @
Economic	39.496	6.812	39.547	5.869	38.562	6.656	2.661 @
Democratic	44.306	4.919	43.927	5.507	44.516	4.776	1.237 @
Knowledge	44.135	5.070	43.687	4.497	44.338	4.624	1.749 @
Power	38.667	7.219	38.753	6.843	39.270	6.992	0.755 @
Hedonistic	43.775	4.829	44.053	4.224	44.137	4.934	0.430 @
Aesthetic	41.117	6.442	42.607	4.998	42.635	5.252	6.454 **
Health	46.523	4.340	46.453	4.460	47.018	4.163	1.867 @
Total	**375.387**	**25.294**	**376.953**	**23.952**	**378.461**	**23.248**	**1.253 @**

@ not significant at 0.05 level
* significant at 0.05 level
** significant at 0.01 level

It is evident from Table 5.33 that the total mean practice scores differ significantly for three personality groups *viz.*, Low scorers (Mean =359.392), Moderate scorers (Mean = 359.917) and High scorers (Mean = 370.331), See vide Figure 5.32. (*on page 143*) It is evident from the F-ratios that all the values differ significantly at 0.01 level except for Economic, Democratic and Aesthetic Values, which are significant at 0.05 level. Also, it could be seen that the relationship between overall value practices and Factor—C was significant. Hence it is clear that emotionally more stable B.Ed. students practice values better than the emotionally less stable B.Ed. students.

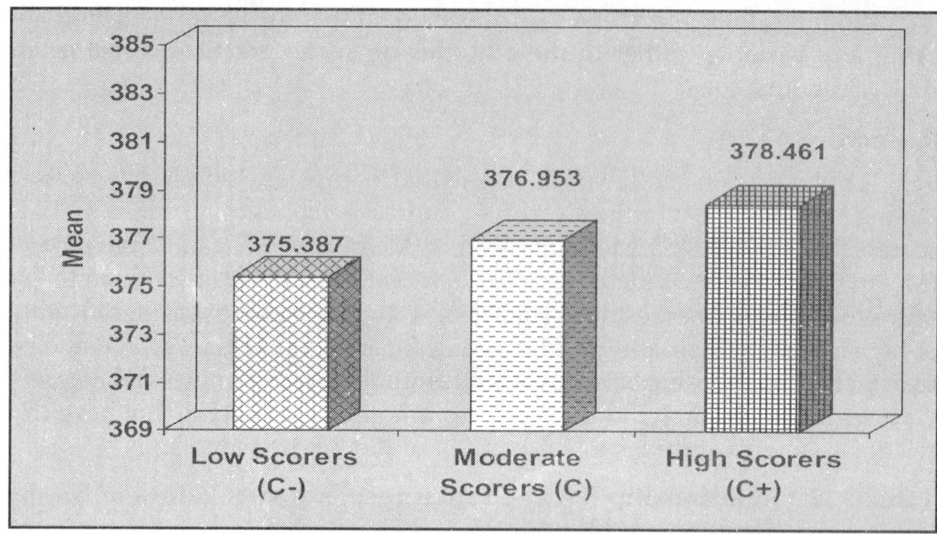

Figure 5. 31 Histogram Showing the Relationship Between Overall Attitudes Towards Values of B.Ed., Students and Factor—C

Table 5.33 Relationship Between Value Practices of B.Ed. Students and Factor—C

Values	Low Scorers (C-) (222)		Moderate Scorers (C) (300)		High Scorers (C+) (438)		F-value (2,957 d.f.)
	Mean	S.D.	Mean	S.D.	Mean	S.D.	
Social	42.117	5.866	41.533	7.245	43.813	6.123	12.36 **
Religious	38.694	6.062	38.917	6.549	40.617	6.216	9.778 **
Economic	34.910	6.053	36.333	5.917	35.400	6.238	3.821 *
Democratic	43.041	6.785	44.367	5.821	44.292	6.215	3.603 *
Knowledge	41.036	7.059	40.517	7.801	42.740	6.876	9.490 **
Power	38.131	7.150	36.150	7.018	37.306	6.510	5.628 **
Hedonistic	42.207	5.852	42.800	5.883	43.927	5.337	7.849 **
Aesthetic	39.440	6.695	39.667	7.146	40.811	6.721	3.974 *
Health	39.820	7.320	39.633	7.179	41.427	7.424	6.562 **
Total	**359.392**	**28.264**	**359.917**	**29.498**	**370.331**	**28.563**	**16.279 ****

@ not significant at 0.05 level
* significant at 0.05 level
** significant at 0.01 level.

From the results of Tables 5.32 and 5.33, it is evident that in general, the emotionally stable B.Ed. Students though not have high attitudes but they practice very well than the less stable B.Ed. Students.

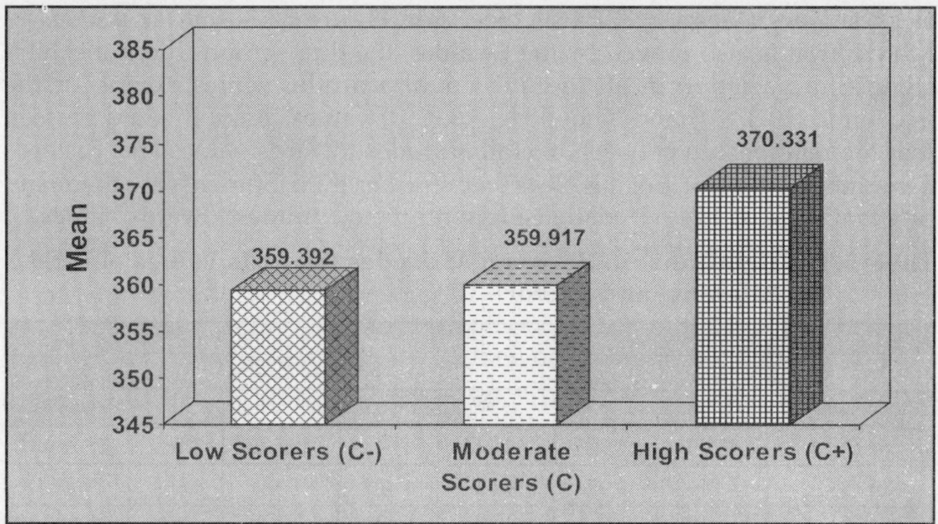

Figure 5.32 Histogram Showing the Relationship Between Overall Values Practices of B.Ed., Students and Factoıs—C

Table 5.34 Relationship Between Attitudes Towards Values of B.Ed. Students and Factor—E

Values	Low Scorers (E-) (412)		Moderate Scorers (E)(355)		High Scorers (E+) (193)		F-value (2,957 d.f.)
	Mean	S.D.	Mean	S.D.	Mean	S.D.	
Social	43.209	4.532	43.538	4.461	42.808	4.947	1.612 @
Religious	34.384	7.091	34.518	6.592	35.088	7.700	0.686 @
Economic	38.228	6.387	39.166	6.454	40.767	6.363	10.378 **
Democratic	44.733	4.662	43.87	5.205	44.083	5.480	2.974 @
Knowledge	43.850	4.504	44.569	4.806	43.710	4.839	3.029 *
Power	38.685	7.051	39.290	6.892	38.985	7.086	0.714 @
Hedonistic	43.854	4.458	44.383	5.126	43.741	4.334	1.658 @
Aesthetic	42.607	4.775	42.259	5.809	41.596	6.303	2.232 @
Health	46.418	4.343	47.110	4.286	46.684	4.212	2.466 @
Total	**375.966**	**22.384**	**378.704**	**24.957**	**377.461**	**25.280**	**1.253 @**

@ not significant at 0.05 level
* significant at 0.05 level
** significant at 0.01 level

4. Factor—E

An observation into Table 5.38 reveals that there was no significant variation among the total mean attitude scores of three personality groups *viz.*, Low scorers (Mean =375.966), Moderate scorers (Mean = 378.704) and

High scorers (Mean = 377.461), See vide Figure 5.33. (*on the next page*) Moreover, it is also proved by the F-values, the three groups did not exhibit significant variation in all the individual attitudes scores except for the Economic (10.378**) and Knowledge (3.029*) values. Also, it could be seen that the relationship between overall attitudes towards values and Factor—E was not significant. So, it is clear that whether B.Ed. Students are dominant or submissive, it has no relationship with their attitudes towards values.

Table 5.35 Relationship Between Attitudes towards Values of B.Ed. Students and Factor—E

Values	Low Scorers (E-) (412)		Moderate Scorers (E)(355)		High Scorers (E+) (193)		F-Value (2,957 d.f.)
	Mean	S.D.	Mean	S.D.	Mean	S.D.	
Social	43.932	5.966	42.437	6.448	40.596	7.165	18.369 **
Religious	40.498	5.934	39.437	6.485	38.187	6.660	9.172 **
Economic	34.854	6.009	35.873	6.102	36.580	6.205	5.959 **
Democratic	45.085	5.965	43.606	6.114	42.539	6.714	12.463 **
Knowledge	42.864	6.927	41.761	7.046	38.860	7.722	20.752 **
Power	36.384	6.405	37.310	7.191	38.420	6.976	6.042 **
Hedonistic	43.981	5.363	43.254	5.579	41.321	6.076	14.918 **
Aesthetic	39.648	7.161	40.380	6.738	40.725	6.434	1.974 @
Health	41.299	7.059	40.394	7.692	38.964	7.178	6.732 **
Total	**368.544**	**27.78**	**364.451**	**30.146**	**356.192**	**28.982**	**11.995 ****

@ not significant at 0.05 level
* significant at 0.05 level
** Significant at 0.01 level

It is evident from Table 5.35 that the total mean practice scores differ significantly for three personality groups *viz.*, Low scorers (Mean =364.482), Moderate scorers (Mean = 364.534) and High scorers (Mean = 364.732), See vide Figure 5.34. (*on next page*) Moreover, the F-ratios also reveal that the variations are significant at 0.01 level of probability, except for Aesthetic Value. Hence it can be said that Factor—E does have significant relationship with the value practices of the B.Ed. Students. It is concluded that B.Ed. students with submissive nature practice values better than the B.Ed. students with dominant nature.

From the results of Tables 5.34 and 5.35, it is evident that in general, the dominant B.Ed. Students though not have high attitudes but they practice very well than the submissive B.Ed. Students. The dominant or submissive B.Ed. Students attitudes are high regarding economic and knowledge values and they do practice those values more. Moreover, it is only for the aesthetic value, where the B.Ed. Students or not high regarding attitudes and they also do not practice well.

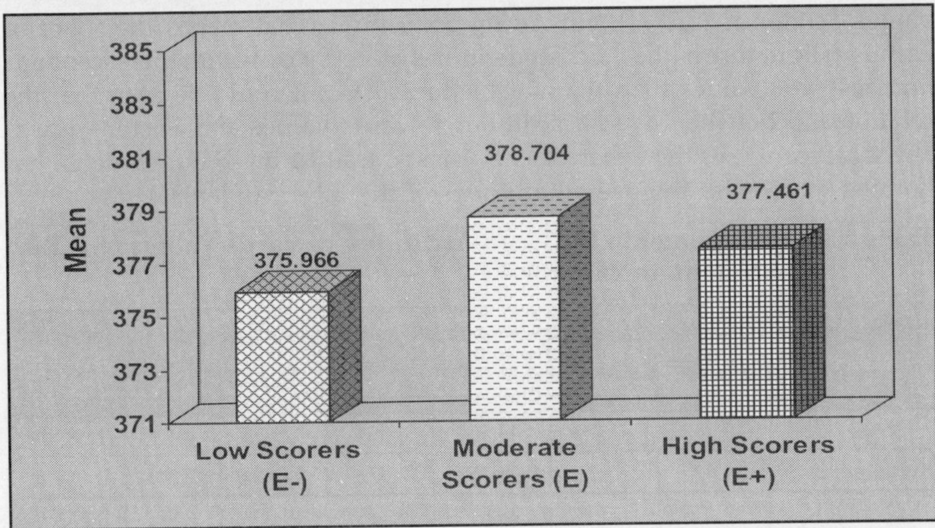

Figure 5.33 **Histogram Showing the Relationship Between Overall Attitudes Towards Values of B.Ed., Students and Factor—E**

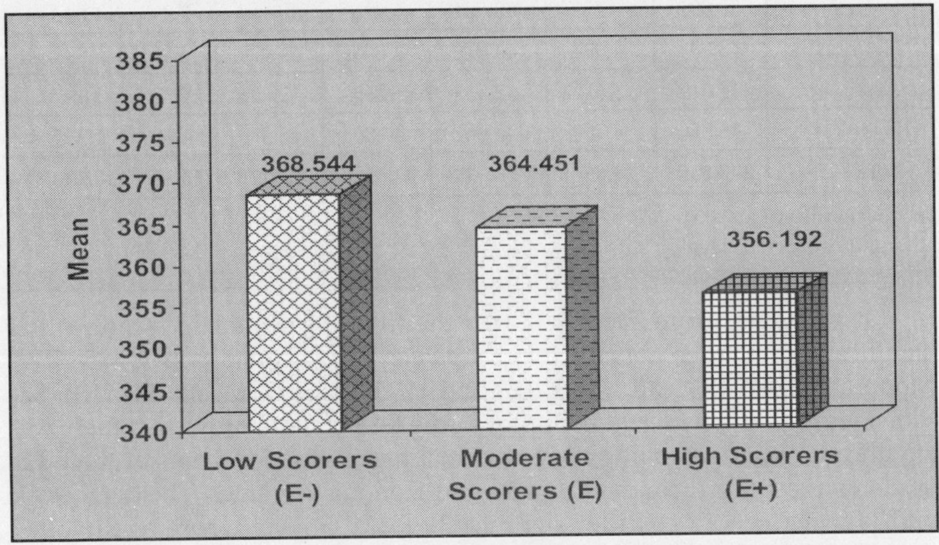

Figure 5.34 **Histogram Showing the Relationship Between Overall Value Practices of B.Ed., Students and Factor—E**

5. Factor—F

An observation into Table 5.36 reveals that there was no significant variation among the total mean attitude scores of three personality groups *viz.*, Low scorers (Mean =377.819), Moderate scorers (Mean = 376.912) and High scorers (Mean = 377.170), See vide Figure 5.35. (*on page 147*) Moreover, the F-ratios also reveal that the variations are not significant, except for the values Economic (3.277*) and Aesthetic (3.497*). That means the sober or enthusiastic nature of the B.Ed. students has more concern with their economic and aesthetic values than the other values. Also, it could be seen that the relationship between overall attitudes towards values and Factor—F was not significant. So, the sober or enthusiastic trait of the B.Ed. students has nothing to do with the overall attitudes of the B.Ed. students.

Table 5.36 Relationship Between Attitudes Towards Values of B.Ed. Student and Factor—F

Values	Low Scorers (E-) (412)		Moderate Scorers (E)(355)		High Scorers (E+) (193)		F-value (2,957 d.f.)
	Mean	S.D.	Mean	S.D.	Mean	S.D.	
Social	43.269	4.879	43.501	4.454	42.815	4.421	1.683 @
Religious	34.625	6.972	34.358	6.926	34.864	7.318	0.413 @
Economic	39.775	6.301	38.534	6.358	39.078	6.801	3.277 *
Democratic	44.388	4.837	44.312	5.018	44.099	5.377	0.235 @
Knowledge	44.025	4.801	44.146	4.728	44.074	4.518	0.068 @
Power	39.331	6.789	38.584	6.976	39.119	7.295	1.093 @
Hedonistic	43.931	4.994	44.076	4.604	44.074	4.451	0.091 @
Aesthetic	41.619	5.672	42.539	5.563	42.708	5.123	3.497 *
Health	46.856	4.190	46.862	4.285	46.338	4.469	1.352 @
Total	**377.819**	**24.66**	**376.912**	**22.63**	**377.170**	**25.19**	**0.130 @**

@ not significant at 0.05 level
* significant at 0.05 level
** significant at 0.01 level

It is evident from Table 5.37 that the total mean practice scores differ significantly for three personality groups *viz.*, Low scorers (Mean =358.734), Moderate scorers (Mean = 369.106) and High scorers (Mean=364.753), See vide Figure 5.36. (*on page 148*) Moreover, the F-ratios also prove that there was significant variation among the individual mean practice scores of the B.Ed. students except for Economic, Power and Hedonistic values. The democratic and knowledge values differ significantly at 0.05 level where as the other values social, religious, aesthetic and health values differ significantly at 0.01 level. Also, it could be seen that the relationship between overall value practices and Factor—F was significant. It was concluded that B.Ed. students with enthusiastic nature practice values better than B.Ed. students with sober nature.

It can be interpreted from the F-values of the two tables 5.36 and 5.37 of Factor—F that, even though the sober or enthusiastic B.Ed. Students attitudes are high regarding their economic value they do not practice that value as per their attitudes. The sober or enthusiastic B.Ed. Students attitudes are high for aesthetic value and they do practice that value more.

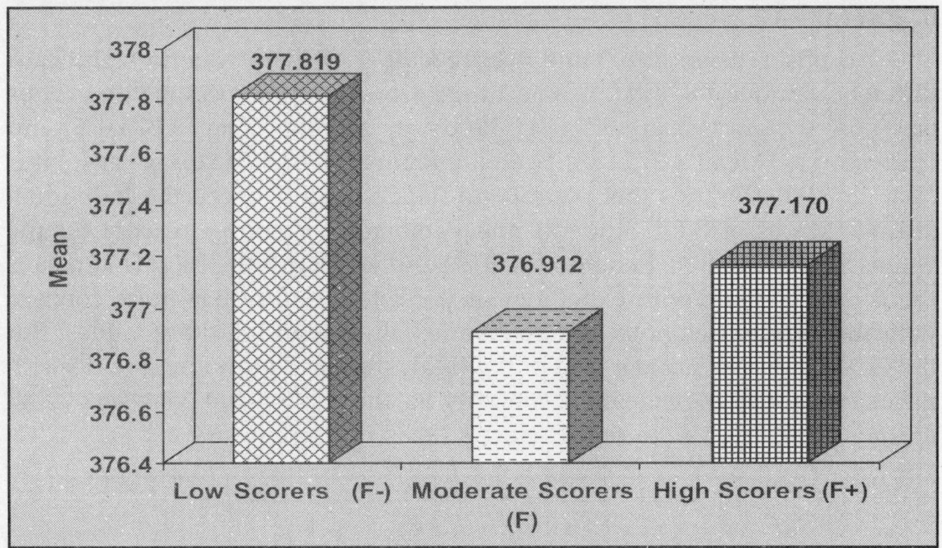

Figure 5.35 Histogram Showing the Relationship Between Overall Attitudes Towards Values of B.Ed., Students and Factor—F

Table 5.37 Relationship Between Value Practices of B.Ed. Students and Factor—F

Values	Low Scorers (F-) (320)		Moderate Scorers (F) (397)		High Scorers (F+) (243)		F-value (2,957 d.f.)
	Mean	S.D.	Mean	S.D.	Mean	S.D.	
Social	42.016	6.378	43.539	6.267	42.263	6.955	5.649 **
Religious	39.234	6.156	40.378	6.133	38.971	6.816	4.732 **
Economic	35.984	6.150	35.214	5.958	35.638	6.307	1.419 @
Democratic	43.391	6.468	44.647	5.752	43.848	6.658	3.733 *
Knowledge	40.969	7.004	42.355	7.057	41.399	7.906	3.421 *
Power	37.609	7.114	36.788	6.567	37.078	6.961	1.288 @
Hedonistic	42.813	5.810	43.463	5.599	43.189	5.605	1.166 @
Aesthetic	38.219	7.068	41.058	6.572	41.152	6.580	19.396 **
Health	38.500	7.144	41.662	7.045	41.214	7.651	18.529 **
Total	**358.734**	**26.500**	**369.106**	**28.13**	**364.753**	**33.01**	**11.995 ****

@ not significant at 0.05 level
* significant at 0.05 level
** significant at 0.01 level

6. Factor—G

An observation into Table 5.38 reveals that there was no significant difference among the total mean attitude scores of three personality groups *viz.*, Low scorers (Mean =379.631), Moderate scorers (Mean = 373.035) and High scorers (Mean = 377.188), See vide Figure 5.37. (*on next page*) Also, it is clear from the F-ratios that there is no relationship between the individual attitude scores of B.Ed. students and Personality Factor—G except for the values Social (3.858**), Religious (3.062*) and Economic (8.308*). That means the B.Ed. Students with expedient or persistent nature has more concern with their social, religious and economic values than the other values. But the expedient or persistent trait of the B.Ed. students has nothing to do with the overall attitudes of the B.Ed. students. So, the relationship between overall attitudes towards values and Factor—G was not significant.

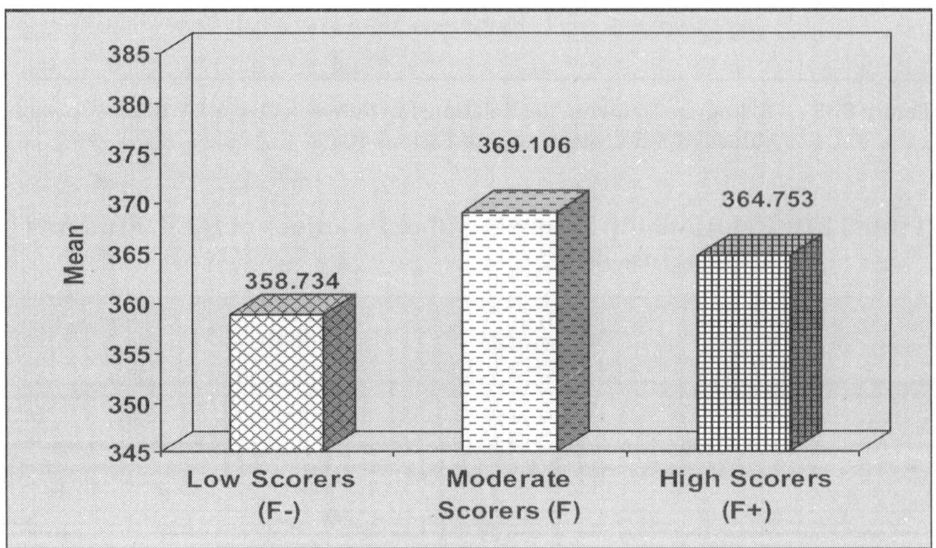

Figure 5.36 Histogram Showing the Relationship Between Overall Value Practices of B.Ed., Students and Factor—F

It is evident from Table 5.39 that the total mean practice scores differ significantly for three personality groups *viz.*, Low scorers (Mean =352.318), Moderate scorers (Mean = 367.931) and High scorers (Mean = 368.567), See vide Figure 5.38. (*on page 150*) Moreover, the F-ratios also prove that there was relationship between the value practices of B.Ed. Students and Factor—G, except for the aesthetic value. Also, it could be seen that the relationship between overall value practices and Factor—G was significant. Therefore the expedient and persistent nature of B.Ed. students do possesses relationship with their value practices. It is also concluded that B.Ed. students with persistent nature practice values better than the B.Ed. students with expedient nature.

Table 5.38 Relationship Between Attitudes Towards Values of B.Ed. and Factor—G

Values	Low Scorers (G-) (233)		Moderate Scorers (G) (116)		High Scorers (G+) (611)		F-value (2,957 d.f.)
	Mean	S.D.	Mean	S.D.	Mean	S.D.	
Social	43.124	4.455	42.224	4.954	43.493	4.556	3.858 **
Religious	35.442	7.466	33.586	6.961	34.432	6.859	3.062 *
Economic	40.575	6.031	38.724	6.011	38.586	6.636	8.308 **
Democratic	44.403	4.891	44.328	4.805	44.229	5.158	0.118 @
Knowledge	43.991	4.696	44.103	4.598	44.121	4.721	0.068 @
Power	39.416	6.441	37.741	7.392	39.031	7.109	2.293 @
Hedonistic	43.742	4.643	44.052	4.670	44.131	4.724	0.589 @
Aesthetic	41.871	5.748	41.828	5.383	42.514	5.430	1.585 @
Health	47.064	3.860	46.448	4.179	46.651	4.481	1.027 @
Total	**379.631**	**22.209**	**373.035**	**24.547**	**377.188**	**24.409**	**2.959 @**

@ not significant at 0.05 level
* significant at 0.05 level
** significant at 0.01 level

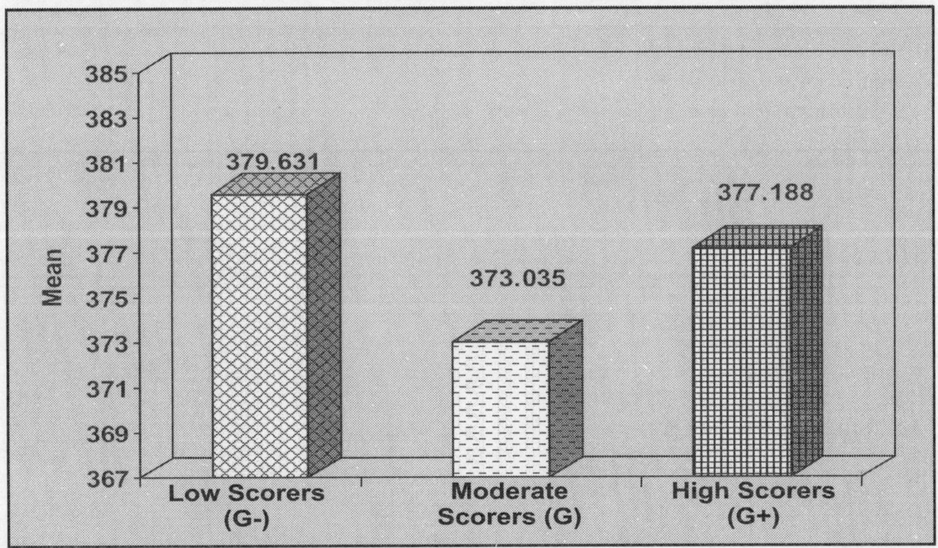

Figure 5.37 Histogram Showing the Relationship Between Overall Attitude Towards Values of B.Ed., Students and Factor—G

It can be interpreted from Tables 5.38 and 5.39, that expedient or persistent nature of the B.Ed. Students do not possess any significant relationship with their attitudes towards values, but they do possess significant relationship with their value practices. But social, religious and economic values indicate variation with B.Ed. student's attitudes towards values and also with their practices. It is only the aesthetic value that does not possess significant relationship with both attitudes and practices.

Table 5.39 Relationship Between Value Practices of B.Ed. Students and Factor—G

Values	Low Scorers (G-) (233)		Moderate Scorers (G) (116)		High Scorers (G+) (611)		F-value (2,957 d.f.)
	Mean	S.D.	Mean	S.D.	Mean	S.D.	
Social	39.700	7.494	43.793	5.847	43.650	5.862	35.167 **
Religious	37.854	7.095	39.828	6.253	40.286	5.926	12.765 **
Economic	36.695	6.265	35.517	6.128	35.164	6.010	5.344 **
Democratic	42.124	6.687	44.612	5.829	44.640	6.015	14.651 **
Knowledge	38.197	8.119	42.845	6.667	42.741	6.626	37.226 **
Power	38.026	7.425	35.948	6.818	37.021	6.601	3.799 *
Hedonistic	41.352	6.035	43.534	5.517	43.805	5.414	16.555 **
Aesthetic	40.172	7.190	40.690	6.557	40.016	6.811	0.465 @
Health	38.197	7.294	41.164	7.113	41.244	7.272	15.414 **
Total	**352.318**	**29.773**	**367.931**	**27.395**	**368.567**	**28.116**	**28.466 ****

@ not significant at 0.05 level
* significant at 0.05 level
** significant at 0.01 level

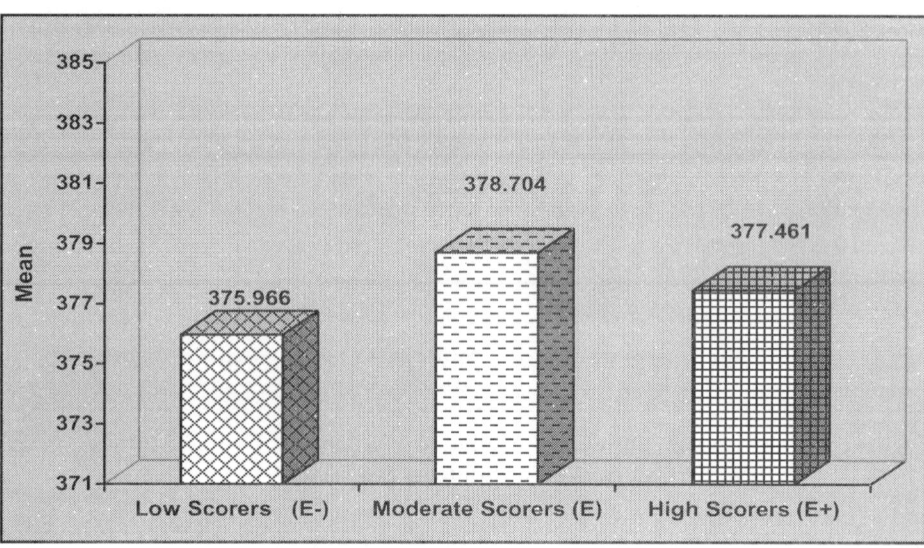

Figure 5.38 **Histogram Showing the Relationship Between Overall Value Practices of B.Ed., Students and Factor—G**

7. Factor—H

An observation into Table 5.41 reveals that there was no significant difference among the total mean attitude scores of three personality groups *viz.*, Low scorers (Mean =374.414), Moderate scorers (Mean = 377.209) and High scorers (Mean = 379.120), See vide Figure 5.39. (*on page 152*) The 'F' ratios calculated also discloses that they do not show significant variation, except for the values Economic (5.292**), Knowledge (3.212*), and aesthetic (3.304*). Also, it could be seen that the relationship between overall attitudes towards values and Factor-H was significant. It indicates that either shyness or venturesome B.Ed. Students do not possess any relationship with their attitudes towards values.

Table 5.40 Relationship Between Attitudes Towards Values of B.Ed. Students and Factor—H

Values	Low Scorers (H-) (203)		Moderate Scorers (H) (425)		High Scorers (H+) (332)		F-value (2,957 d.f.)
	Mean	S.D.	Mean	S.D.	Mean	S.D.	
Social	43.113	4.396	43.289	4.520	43.283	4.817	0.142 @
Religious	34.473	6.952	34.240	7.264	35.066	6.784	1.323 @
Economic	37.833	6.127	39.233	6.251	39.663	6.853	5.292 **
Democratic	44.089	5.133	44.278	5.193	44.410	4.814	0.274 @
Knowledge	43.389	4.623	44.400	4.449	44.114	5.006	3.212 *
Power	39.429	7.689	38.767	6.652	38.946	6.995	0.612 @
Hedonistic	43.517	4.661	43.878	4.903	44.530	4.404	3.304 *
Aesthetic	42.424	4.927	42.329	5.502	42.114	5.850	0.214 @
Health	46.148	4.620	46.795	4.245	46.994	4.153	2.520 @
Total	**374.415**	**24.201**	**377.209**	**22.867**	**379.120**	**25.053**	**2.442 @**

@ not significant at 0.05 level
* significant at 0.05 level
** significant at 0.01 level

It is evident from Table 5.41 that the total mean practice scores differ significantly for three personality groups *viz.*, Low scorers (Mean =370.714), Moderate scorers (Mean = 363.424) and High scorers (Mean = 362.214), See vide Figure 5.40. (*on page 153*) Moreover, the F-ratios also prove that there was significant relationship between the value practices of B.Ed. Students and Factor—H, except for economic, aesthetic and health values. Also, it could be seen that the relationship between overall value practices and Factor—H was significant. Therefore the shyness or venturesome nature of B.Ed. students does possess relationship with their value practices. It is concluded that B.Ed. students with shy nature practice values better than the B.Ed. students with adventurous nature.

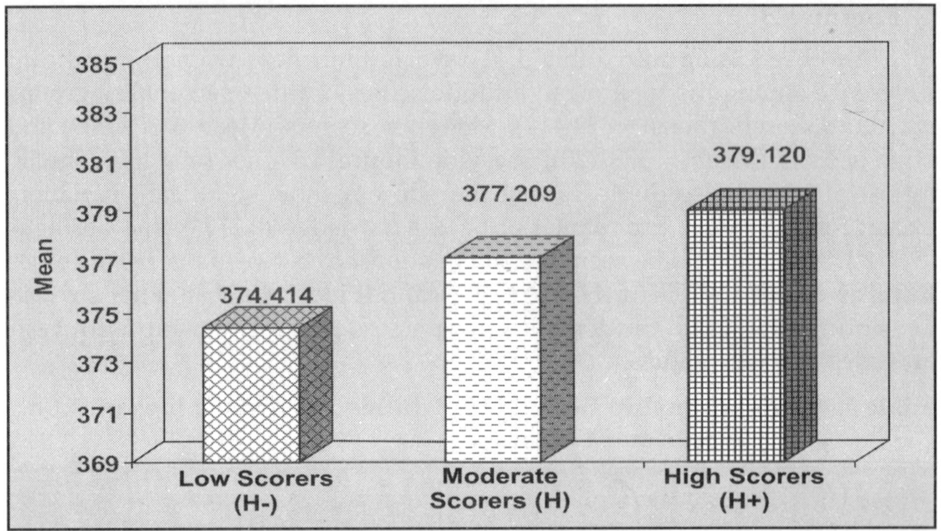

Figure 5.39 Histogram Showing the Relationship Between Overall Attitude Towards Values of B.Ed., Students and Factor—H

Table 5.41 Relationship Between Value Practices of B.Ed. Students and Factor—H

Values	Low Scorers (H-) (203)		Moderate Scorers (H) (425)		High Scorers (H+) (332)		F-value (2,957 d.f.)
	Mean	S.D.	Mean	S.D.	Mean	S.D.	
Social	43.867	6.048	42.588	6.633	42.154	6.569	4.520 *
Religious	40.443	5.828	39.918	6.223	38.795	6.713	5.023 **
Economic	35.345	5.770	35.918	6.045	35.286	6.398	1.177 @
Democratic	46.108	4.027	43.835	6.181	42.997	7.112	16.476 **
Knowledge	43.448	6.539	41.341	7.290	40.949	7.542	8.240 **
Power	35.591	6.868	36.835	6.689	38.464	6.836	12.060 **
Hedonistic	44.901	4.532	42.965	5.831	42.395	5.887	13.176 **
Aesthetic	39.877	7.269	39.588	6.860	40.994	6.566	4.103 @
Health	41.133	7.525	40.435	7.186	40.181	7.494	1.087 @
Total	**370.714**	**27.774**	**363.424**	**28.274**	**362.214**	**30.868**	**5.945 ****

@ not significant at 0.05 level
* significant at 0.05 level
** significant at 0.01 level

It can be interpreted from Tables 5.40 and 5.41, that shyness or venturesome nature of the B.Ed. Students do not possess any significant relationship with their attitudes towards values, but they do possess significant relationship with their value practices. Economic and aesthetic values indicate variation with B.Ed. student's attitudes towards values but they do not possess any significant variation with their practices.

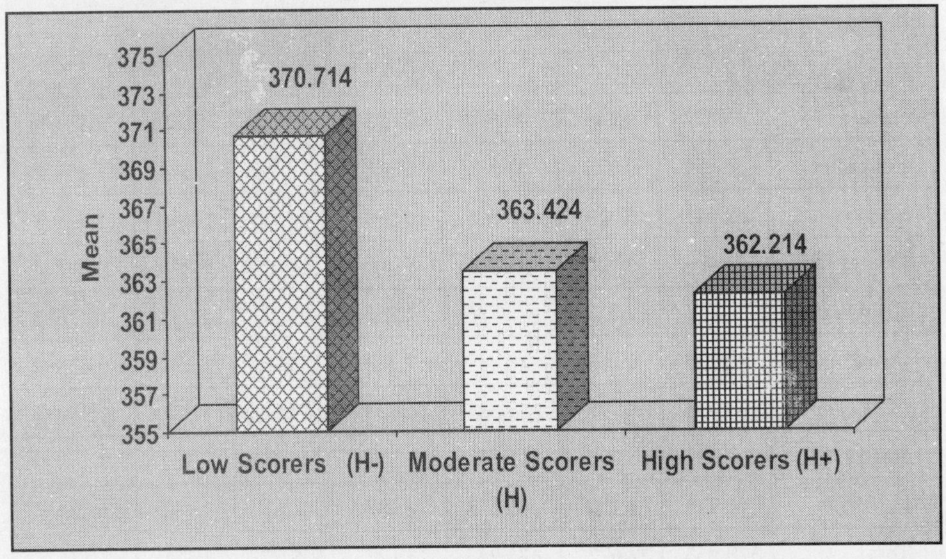

Figure 5.40 **Histogram Showing the Relationship Between Overall Value Practices of B.Ed., Students and Factor—H**

8. Factor—I

An observation into Table 5.40 reveals that there was significant difference among the total mean attitude scores of three personality groups *viz.*, Low scorers (Mean =378.953), Moderate scorers (Mean = 374.947) and High scorers (Mean = 378.773), See vide Figure 5.41. (*on next page*) But the 'F' ratios calculated discloses that the variation was not significant, except for the aesthetic value (9.447**). Also, it could be seen that the relationship between overall attitudes towards values and Factor—I was significant. So, it may be concluded that tough-minded B.Ed. students have better attitudes towards values than tender-minded B.Ed. students.

It is evident from Table 5.43 that the total mean practice scores differ significantly for three personality groups *viz.*, Low scorers (Mean =367.538), Moderate scorers (Mean = 366.221) and High scorers (Mean = 354.530), See vide Figure 5.42. (*on the page 154*) Moreover, the F-ratios also prove that there was relationship between the value practice of B.Ed. Students and Factor—I, except for religious and economic values. Also, it could be seen that the relationship between overall value practices and Factor-I was significant. It may be concluded that tough-minded B.Ed. students practice values better than tender-minded B.Ed. students.

Table 542 Relationship Between Attitudes Towards Values of B.Ed. Students and Factor—I

Values	Low Scorers (I-) (386)		Moderate Scorers (I) (393)		High Scorers (I+) (181)		F-value (2,957 d.f.)
	Mean	S.D.	Mean	S.D.	Mean	S.D.	
Social	43.627	4.446	42.972	4.695	43.050	4.660	2.184 @
Religious	34.451	6.923	34.336	6.898	35.359	7.548	1.404 @
Economic	39.041	6.328	38.809	6.594	39.779	6.480	1.411 @
Democratic	44.409	4.986	44.285	5.000	44.011	5.298	0.392 @
Knowledge	44.285	4.523	43.776	4.735	44.343	4.952	1.476 @
Power	39.036	6.609	38.748	7.263	39.304	7.234	0.428 @
Hedonistic	43.964	4.716	43.837	4.823	44.575	4.344	1.589 @
Aesthetic	43.202	5.097	41.730	5.488	41.481	6.104	9.447 **
Health	46.938	4.120	46.453	4.637	46.873	3.900	1.379 @
Total	**378.953**	**22.677**	**374.947**	**25.177**	**378.773**	**23.624**	**3.171 ***

@ not significant at 0.05 level
* significant at 0.05 level
** significant at 0.01 level

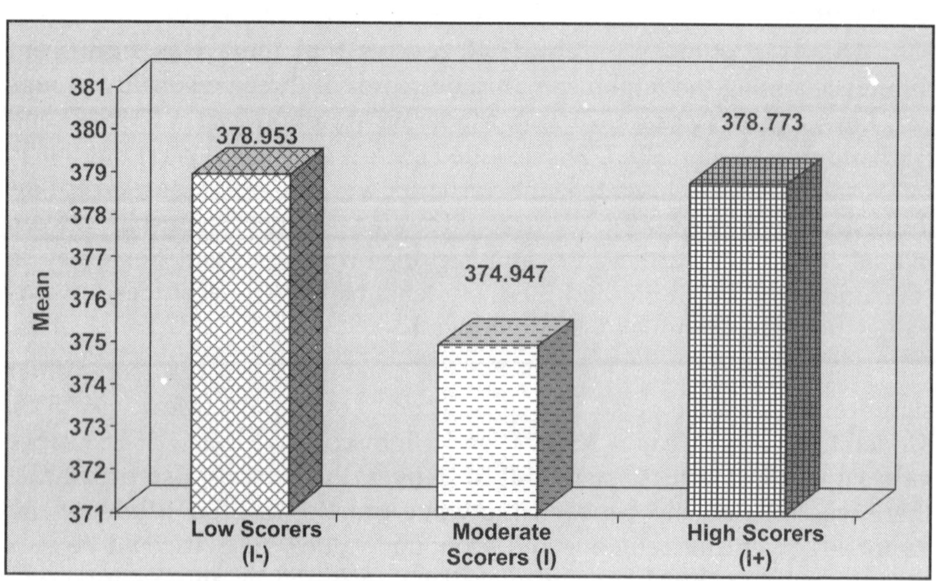

Figure 5.41 Histogram Showing the Relationship Between Overall Attitude Towards Values of B.Ed., Students and Factor—I

Table 5.43 Relationship Between Value Practices of B.Ed. Student and Factor—I

Values	Low Scorers (I-) (386)		Moderate Scorers (I) (393)		High Scorers (I+) (181)		F-value (2,957 d.f.)
	Mean	S.D.	Mean	S.D.	Mean	S.D.	
Social	42.927	6.721	43.041	6.447	41.519	6.104	3.767 *
Religious	39.430	6.411	39.962	6.191	39.392	6.533	0.857 @
Economic	35.155	6.374	35.827	5.660	35.939	6.472	1.567 @
Democratic	44.832	6.129	44.186	5.995	41.961	6.616	13.554 **
Knowledge	41.813	7.590	42.176	6.928	40.166	7.205	4.914 **
Power	37.085	7.098	36.578	6.705	38.453	6.505	4.685 **
Hedonistic	43.472	5.606	43.524	5.403	41.796	6.188	6.714 **
Aesthetic	41.334	6.691	40.051	6.710	37.762	7.000	17.254 **
Health	41.490	7.528	40.878	7.174	37.541	6.680	19.314 **
Total	**367.538**	**32.025**	**366.221**	**26.874**	**354.530**	**25.770**	**13.630 ****

@ not significant at 0.05 level
* significant at 0.05 level
** significant at 0.01 level

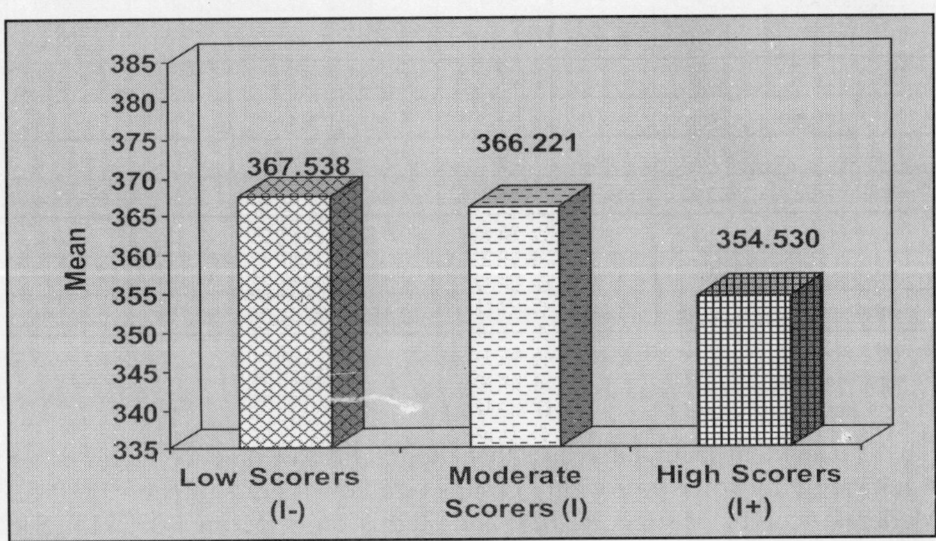

Figure 5.42 Histogram Showing the Relationship Between Overall Value Practices of B.Ed., Students and Factor—I

It can be interpreted from Tables 5.42 and 5.43, that tough-minded or tender-minded nature of the B.Ed. Students do not possess any significant relationship with their attitudes towards values, but they do possess significant relationship with their value practices. It is religious and economic values that do not indicate variation with B.Ed. student's attitudes towards values and also with their practices. It is only the aesthetic value that possesses significant relationship with both attitudes and practices.

9. Factor—L

An observation into Table 5.44 reveals that there was no significant difference among the total mean attitude scores of three personality groups *viz.*, Low scorers (Mean =378.331), Moderate scorers (Mean = 377.083) and High scorers (Mean = 372.250), See vide Figure 5.43. (*on next page*) The 'F' ratios calculated also discloses that the variation was not significant, except for the democratic value (4.965**). Also, it could be seen that the relationship between overall attitudes towards values and Factor—L was not significant. Hence it is clear that whether the B.Ed. Students have trusting or suspecting nature they do not vary in their attitudes towards values.

Table 5.44 Relationship Between Attitudes Towards Values of B.Ed. Students and Factor—L

Values	Low Scorers (L-) (351)		Moderate Scorers (L) (473)		High Scorers (L+) (136)		F-value (2,957 d.f.)
	Mean	S.D.	Mean	S.D.	Mean	S.D.	
Social	43.425	4.677	43.302	4.578	42.618	4.419	1.565 @
Religious	34.262	7.258	34.939	6.798	34.118	7.261	1.273 @
Economic	38.781	6.400	39.112	6.568	39.779	6.290	1.183 @
Democratic	44.781	4.657	44.228	5.225	43.191	5.246	4.965 **
Knowledge	43.966	4.716	44.258	4.644	43.809	4.831	0.680 @
Power	39.419	7.405	38.651	6.713	38.912	6.872	1.226 @
Hedonistic	44.194	4.473	43.911	4.942	44.000	4.389	0.362 @
Aesthetic	42.547	5.421	42.097	5.542	42.191	5.614	0.692 @
Health	46.957	4.173	46.584	4.440	46.632	4.151	0.783 @
Total	**378.331**	**23.882**	**377.083**	**24.353**	**375.250**	**22.779**	**0.841 @**

@ not significant at 0.05 level
* significant at 0.05 level
** significant at 0.01 level

It is evident from Table 5.45 that the total mean practice scores differ significantly for three personality groups *viz.*, Low scorers (Mean =365.085), Moderate scorers (Mean = 365.824) and High scorers (Mean = 358.713), See vide Figure 5.44. (*on page 158*) Moreover, the F-ratios calculated discloses that there was significant variation between the value practice of B.Ed. Students and Factor—L, for the values Social (4.173**), Democratic (3.085*), Hedonistic (3.845*). Also, it could be seen that the relationship between overall value practices and Factor—L was significant. It may be concluded that the B.Ed. students with trusting nature practice values better than the B.Ed. students with suspecting nature.

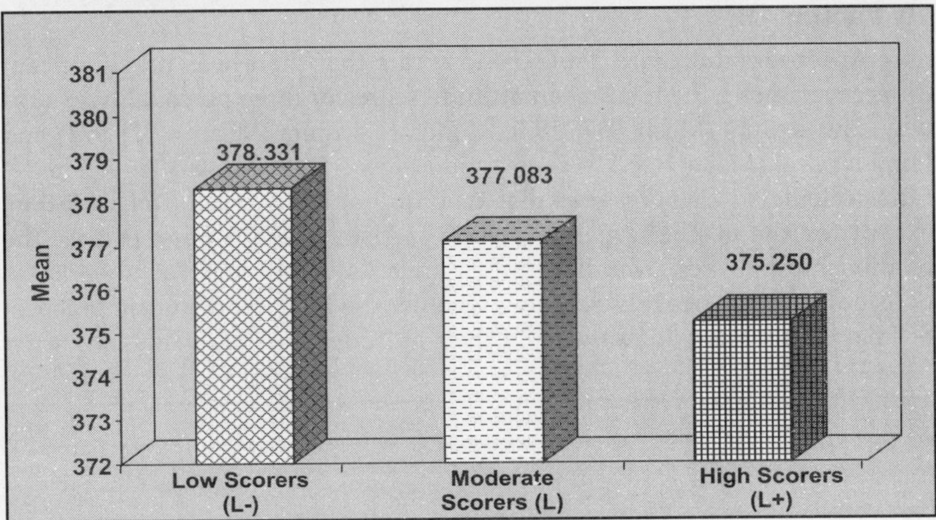

Figure 5.43 Histogram Showing the Relationship Between Overall Attitud Towards Values of B.Ed., Students and Factor—L

Table 5.45 Relationship Between Value Practices of B.Ed. Students and Factor—L

Values	Low Scorers (L-) (351)		Moderate Scorers (L) (473)		High Scorers (L+) (136)		F-value (2,957 d.f.)
	Mean	S.D.	Mean	S.D.	Mean	S.D.	
Social	42.792	6.202	43.066	6.591	41.250	6.879	4.173 **
Religious	39.501	6.367	39.789	6.282	39.485	6.534	0.248 @
Economic	35.399	6.278	35.909	5.941	34.890	6.250	1.757 @
Democratic	44.245	6.262	44.218	6.100	42.794	6.632	3.085 *
Knowledge	41.852	7.568	41.892	7.091	40.294	7.091	2.773 @
Power	36.909	6.902	37.019	6.717	38.125	7.173	1.673 ©
Hedonistic	43.490	5.769	43.298	5.544	41.949	5.747	3.845 *
Aesthetic	40.313	6.807	39.852	6.887	40.662	6.987	0.921 @
Health	40.584	7.330	40.782	7.316	39.265	7.565	2.291 @
Total	**365.085**	**28.980**	**365.824**	**29.298**	**358.713**	**29.263**	**3.232 ***

@ not significant at 0.05 level
* significant at 0.05 level
** significant at 0.01 level

It can be interpreted from Tables 5.44 and 5.45, that trusting or suspecting nature of B.Ed. students could not bring variation in the attitudes towards values of B.Ed. Students, but it could bring difference in the value practices of them. It is only the democratic value that possesses significant relationship with both attitudes and practices.

10. Factor—M

An observation into Table 5.46 reveals that there was no significant difference among the total mean attitude scores of three personality groups *viz.*, Low scorers (Mean =376.197), Moderate scorers (Mean = 376.974) and High scorers (Mean = 363.348), See vide Figure 5.45. (*on next page*) The 'F' ratios calculated also discloses that they do not show significant variation, except for the aesthetic value (4.703**). Also, it could be seen that the relationship between overall attitudes towards values and Factor—M was not significant. Hence it is clear that whether the B.Ed. Students are practical or imaginative they do not vary in their attitudes towards values.

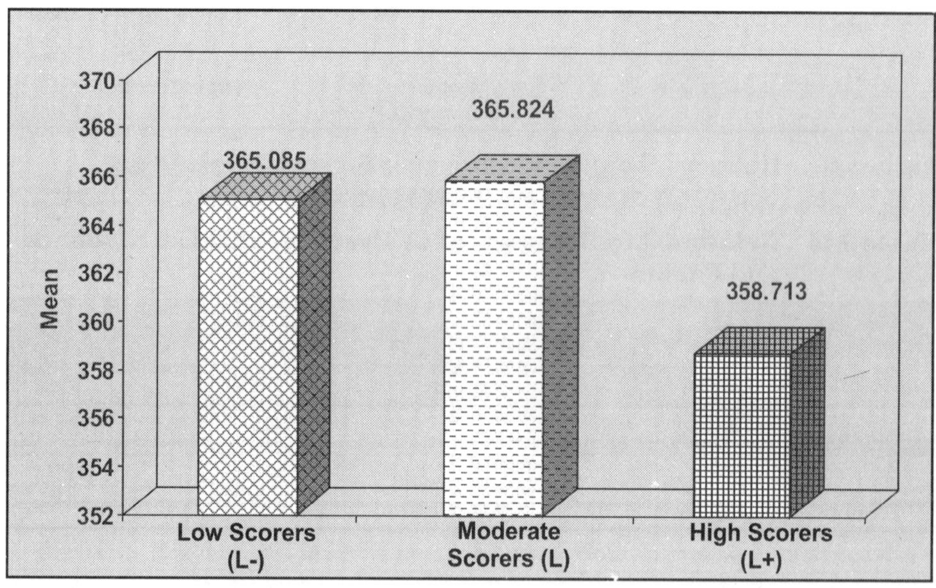

Figure 5.44 **Histogram Showing the Relationship Between Overall Value Practices of B.Ed., Students and Factor—L**

It is evident from Table 5.41 that the total mean practice scores do not differ significantly for three personality groups *viz.*, Low scorers (Mean =363.266), Moderate scorers (Mean = 365.921) and High scorers (Mean = 379.174), See Vide Figure 5.46. (*on page 159*) Moreover, the F-ratios also prove that there was no significant relationship between the value practice of B.Ed. Students and Factor—M, except for the values Social (6.614**), Democratic (5.125**), Aesthetic (10.452**), Health (3.837*) Also, it could be seen that the relationship between overall value practices and Factor—M was not significant.. Therefore the practical or imaginative nature of B.Ed. students does not possess relationship with their value practices.

Table 5.46 Relationship Between Value Practices of B.Ed. Students and Factor—M

Values	Low Scorers (M-) (274)		Moderate Scorers (M) (456)		High Scorers (M+) (230)		F-value (2,957 d.f.)
	Mean	S.D.	Mean	S.D.	Mean	S.D.	
Social	43.255	4.682	43.132	4.654	41.413	7.014	0.449 @
Religious	34.555	6.861	34.250	7.021	39.174	6.753	1.536 @
Economic	38.693	6.120	39.070	6.556	35.957	5.719	1.183 @
Democratic	44.518	4.514	44.237	5.002	44.500	5.496	0.490 @
Knowledge	44.029	4.836	44.162	4.559	40.652	7.270	0.113 @
Power	38.891	7.014	39.154	7.204	37.087	6.883	0.347 @
Hedonistic	44.270	4.529	43.908	4.904	43.152	5.870	0.521 @
Aesthetic	41.431	5.850	42.526	5.259	40.978	6.610	4.703 **
Health	46.555	4.063	46.535	4.581	40.435	7.765	2.820 @
Total	**376.197**	**22.846**	**376.974**	**24.428**	**363.348**	**30.263**	**1.036 @**

@ not significant at 0.05 level
* significant at 0.05 level
** significant at 0.01 level

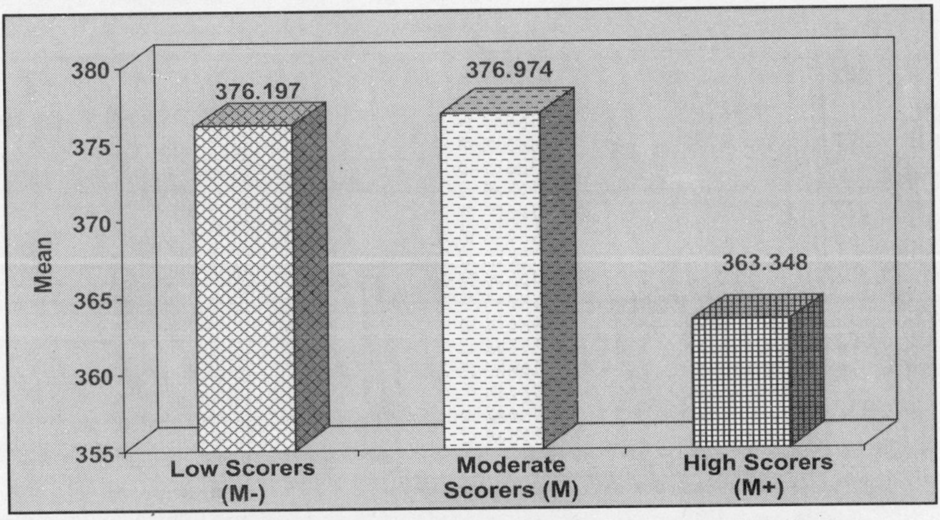

Figure 5.45 Histogram Showing the Relationship Between Overall Attitude Towards Values of B.Ed., Students and Factor—M

It can be interpreted from Tables 5.46 and 5.47, that the imaginative or practical nature of the B.Ed. students could not bring any variation either in the attitudes or in the practice of values of B.Ed. Students. It is only the aesthetic value that possesses significant relationship with both attitudes and practices, at 0.01 level.

Table 5.47 Relationship Between Value Practices of B.Ed. Student and Factor—M

Values	Low Scorers (M-) (274)		Moderate Scorers (M) (456)		High Scorers (M+) (230)		F-value (2,957 d.f.)
	Mean	S.D.	Mean	S.D.	Mean	S.D.	
Social	43.449	5.763	42.917	6.600	43.478	4.380	6.614 **
Religious	40.146	6.081	39.572	6.279	35.243	7.258	1.517 @
Economic	36.004	6.504	35.132	6.048	39.583	6.692	2.320 @
Democratic	43.011	6.951	44.397	6.105	44.096	5.713	5.125 **
Knowledge	42.007	6.819	41.941	7.524	44.009	4.811	2.868 @
Power	37.628	6.673	36.864	6.948	38.696	6.569	1.064 @
Hedonistic	42.920	5.825	43.344	5.482	43.974	4.472	0.481 @
Aesthetic	38.558	6.942	40.658	6.818	42.783	5.476	10.452 **
Health	39.544	7.317	41.096	7.141	47.313	3.960	3.837 *
Total	**363.266**	**28.037**	**365.921**	**29.437**	**379.174**	**24.312**	**0.960 @**

@ not significant at 0.05 level
* significant at 0.05 level
** significant at 0.01 level

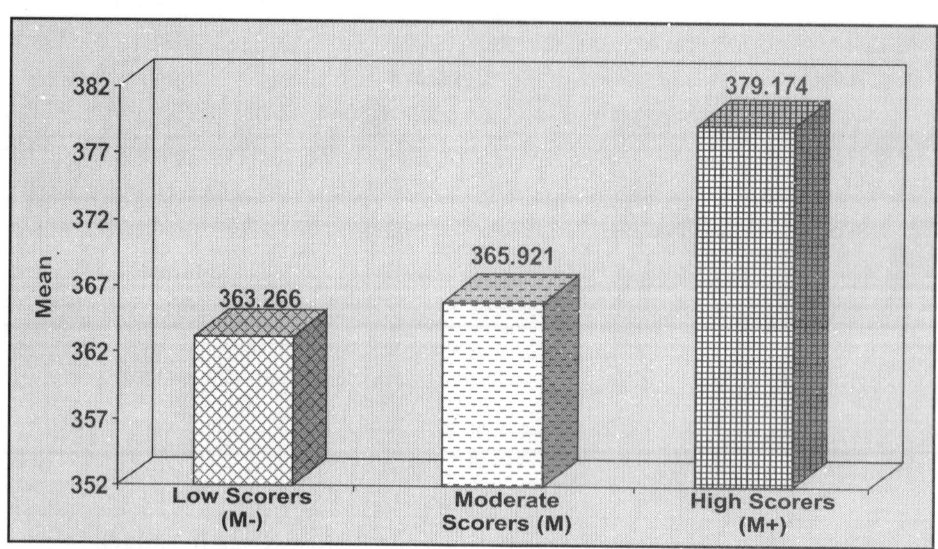

Figure 5.46 Histogram Showing the Relationship Between Overall Value Practices of B.Ed., Students and Factor—M

11. Factor—N

An observation into Table 5.48 reveals that there was no significant difference among the total mean attitude scores of three personality groups *viz.,* Low scorers (Mean =377.365). Moderate scorers (Mean = 376.960) and

High scorers (Mean = 377.752), See vide Figure 5.47. The 'F' ratios calculated also discloses that difference was not significant, except for the values Economic (9.211**) and Aesthetic (7.859**). Also, it could be seen that the relationship between overall attitudes towards values and Factor—N was not significant. Hence it is clear that whether the B.Ed. Students are forthright or polished they do not vary in their attitudes towards values.

Table 5.48 Relationship Between Attitudes towards Values of B.Ed. Students and Factor—N

Values	Low Scorers (N-) (315)		Moderate Scorers (N) (419)		High Scorers (N+) (226)		F-value (2,957 d.f.)
	Mean	S.D.	Mean	S.D.	Mean	S.D.	
Social	43.517	4.764	43.160	4.326	43.044	4.838	0.805 @
Religious	34.629	6.719	34.353	7.504	34.912	6.578	0.484 @
Economic	37.816	6.748	39.747	6.243	39.628	6.251	9.211 **
Democratic	44.305	4.876	44.573	4.895	43.717	5.519	2.124 @
Knowledge	44.248	4.925	44.048	4.412	43.938	4.890	0.317 @
Power	38.673	7.124	38.788	7.154	39.717	6.485	1.718 @
Hedonistic	44.248	4.687	43.661	4.705	44.398	4.665	2.319 @
Aesthetic	43.232	4.928	41.952	5.509	41.540	6.078	7.589 **
Health	46.698	4.601	46.678	4.120	46.858	4.219	0.162 @
Total	**377.365**	**24.945**	**376.960**	**22.559**	**377.752**	**25.154**	**0.084 @**

@ not significant at 0.05 level
* significant at 0.05 level
** significant at 0.01 level

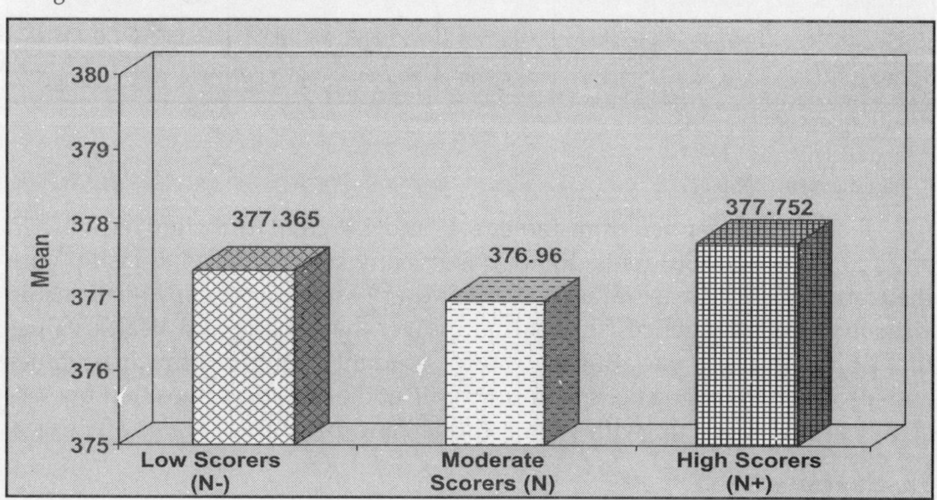

Figure 5.47 Histogram Showing the Relationship Between Overall Attitude Towards Values of B.Ed., Students and Factor—N

It is evident from Table 5.49 that the total mean practice scores differ significantly for three personality groups *viz.*, Low scorers (Mean =366.381), Moderate scorers (Mean = 365.484) and High scorers (Mean = 360.243), See vide Figure 5.48. (*on next page*) Moreover, the F-ratios also prove that there was relationship between the value practice of B.Ed. Students and Factor—N, for the values Religious (4.593**), Economic (7.744**), Democratic (6.998**), Knowledge (10.372**), Aesthetic (3.652*) Also, it could be seen that the relationship between overall value practices and Factor—N was significant. Therefore the forthright or polished nature of B.Ed. students does possess relationship with their value practices. Moreover, B.Ed. students with forthright nature possess better value practices than B.Ed. students with polished nature.

Table 5.49 Relationship Between Value Practices of B.Ed. Students and Factor—N

Values	Low Scorers (N-) (315)		Moderate Scorers (N) (419)		High Scorers (N+) (226)		F-value (2,957 d.f.)
	Mean	S.D.	Mean	S.D.	Mean	S.D.	
Social	42.984	6.142	42.959	6.467	41.858	7.046	2.529 @
Religious	40.381	6.079	39.582	6.312	38.717	6.659	4.593 **
Economic	34.476	5.848	36.074	6.248	36.195	6.047	7.744 **
Democratic	45.095	5.485	43.556	6.733	43.407	6.156	6.998 **
Knowledge	42.968	6.748	41.480	7.567	40.133	7.163	10.372 **
Power	36.778	6.820	37.458	6.754	37.035	7.091	0.915 @
Hedonistic	43.810	5.465	42.852	5.832	42.898	5.608	2.917 @
Aesthetic	39.476	7.136	40.800	6.752	39.823	6.631	3.652 *
Health	40.413	7.433	40.728	7.386	40.177	7.255	0.442 @
Total	**366.381**	**28.311**	**365.489**	**29.652**	**360.243**	**29.470**	**3.300 ***

@ not significant at 0.05 level
* significant at 0.05 level
** significant at 0.01 level

It can be interpreted from Tables 5.48 and 5.49, that forthright or polished nature of the B.Ed. Students do not possess any significant relationship with their attitudes towards values, but they do possess significant relationship with their value practices. It is social, power, hedonistic and health values that do not indicate variation with B.Ed. student's attitudes towards values and also with their practices. It is economic and aesthetic values that possess significant relationship with both attitudes and practices.

12. Factor—O

An observation into Table 5.50 reveals that there was no significant difference among the total mean attitude scores of three personality groups *viz.*, Low scorers (Mean =379.437), Moderate scorers (Mean = 377.641) and High scorers (Mean = 375.149), See vide Figure 5.49. (*on next page*) The 'F' ratios calculated also discloses that they do not show significant variation, except for the Democratic (4.525**) and Power (6.528**) values. Also, it could be seen that the relationship between overall attitudes towards values and Factor—O was not significant. Hence it is clear that whether the B.Ed. Students are secure or insecure they do not vary in their attitudes towards values.

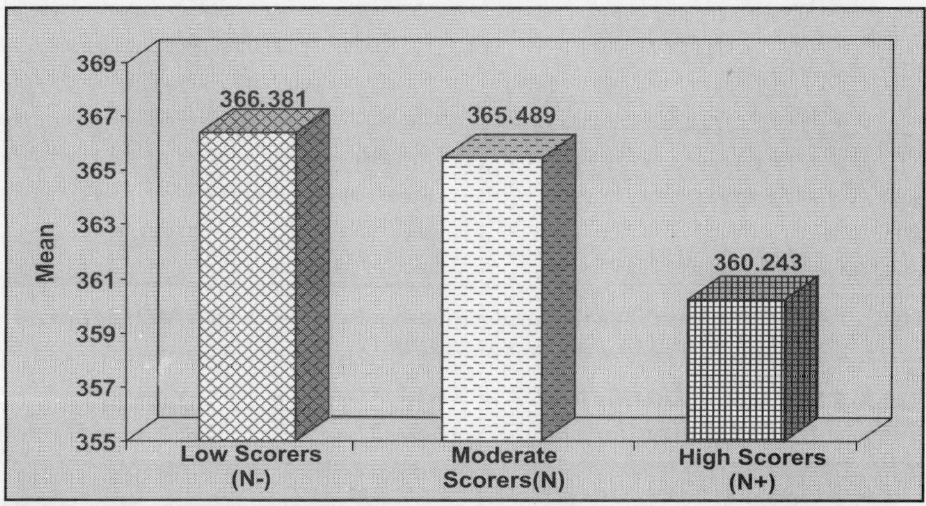

Figure 5.48 **Histogram Showing the Relationshp Between Overall Value Practices of B.Ed., Students and Factor—N**

Table 5.50 Relationship Between Attitudes towards Values of B.Ed. Students and Factor—O

Values	Low Scorers (O-) (263)		Moderate Scorers (O) (368)		High Scorers (O+) (329)		F-Value (2,957 d.f.)
	Mean	S.D.	Mean	S.D.	Mean	S.D.	
Social	43.643	4.320	43.185	4.564	43.009	4.832	1.469 @
Religious	35.057	6.976	34.668	7.219	34.085	6.869	1.455 @
Economic	38.996	6.686	39.495	6.267	38.699	6.510	1.351 @
Democratic	44.441	5.221	44.755	4.780	43.629	5.146	4.525 **
Knowledge	44.403	5.065	44.109	4.585	43.812	4.505	1.180 @
Power	39.513	7.124	38.587	7.182	38.96	6.672	6.528 **
Hedonistic	44.297	4.697	43.788	4.616	44.079	4.784	0.930 @
Aesthetic	42.433	5.725	42.272	5.371	42.152	5.492	0.181 @
Health	46.654	4.646	46.783	3.956	46.723	4.401	0.054 @
Total	**379.437**	**25.558**	**377.641**	**22.228**	**375.149**	**24.403**	**2.415 @**

@ not significant at 0.05 level
* significant at 0.05 level
** significant at 0.01 level

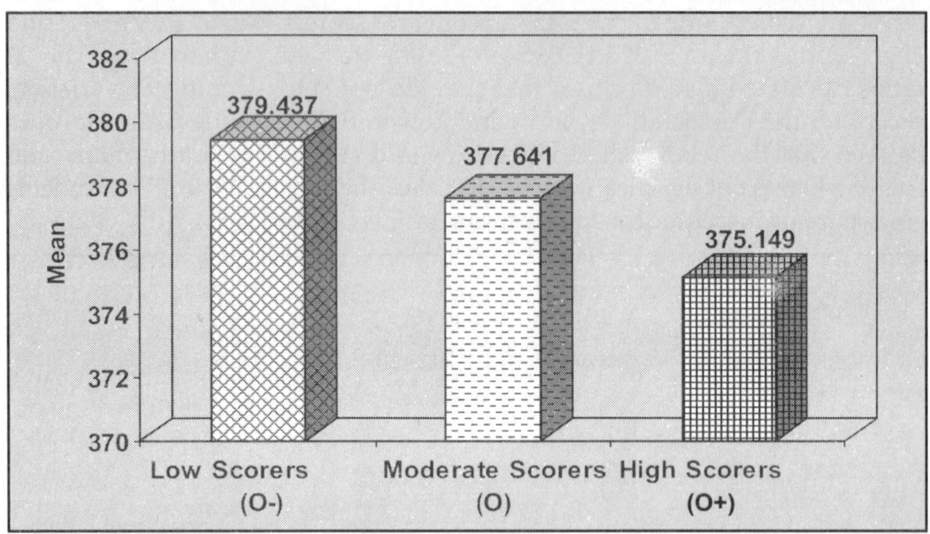

Figure 5.49 Histogram Showing the Relationship Between Overall AttitudeToward Values of B.Ed., Students and Factor-O

Table 5.51 Relationship Between Attitudes towards Values of B.Ed. Students and Factor—O

Values	Low Scorers (O-) (263)		Moderate Scorers (O) (368)		High Scorers (O+) (329)		F-value (2,957 d.f.)
	Mean	S.D.	Mean	S.D.	Mean	S.D.	
Social	41.654	6.407	42.541	6.674	43.739	6.284	7.801 **
Religious	38.954	6.220	39.416	6.339	40.441	6.382	4.429 **
Economic	35.209	6.289	35.788	6.148	35.638	5.938	0.722 @
Democratic	42.757	6.575	44.008	6.385	45.061	5.631	10.121 **
Knowledge	40.856	7.486	41.454	7.582	42.508	6.685	4.013 **
Power	38.194	7.366	37.079	6.753	36.353	6.445	5.335 **
Hedonistic	42.129	6.180	43.003	5.696	44.210	5.029	10.312 **
Aesthetic	39.373	6.968	40.041	7.133	40.851	6.430	3.459 *
Health	39.106	7.482	40.082	7.528	42.067	6.806	13.073 **
Total	**358.232**	**29.181**	**363.410**	**29.845**	**370.866**	**27.393**	**14.486 ****

@ not significant at 0.05 level
* significant at 0.05 level
** significant at 0.01 level

It is evident from Table 5.51 that the total mean practice scores differ significantly for three personality groups *viz.,* Low scorers (Mean =358.332), Moderate scorers (Mean = 363.410) and High scorers (Mean = 370.866), See vide Figure 5.50. (*on next page*) Moreover, the F-ratios also prove that there was relationship between the value practice of B.Ed. Students and Factor—O, except for economic value. Also, it could be seen that the relationship between overall value practices and Factor—O was significant. Therefore the secured or unsecured nature of B.Ed. students does possess relationship with their value practices. Moreover, it is the secured students who practice well than the unsecured students.

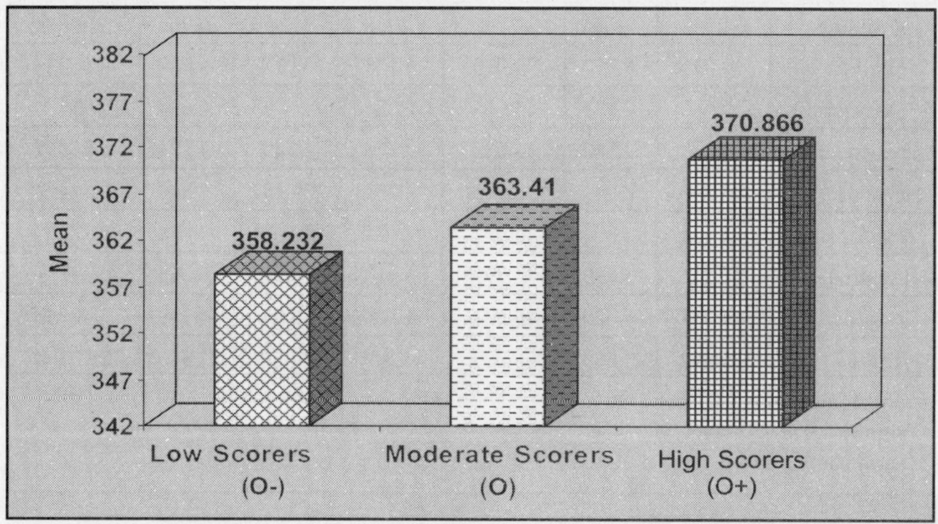

Figure 5.50 Histogram Showing the Relationship Between Overall Value Practices of B.Ed., Students and Factor—O

It can be interpreted from Tables 5.50 and 5.51, that secure or insecure nature of the B.Ed. Students do not possess any significant relationship with their attitudes towards values, but they do possess significant relationship with their value practices. It is economic value that does not indicate variation with B.Ed. student's attitudes towards values and also with their practices. It is democratic and power values that possess significant relationship with both attitudes and practices at 0.01 level.

13. Factor—Q1

An observation into Table 5.52 reveals that there was no significant difference among the total mean attitude scores of three personality groups *viz.*, Low scorers (Mean =375.892), Moderate scorers (Mean = 376.330) and High scorers (Mean = 379.566), See vide Figure 5.51. (*on next page*) The 'F' ratios calculated also discloses that the variation was not significant, except for the Democratic value (4.965**). Also, it could be seen that the relationship between overall attitudes towards values and Factor—Q1 was not significant. Hence it is clear that whether the B.Ed. Students are conservative or experimenting they do not vary in their attitudes towards values.

Table 5.52 Relationship Between Attitudes towards Values of B.Ed. Students and Factor—Q1

Values	Low Scorers (Q1-) (203)		Moderate Scorers (Q1) (448)		High Scorers (Q1+) (309)		F-value (2,957 d.f.)
	Mean	S.D.	Mean	S.D.	Mean	S.D.	
Social	43.271	4.434	43.165	4.600	43.359	4.703	0.166 @
Religious	34.759	7.183	34.299	7.067	34.854	6.905	0.666 @
Economic	39.094	6.957	39.018	6.158	39.178	6.597	0.060 @
Democratic	43.862	4.937	43.964	5.321	45.023	4.634	4.965 **
Knowledge	44.236	4.580	44.013	4.736	44.097	4.724	0.519 @
Power	38.236	7.099	38.946	7.252	39.482	6.516	1.944 @
Hedonistic	43.813	4.804	44.094	4.825	44.071	4.438	0.272 @
Aesthetic	41.862	5.690	42.299	5.310	42.511	5.665	0.857 @
Health	46.759	4.520	46.531	4.305	46.990	4.149	1.027 @
Total	**375.892**	**23.586**	**376.330**	**24.147**	**379.566**	**23.846**	**2.104 @**

@ not significant at 0.05 level
* significant at 0.05 level
** significant at 0.01 level

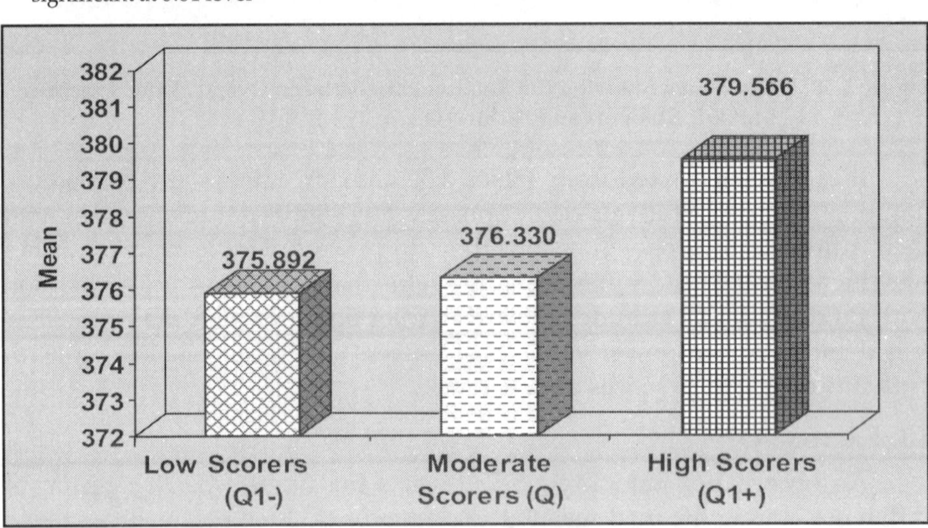

Figure 5.51 Histogram Showing the Relationship Between Overall Attitude Towards Values of B.Ed., Students and Factor—Q1

It is evident from Table 5.53 that the total mean practice scores do differ significantly for three personality groups *viz.*, Low scorers (Mean =359.310), Moderate scorers (Mean = 365.380) and High scorers (Mean = 366.780), See vide Figure 5.52. (*on next page*) The F-ratios discloses that there was no significant relationship between the value practice of B.Ed. Students and

Factor—Q1, except for Aesthetic (7.753**) and Health (5.074**) values. Also, it could be seen that the relationship between overall value practices and Factor—Q1 was significant. Therefore the conservative or experimenting nature of B.Ed. students possesses relationship with their value practices. It can be concluded that B.Ed. students with experimenting nature possess better value practices than the B.Ed. students with conservative nature.

Table 5.53 Relationship Between Value Practices of B.Ed. Students and Factor—Q1

Values	Low Scorers (Q1-) (203)		Moderate Scorers (Q1) (448)		High Scorers (Q1+) (309)		F-value (2,957 d.f.)
	Mean	S.D.	Mean	S.D.	Mean	S.D.	
Social	42.635	5.851	42.734	6.533	42.718	6.912	0.024 @
Religious	38.966	6.345	39.821	6.164	39.822	6.587	1.455 @
Economic	35.443	6.716	35.391	5.918	35.939	5.984	0.789 @
Democratic	43.522	5.868	44.319	5.949	43.932	6.884	1.178 @
Knowledge	40.591	7.203	41.920	7.079	41.958	7.579	2.744 @
Power	37.709	6.986	37.109	6.851	36.796	6.773	1.085 @
Hedonistic	42.660	5.411	43.103	5.896	43.625	5.492	1.868 @
Aesthetic	38.744	6.489	40.056	6.915	41.165	6.904	7.753 **
Health	39.039	7.508	40.926	7.341	40.825	7.211	5.074 **
Total	**359.310**	**27.214**	**365.380**	**28.998**	**366.780**	**30.543**	**4.368 ****

@ not significant at 0.05 level
* significant at 0.05 level
** significant at 0.01 level

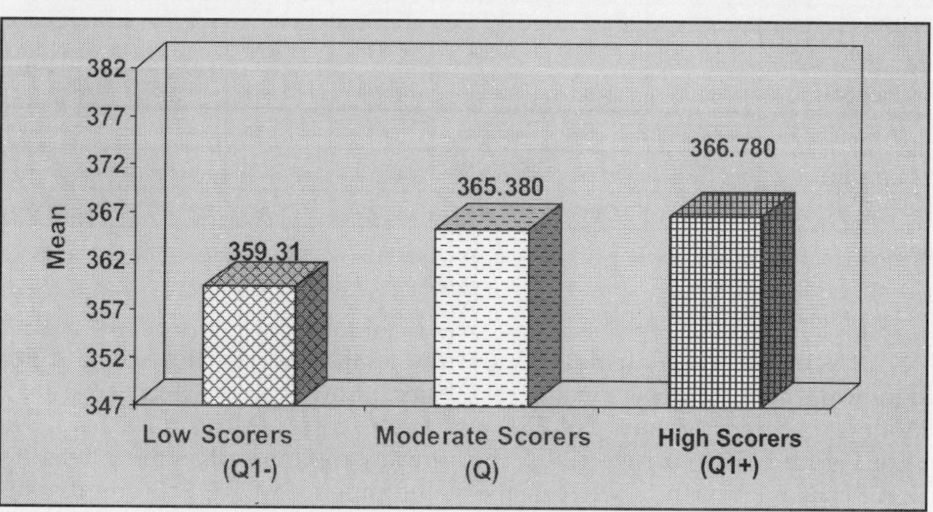

Figure 5.52 Histogram Showing the Relationship Between Overall Value Practices Students of B.Ed., and Factor—Q1

It can be interpreted from Tables 5.52 and 5.53, it is evident that the Factor—Q1 could not bring any variation in the attitudes but the practice of values show significant variation of B.Ed. Students. It is only the democratic value that possesses significant relationship with attitudes and aesthetic and health values that possesses significant relationship with practices, at 0.01 level.

14. Factor—Q2

An observation into Table 5.54 reveals that there was no significant difference among the total mean attitude scores of three personality groups *viz.*, Low scorers (Mean =377.006), Moderate scorers (Mean = 377.440) and High scorers (Mean = 377.381), See vide Figure 5.53. (*on next page*) The 'F' ratios calculated also discloses that they do not show significant variation, except for the Economic (9.942**) and Health (6.087**) values. Also, it could be seen that the relationship between overall attitudes towards values and Factor—Q2 was not significant. Hence it is clear that whether the B.Ed. Students are dependent or self-sufficient they do not vary in their attitudes towards values.

Table 5.54 Relationship Between Attitudes towards Values of B.Ed. Students and Factor—Q2

Values	Low Scorers (Q2-) (338)		Moderate Scorers (Q2) (496)		High Scorers (Q2+) (126)		F-value (2,957 d.f.)
	Mean	S.D.	Mean	S.D.	Mean	S.D.	
Social	43.408	4.623	43.218	4.650	42.952	4.313	0.473 @
Religious	34.373	6.885	34.706	7.080	34.603	7.316	0.222 @
Economic	37.911	6.368	39.524	6.398	40.508	6.567	9.942 **
Democratic	44.213	4.914	44.290	5.051	44.444	5.419	0.098 @
Knowledge	44.231	4.900	44.161	4.540	43.413	4.720	1.544 @
Power	38.976	6.896	38.927	6.848	39.111	7.857	0.041 @
Hedonistic	44.266	4.748	43.960	4.698	43.651	4.547	0.884 @
Aesthetic	42.254	5.363	42.226	5.606	42.524	5.526	0.148 @
Health	47.373	3.862	46.427	4.525	46.175	4.353	6.087 **
Total	**377.006**	**23.485**	**377.440**	**24.325**	**377.381**	**23.959**	**0.034 @**

@ not significant at 0.05 level
* significant at 0.05 level
** significant at 0.01 level

It is evident from Table 5.55 that the total mean practice scores differ significantly for three personality groups *viz.*, Low scorers (Mean =366.465), Moderate scorers (Mean = 366.351) and High scorers (Mean = 352.302), See vide Figure 5.54. (*on page 170*) The F-ratios discloses that there was no significant relationship between the value practice of B.Ed. Students and Factor—Q2, except for Social (12.917**), Religious (14.009**) and Health (11.343**) values. Also, it could be seen that the relationship between overall value practices and Factor—Q2 was significant. Therefore the dependent or self-sufficient nature of B.Ed. students does not possess relationship with their value practices, except for social, religious and health values. It can be concluded that B.Ed. students with dependent nature possess better value practices than the B.Ed. students with self-sufficient nature. I

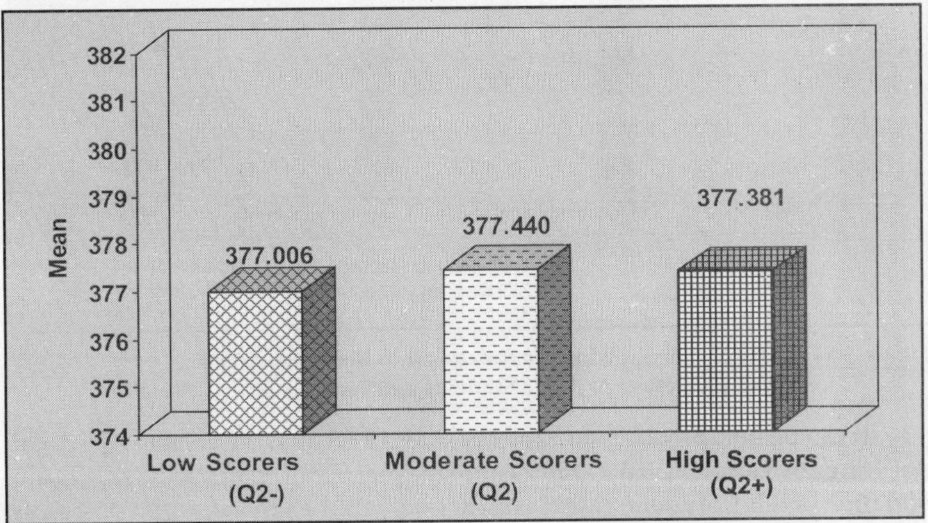

Figure 5.53 **Histogram Showing the Relationship Between Overall Attitude Towards Values of B.Ed., Students and Facto—Q2**

Table 5.55 Relationship Between Value Practices of B.Ed. Students and Factor—1Q2

Values	Low Scorers (Q2-) (338)		Moderate Scorers (Q2) (496)		High Scorers (Q2+) (126)		F-value (2,957 d.f.)
	Mean	S.D.	Mean	S.D.	Mean	S.D.	
Social	43.225	5.988	43.044	6.436	40.000	7.510	12.917 **
Religious	40.325	5.983	39.859	6.234	36.944	7.042	14.009 **
Economic	35.607	6.235	35.343	5.995	36.429	6.224	1.629 @
Democratic	44.157	6.159	44.163	6.216	43.135	6.595	1.461 @
Knowledge	42.056	6.890	42.067	7.199	38.929	8.065	0.707 @
Power	37.396	6.773	36.956	6.742	37.143	7.521	0.414 @
Hedonistic	43.284	5.649	43.347	5.513	42.222	6.279	2.071 @
Aesthetic	39.586	6.985	40.575	6.714	39.881	7.112	2.187 @
Health	40.828	7.251	40.998	7.362	37.619	7.091	11.343 **
Total	**366.465**	**27.111**	**366.351**	**29.491**	**352.302**	**31.020**	**13.035 ****

@ not significant at 0.05 level
* significant at 0.05 level
** significant at 0.01 level

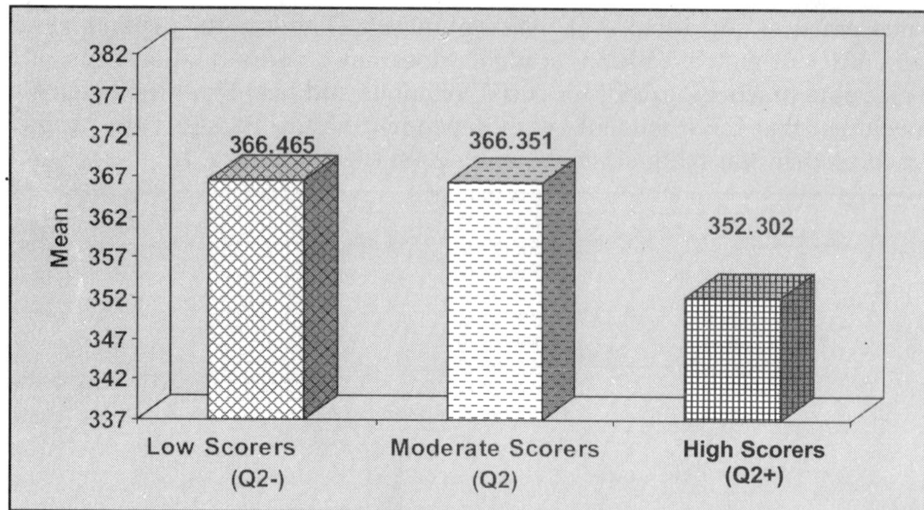

Figure 5.54 Histogram Showing the Relationship Between Overall Value Practices of B.Ed., Students and Factor—Q2

It can be interpreted from Tables 5.54 and 5.55, that the Factor—Q1 could not bring any variation in the attitudes but the practice of values show significant variation of B.Ed. Students. Moreover, it is only the health value that possesses significant relationship with attitudes and practices at 0.01 level.

Table 5.56 Relationship Between Attitudes towards Values of B.Ed. Students and Factor—Q3

Values	Low Scorers (Q3-) (189)		Moderate Scorers (Q3) (364)		High Scorers (Q3+) (407)		F-value (2,957 d.f.)
	Mean	S.D.	Mean	S.D.	Mean	S.D.	
Social	42.656	4.528	42.879	4.876	43.857	4.298	6.369 **
Religious	33.926	7.318	35.363	6.802	34.172	7.065	3.777 *
Economic	39.619	6.357	39.692	6.013	38.295	6.836	5.328 **
Democratic	44.402	4.714	44.016	5.376	44.467	4.896	0.843 @
Knowledge	44.593	4.716	43.780	4.602	44.128	4.759	1.909 @
Power	39.354	7.037	38.945	6.776	38.811	7.182	0.398 @
Hedonistic	43.947	4.738	43.725	4.754	44.334	4.616	1.680 @
Aesthetic	41.566	6.165	42.533	5.152	42.373	5.476	2.033 @
Health	46.265	3.989	46.874	4.463	46.811	4.292	1.379 @
Total	**376.328**	**23.336**	**377.808**	**23.897**	**377.248**	**24.344**	**0.237 @**

@ not significant at 0.05 level
* significant at 0.05 level
** significant at 0.01 level

15. Factor—Q3

An observation into Table 5.56 reveals that there was no significant difference among the total mean attitude scores of three personality groups *viz.*, Low scorers (Mean =376.328), Moderate scorers (Mean = 377.808) and High scorers (Mean = 377.248), See vide Figure 5.55. The 'F' ratios calculated also discloses that they do not show significant variation, except for the Social (6.369**), Religious (3.777*) and Economic (5.328**) values. Also, it could be seen that the relationship between overall attitudes towards values and Factor—Q3 was not significant. Hence it is clear that whether the B.Ed. Students are uncontrolled or controlled they do not vary in their attitudes towards values.

It is evident from Table 5.57 that the total mean practice scores do not differ significantly for three personality groups *viz.*, Low scorers (Mean =360.556), Moderate scorers (Mean = 366.003) and High scorers (Mean = 365.098), See vide Figure 5.56. (*on next page*) Moreover, the F-ratios also prove that there was significant relationship between the value practice of B.Ed. Students and Factor—Q3, except for the values Economic (5.030**), Democratic (11.215**), Power (4.079*), Hedonistic (4.350*), Health (3.763*) and the Social, Religious, Knowledge, Aesthetic do not possess significant relationship. Also, it could be seen that the relationship between overall value practice scores and Factor—Q3 was not significant. Therefore the uncontrolled or controlled nature of B.Ed. students does not possess relationship with their value practice.

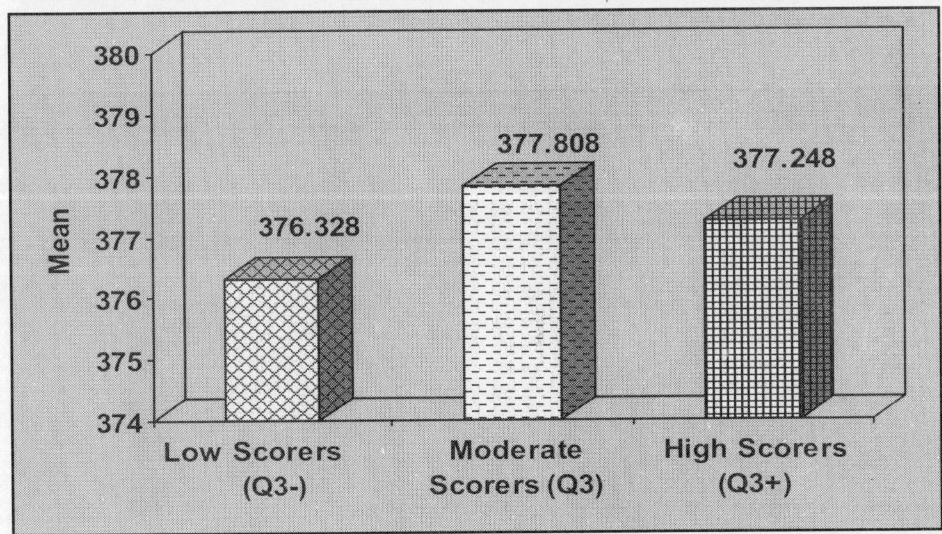

Figure 5.55 Histogram Showing the Relationship Between Overall Attitude Towards Values of B.Ed. Students and Factor—Q3

It can be interpreted from Tables 5.56 and 5.67, uncontrolled or controlled nature of the B.Ed. Students do not possess any significant relationship with their attitudes towards values and value practices. But, it is economic value that possesses significant relationship with both attitudes and practices at 0.01 level.

Table 5.57 Relationship Between Value Practices of B.Ed. Students and Factor—Q3

Values	Low Scorers (Q3-) (189)		Moderate Scorers (Q3) (364)		High Scorers (Q3+) (407)		F-value (2,957 d.f.)
	Mean	S.D.	Mean	S.D.	Mean	S.D.	
Social	42.275	6.512	42.473	6.529	43.120	6.497	1.462 @
Religious	39.683	5.984	39.684	6.118	39.582	6.710	0.025 @
Economic	36.561	6.259	35.797	6.023	34.926	6.068	5.030 **
Democratic	42.116	6.920	44.505	6.078	44.484	5.912	11.215 **
Knowledge	40.926	7.057	41.868	7.288	41.794	7.376	1.170 @
Power	38.386	6.597	36.964	6.908	36.708	6.875	4.079 *
Hedonistic	42.116	5.882	43.571	5.380	43.317	5.782	4.350 *
Aesthetic	39.233	6.769	40.082	6.792	40.602	6.962	2.592 @
Health	39.259	6.879	41.058	7.699	40.565	7.230	3.763 *
Total	**360.556**	**27.212**	**366.003**	**28.669**	**365.098**	**30.543**	**2.290 @**

@ not significant at 0.05 level
* significant at 0.05 level
** significant at 0.01 level

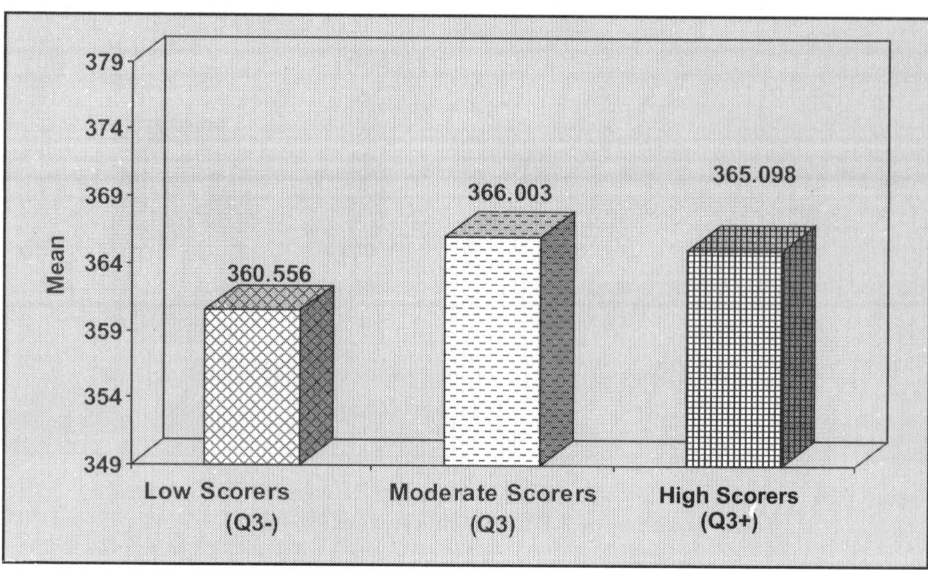

Figure 5.56 **Histogram Showing the Relationship Between Overall Value Practices of B.Ed. Students and Factor—Q3**

16. Factor—Q4

An observation into Table 5.58 reveals that there was no significant difference among the total mean attitude scores of three personality groups *viz.*, Low scorers (Mean =377.325), Moderate scorers (Mean = 375.530) and High scorers (Mean = 379.986), See vide Figure 5.57. (*on next page*) The 'F' ratios calculated also discloses that they do not show significant variation, except for Economic (4.890 **), Knowledge (7.096**) and Power (3.097*) values. Also, it could be seen that the relationship between overall attitudes towards values and Factor—Q4 was not significant. Hence it is clear that whether the B.Ed. Students whether relaxed or tensed they do not vary in their attitudes towards values.

Table 5.58 Relationship Between Attitudes towards Values of B.Ed. Students and Factor—Q4

Values	Low Scorers (Q4-) (243)		Moderate Scorers (Q4) (438)		High Scorers (Q4+) (279)		F-value (2,957 d.f.)
	Mean	S.D.	Mean	S.D.	Mean	S.D.	
Social	42.922	4.502	43.205	4.543	43.606	4.747	1.493 @
Religious	34.955	6.898	34.370	6.681	34.566	7.687	0.555 @
Economic	38.650	7.270	38.680	6.150	40.100	6.120	4.890 **
Democratic	44.115	4.887	44.374	4.834	44.287	5.510	0.215 @
Knowledge	44.749	4.168	43.479	4.717	44.466	4.986	7.096 **
Power	38.412	7.481	38.735	6.807	39.821	6.803	3.097 *
Hedonistic	44.082	4.761	43.836	4.537	44.280	4.884	0.793 @
Aesthetic	42.626	5.379	42.425	5.254	41.735	5.966	1.999 @
Health	46.815	4.323	46.425	4.433	47.125	4.048	2.302 @
Total	**377.325**	**24.772**	**375.530**	**23.732**	**379.986**	**23.425**	**2.960 @**

@ not significant at 0.05 level
* significant at 0.05 level
** significant at 0.01 level

It is evident from Table 5.59 that the total mean practice scores do not differ significantly for three personality groups *viz.*, Low scorers (Mean =362.922), Moderate scorers (Mean = 364.932) and High scorers (Mean = 365.358), See vide Figure 5.58. (*on page 175*) Moreover, the F-ratios also prove that there was no significant relationship between the value practice of B.Ed. Students and Factor—Q4, except for Economic (3.265*) and Power (5.086**) values. Also, it could be seen that the relationship between overall value practices and Factor—Q4 was not significant. Therefore the relaxed or tensed nature of B.Ed. students does not possess relationship with their value practices.

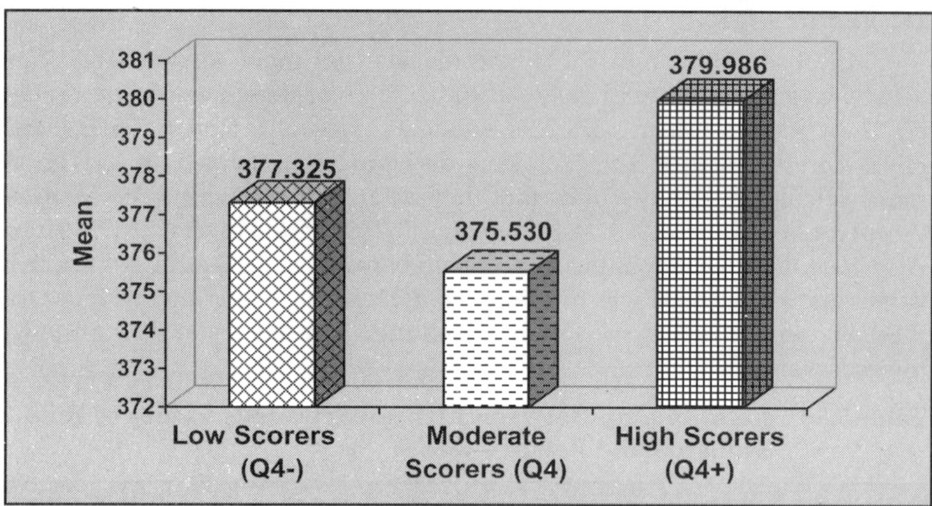

Figure 5.57 Histogram Showing the Relationship Between Overall Attitude Towards Values of B.Ed. Students and Factor—Q4

Table 5.59 Relationship Between Value Practices of B.Ed. Students and Factor—Q4

Values	Low Scorers (Q1-) (243)		Moderate Scorers (Q1) (438)		High Scorers (Q1+) (279)		F-value (2,957 d.f.)
	Mean	S.D.	Mean	S.D.	Mean	S.D.	
Social	42.181	6.601	42.854	6.617	42.939	6.273	1.072 @
Religious	39.156	6.572	40.057	6.440	39.409	5.961	1.842 @
Economic	35.782	5.979	35.057	5.989	36.219	6.371	3.265 *
Democratic	43.848	6.324	44.521	5.975	43.405	6.561	2.865 @
Knowledge	41.399	7.462	41.667	7.485	41.846	6.805	0.254 @
Power	37.716	6.652	36.370	6.961	37.832	6.762	5.086 **
Hedonistic	42.942	6.072	43.527	5.438	42.832	5.662	1.571 @
Aesthetic	39.918	7.441	40.228	6.719	40.179	6.609	0.169 @
Health	39.979	7.586	40.651	7.253	40.699	7.355	0.801 @
Total	**362.922**	**29.491**	**364.932**	**28.413**	**365.358**	**30.350**	**0.520 @**

@ not significant at 0.05 level
* significant at 0.05 level
** significant at 0.01 level

It can be interpreted from Tables 5.58 and 5.59, that relaxed or tense nature of the B.Ed. Students does not possess any significant relationship with their attitudes towards values or value practices. It is only the economic and power value that possesses significant relationship with both attitudes and practices.

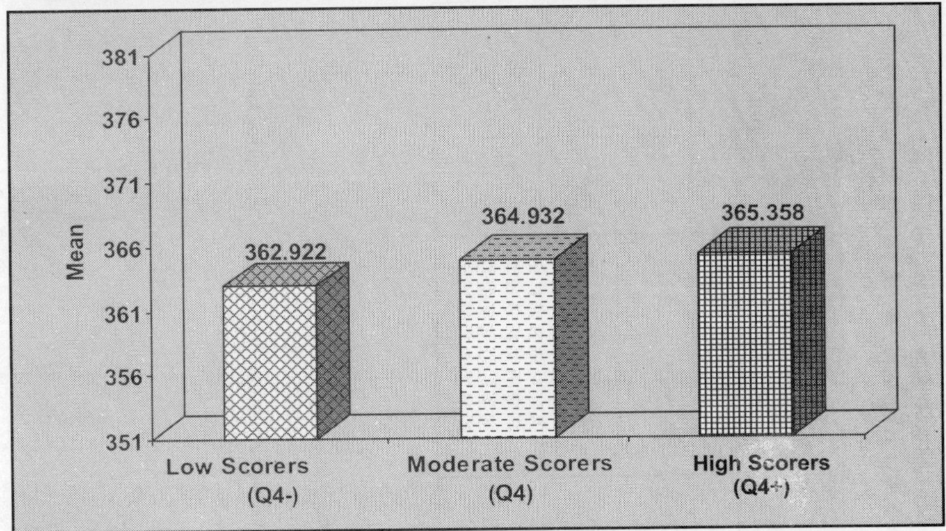

Figure 5.58 **Histogram Showing the Relationship Between Overall Value Practices of B.Ed. Students and Factor—Q4**

SECTION—IV

PREDICTION OF ATTITUDES TOWARDS VALUES AND VALUE PRACTICES OF B.ED. STUDENTS THROUGH STEPWISE REGRESSION ANALYSIS

Attitudes towards Values (A.T.V.) and Value Practices (V.P.) of the B.Ed. students depend upon many factors. Apart from the fact that innumerable variables may contribute to Attitudes towards Values and their Practices, the contribution of each (variable) factor may vary widely. So to find out a set of independent variables and the relative contribution of each of them to the dependent variables, multiple regression analysis has been employed.

In the present study step-wise multiple regression analysis was carried out, with 16 personality factors and some of the demographic variables which showed significant differences in their attitudes towards values and their practices namely gender, age, caste, region, religion, methodology, educational qualifications, marital status, father's occupation, mother's occupation as the independent variables to find out the contribution of these variables for the B.Ed. Students Attitudes towards Values (A.T.V.) and Value Practices (V.P.)

Prediction of Attitudes Towards Value (A.T.V.) With Demographic Variables and 16 Personality Factor

From Table 5.60 it can be seen that the first variable entered into multiple regression analysis was the demographic variable Methodology (M). The multiple correlation (R) obtained was 0.117. The relationship was positive as

Table 5.60 Multiple (Step Wise) Regression Analysis Dependent Variable: Attitudes Towards Values (A.T.V.) Independent Variables: Demographic Variables (Methodology, Region) and 16 P.F. (Factor-A)

Step No.	IV/ (VN)	R	'F' Value for R	R^2	S.E. of R	b (Partial Regression Coefficient)1	't' value for b	Constant	B	r	% of variance
1	2	3	4	5	6	7	8	9	10	11	12
1.	Methodology (7)	0.117	13.918 (1, 958)	0.014	49.663	5.200 (V1)(7)	3.633	134.800	0.117	0.117	1.40
2.	Factor A (15)	0.143	10.046 (2, 957)	0.021	49.513	5.300 (V1)(7) 5.411 (V2)(15)	3.696 2.610	126.808	0.118 0.084	0.081	1.42 0.68
3.	Region (4)	0.161	8.534 (3, 956)	0.026	49.399	5.229 (V1)(7) 6.100 (V2)(15) 4.600 (V3) (4)	3.715 3.027 2.327	116.168	0.119 0.099 0.076	0.056	1.40 0.77 0.43

IV: Independent Variable;
VN: Variable Number;
R: Multiple Correlation;
S.E.: Standard Error;
b: partial regression coefficient;
B: Beta Coefficient;
r: Simple correlation coefficient with the dependent variable;
% of variance in the dependent variable explained by each independent variable.

(The number in the parenthesis in columns 2 and 7, correspond to the serial no. of the independent variables entered into the regression analysis.)

indicated by the positive value of 'b', the partial regression co-efficient. This shows that higher score on locality, higher was the attitude towards values. The value indicated that the strength of the relationship between the two was about 12%. It could also be observed that R was significant beyond 0.01 level (F = 13.198 for 1 and 958 d.f.). The coefficient of multiple determinant (R^2) was 0.014. This shows that 1.40 per cent of the variance in attitudes towards values was accounted for the variable methodology.

The standard error of multiple R (SE of R) was 49.663. Thus nearly 68 per cent of the attitudes towards value scores would lie within + 49.663 points of the attitude towards values predicted with the help of this factor.

The partial regression coefficient or b coefficient presented in column 7 was 5.200 units for every unit of charge in variable methodology. The't' value for b was 3.633 (column 8). The value of the constant that would go into the multiple regression equation to predict attitude towards values at this stage was 134.800.

The general form of the multiple regression equation may be given as:

$$Y = A + b1x1 + b2x2 + b3x3 + \ldots\ldots\ldots\ldots bnxn$$

Where Y is the predicted score on the dependent variable

A is a constant

$b1, b2, b3 \ldots\ldots. bn$ are partial regression coefficients and

$x1, x2, x3 \ldots\ldots.. xn$ are the scores on different independent variables.

Thus the multiple regression equation at the end of the step to predict attitudes towards value (A.T.V.) with the variable Methodology (M) could be written as:

$$ATV = 134.800 + 5.200\ M$$

Factor A (FA) of the 16 PF entered into the step-wise regression analysis as the second most significant variable. The multiple correlation (R) between Attitude towards values on one side and the independent variables, *viz.*, Methodology and Factor A on the other side was about 0.143. Thus the strength of the relationship between Attitude towards values and the two independent variables put together was 14 per cent. R was significant at 0.01 level (F = 10.046 d.f. 2 and 957).

R^2 was equal to 0.021. Hence the two variables put together could explain about 2.1 per cent of the variance in the dependent variable *viz.*, Attitude towards values. Out of this, 1.42 per cent of the variance was explained by the variable methodology and the remaining 0.68 per cent was accounted for by variable Factor A (Column 12). These percentages can be obtained by multiplying the B coefficients or standard partial regression coefficients (column 10) with the corresponding simple correlations between the dependent variable and the respective independent variables given in column 11.

It is evident that by including the variable Factor *A* the contribution of Methodology was gone up from 1.40 to 1.42 per cent due to inter-correlation between the two predictor variables. The standard error of multiple *R* was 49.513 (column 6). Hence 68 per cent of the Attitude towards values scores would lie within one SE limits (+ 49.513).

The partial regression coefficients shown in column 7 shows that when both variables methodology and Factor *A* were included as predictor variables, then the Attitude towards values would change by 5.300 and 5.411 points for every unit of change in Methodology and Factor *A* respectively. Those partial regression coefficients of Methodology were significant at 0.01 level and the partial regression coefficient of Factor *A* was significant at 0.05 level as shown in column 8.

The regression equation to predict Attitude towards values (A.T.V.) with these two variables Methodology (M) and Factor *A* (FA) as predictor variables was

$$ATV = 126.808 + 5.300\ M + 5.411\ FA$$

Where 126.808 was the constant to be considered at this step and 5.300 and 5.411 were partial regression coefficients of methodology and Factor *A*.

Region (R) entered into the third step of the regression analysis. The multiple correlation with the three factors Methodology, Factor *A* and Region was 0.161 which was significant at 0.01 level ('F' = 8.534 for 3 and 956 d.f.). The value of R2 (0.026) shows that 2.60 per cent of variance in Attitude towards values was explained by these three variables. Out of the variance, 1.40 per cent, 0.77 per cent and 0.43 per cent of the variance were explained by the variables methodology, Factor *A* and region respectively. It may be observed that by including region as one more predictor variable the variance accounted for by methodology had brought down from 1.42 per cent to 1.40 per cent and the variance accounted for by Factor *A* had gone up from 0.68 per cent to 0.77 per cent due to inter correlations between the three independent variables.

The obtained partial regression coefficients with these three predictor variables indicate that the change in the Attitude towards values was by 5.229, 6.100 and 4.600 units for every unit of change in methodology, Factor *A* and region respectively.

The regression equation at this step was

$$ATV = 116.168 + 5.229\ (M) + 6.100\ (FA) + 4.600\ (R)$$

The other variables could not enter step-wise regression analysis as their contribution was not significant to predict the Attitude towards values. 2.6 per cent of variance in Attitude towards values was predicted by all the 3 factors and the variables methodology, Factor *A* and region could explain about 2.6 per cent of the variance in the Attitude towards values.

Hence it could be concluded that equation 3 would be the best equation to predict Attitude towards values of B.Ed. students employing demographic variables and 16 PF as the independent variables, although those three variables could not explain the major portion of the variance in the Attitude towards values. So, the hypothesis "It would not be possible to predict significantly the major portion of attitude towards values of B.Ed. Students with the help of the independent variables included in the study" was accepted.

Prediction of Value Practices (V.P.) with Demographic Variables and 16 Personality Factors

This part of the section deals with the prediction (Table 5.61) of practices of values of B.Ed. Students with the help of demographic variables and personality traits. The 27 predictor variables used were the 11 demographic variables *viz.*, Gender, Age, Caste, Region, Religion, Marital Status, Educational Qualifications, Methodology, Locality, Father's Qualification, Mother's Qualification and 16 personality factors of Cattell. As in the earlier analysis, step-wise regression analysis was carried out and the results of the analysis are presented in Table 5.61.

The first variable entered into multiple regression analysis was the demographic variable Region (R). The multiple correlation obtained was 0.305. It could also be observed that R was significant beyond 0.01 level (F = 98.042 for 1 and 958 d.f.). The coefficient of multiple determinant (R^2) was 0.093. Therefore, this variable alone could explain 9.3 per cent of the variance in practices of values of B.Ed. students.

The partial regression coefficient (-18.600) which was significant beyond 0.01 level, shows that for every unit change in this variable, there would be a change of 18.6 units in the practices of values of the B.Ed. students. The regression equation could be written as:

$$VP = 183.000 - 18.600\ (R)$$

Factor F (FF) of the 16 PF entered into the step-wise regression analysis as the second most significant variable. The values of the multiple *R* and multiple R^2 were 0.337 and 0.114 respectively. Thus the two factors region and Factor *F* put together could explain 11 per cent of the variance in the value practices. The equation with these two predictor variables region and Factor *F* would be:

$$VP = 174.000 - 18.800\ (R) + 9.400\ (FF)$$

The third most important variable that entered into the analysis was Factor *E* (FE). The values of the multiple *R* and multiple R^2 were 0.366 and 0.134 respectively. Thus the three factors region, Factor *F* and Factor *E* put together could explain 13 per cent of the variance in the value practices. The equation with these three predictor variables region, Factor *F* and Factor *E* would be:

$$VP = 179.300 - 17.757\ (R) + 10.358\ (FF) - 9.411\ (FE)$$

Table 5.61 Multiple (Step Wise) Regression Analysis Department Variable: Practices of Values (P.O.V.) Independent Variables: Demographic Variables (Region, Marital Status) and 16 PF (Factors F,E)

Step No.	IV/ (VN)	R	'F' Value for R	R^2	S.E. of R	b (Partial Regression Coefficient)	't' value for b	Constant	B	r	% of variance
1	2	3	4	5	6	7	8	9	10	11	12
1.	Region (4)	0.305	98.042 (1, 958)	0.093	47.506	-18.600(V1)(04)	9.902	183.000	-0.305	-0.305	9.30
2.	Factor F(19)	0.337	61.225 (2, 957)	0.114	46.987	-18.756(V1)(04) 9.412(V2)(19)	10.096 4.721	174.700	-0.307 0.144	0.138	9.32 1.99
3.	Factor E(18)	0.366	49.235 (3, 956)	0.134	46.469	-17.757(V1)(04) 10.358(V2)(19) - 9.411(V3)(18)	9.659 5.240 4.738	179.300	-0.292 0.1590 -0.144	-0.158	8.61 2.51 2.28
4.	Marital Status (6)	0.388	42.358 (4, 955)	0.151	46.039	-16.312(V1)(04) 11.858(V2)(19) - 9.360(V3)(18) 14.855(V4)(06)	8.769 5.987 4.781 4.354	149.244	-0.268 0.183 -0.144 0.134	0.157	7.87 2.87 2.26 2.10

IV: Independent Variable; b: partial regression coefficient;
VN: Variable Number; B: Beta Coefficient;
R: Multiple Correlation; r: Simple correlation coefficient with the dependent variable;
S.E.: Standard Error; % of variance in the dependent variable explained by each independent variable.

(The number in the parenthesis in columns 2 and 7, correspond to the serial no. of the independent variables entered into the regression analysis.)

Variable Marital Status (MS) entered into the fourth step of the regression analysis. The values of the multiple *R* and multiple R^2 were 0.388 and 0.151 respectively. Thus the four factors region, Factor *F*, Factor *E* and marital status put together could explain 15 per cent of the variance in the value practices. The equation with these four predictor variables region, Factor *F*, Factor *E* and marital status would be:

$$VP = 149.2214 - 16.312\ (R) + 11.858\ (FF) - 9.360\ (FE) + 14.855\ (MS)$$

The other variables could not enter into the step-wise regression analysis as their contribution was not significant. Thus it could be concluded that 15 per cent of the variance in the value practices of B.Ed. students could be explained with the help of the four independent variables namely region, Factor *F*, Factor *E* and marital status. Hence the hypothesis "It would not be possible to predict significantly the major portion of value practices of B.Ed. Students with the help of the independent variables included in the study" was accepted.

SUMMARY AND CONCLUSION

SUMMARY

An attempt has been made to discuss the major findings of the study to throw more light on the unique findings and also to suggest comprehensive ways and means of utilizing the present information in a fruitful manner. This chapter reports a summary of the study under the headings: introduction, title of the problem, objectives, hypotheses, methodology, tools used, sample, data collection, statistical analysis, conclusions, suggestions for further research and educational implications of the study.

INTRODUCTION

The ultimate aim of education is the total development of personality of the individual. Balanced development of cognitive, affective and psychomotor domains is of utmost importance for fruitful life. In the present day educational system, one can witness a biased emphasis on the cognitive aspect of the personality. Knowledge and technology are developing at a much more rapid pace now than before.

To have a happy and successful life, the educational system should give top priority to the inculcators of values. It is high time to evaluate the present value system prevailing among students and explore the ways and means to internalize the most important values in students.

Even though, many factors such as family, friends, mass media, socioeconomic factors, curricular, co-curricular activities are helping to form certain values in students yet the influence of family and teachers on students is the highest. This is clearly brought out by the Education Commission (1964-66) in its report. It observed, "The school atmosphere, the facilities provided in the school, have a major role in developing a sense of values. It is not only the teachers in charge of moral instruction who are responsible for building character, every teacher, whatever the subject the teacher deals must necessarily accept his responsibility.

Values have different facets such as aesthetic, economic, hedonistic, power, religious, social, knowledge, democratic, health, political, scientific, spiritual and theoretical dimensions. One may not ignore one aspect of value system for the sake of others. A well-balanced personality requires a combination of all these values and such values should be inculcated at the primary to university level. For this the teachers are the real agents. It is natural that unless the teachers are having such value system, he/she may not be able to inculcate such things in students.

Research studies focussing attention on prevailing value system of the student-teachers give base line information which shows the way for development of appropriate strategies to inculcate the desirable value system in student-teachers. Such studies are more warranted in India at present. There are certain studies like Patel (1979), Rathna Kumari (1987), Sombhi (1990), Verma (1996), Taj (1998), Assor Avi (2000), Chaturvedi, Archana (2001), Robert T. Carler and Alex L. Pieterse (2004), Rabindranatha Reddy, C (2006) concentrated on prevailing value system.

Investigations that attempt to identify the attitudes towards different values possessed by B.Ed. students and value practices will give comprehensive idea about the value system prevailing at B.Ed. level. Further studies probing into the relationship between values and personality would help to concentrate on aspects where the emphasis has to be given. Keeping all the above aspects in mind, the present study was formulated. Comprehensive studies covering the attitudes towards different values and their practices possessed by the students generally provide clear perspective about the value system prevailing in the B.Ed. students. The present study the attitudes towards values and their practices in relation to personality factors among B.Ed. students is an attempt in that direction.

STATEMENT OF THE PROBLEM

The problem under investigation is "A Study of Attitudes towards Values and Their Practices in relation to certain Personality Factors among B.Ed. Students in Andhra Pradesh."

Objectives of the Study

The following are the objectives of the study:

- To study the attitudes towards values among B.Ed Students.
- To know the practices of values among B.Ed. Students.
- To ascertain the influence of personal and demographic variables *viz.,*

gender, age, caste, region, religion, marital status, methodology, educational qualifications, nativity, father's occupation, mother's occupation on attitudes towards values and value practices among B.Ed. Students.

- To assess the relationship between attitudes towards values and personality factors among B.Ed. students.
- To assess the relationship between value practices and personality factors among B.Ed. Students.
- To predict attitudes towards values and value practices of B.Ed. Students with the help of independent variables

HYPOTHESES OF THE STUDY

To realize the above objectives the following hypotheses in null form are formulated for testing:

- The attitudes towards various values to be formed by B.Ed. Students would not be different.
- The practices of various values of B.Ed. Students would not be different
- There is no gap between attitudes towards values and their practices for each of the values studied.
- There is no significant difference between gender and attitudes towards values among B.Ed. Students.
- There is no significant difference between gender and value practices among B.Ed. Students.
- There is no significant difference between attitudes towards values and age of B.Ed. Students.
- There is no significant difference between values practices and age of B.Ed. Students.
- There is no significant difference between caste and attitudes towards values among B.Ed. Students.
- There is no significant difference between caste and value practices among B.Ed. Students.
- There is no significant difference between region and attitudes towards values among B.Ed. Students.
- There is no significant difference between region and value practices among B.Ed. Students.
- There is no significant difference between religion and attitudes towards values among B.Ed. Students.
- There is no significant difference between religion and value practices among B.Ed. Students.

- There is no significant difference between marital status and attitudes towards values among B.Ed. Students.
- There is no significant difference between marital status and value practices among B.Ed. Students.
- There is no significant difference between attitudes towards values of B.Ed. Students and qualification.
- There is no significant difference between value practices of B.Ed. Students and qualification.
- There is no significant difference among different Methodology students and attitudes towards values.
- There is no significant difference among different Methodology students and practices on values.
- There is no significant difference between locality and attitudes towards values among B.Ed. Students.
- There is no significant difference between locality and value practices among B.Ed. Students.
- There is no significant difference between father's occupation and attitudes towards values among B.Ed. Students.
- There is no significant difference between father's occupation and value practices among B.Ed. Students.
- There is no significant difference between mother's occupation and attitudes towards values among B.Ed. Students.
- There is no significant difference between mother's occupation and value practices among B.Ed. Students.
- There is no significant difference between personality factors and attitudes towards values among B.Ed. Students.
- There is no significant difference between personality factors and value practices among B.Ed. Students.
- It would not be possible predict significantly the major portion of attitudes towards value and practices of values of B.Ed. Students with the help of the independent variables included in the study.

VARIABLES STUDIED

The list of the variables is given below:

1. **Dependent Variables**

The two dependent variables in the study *viz.,*

(i) Attitudes towards Values

(ii) Practices of Values

2. **Independent Variables**

The independent Variables, which are considered in the study, are grouped under two categories as mentioned below:

a **Personal and Demographic Variables**

(i) Gender

(ii) Age

(iii) Caste

(iv) Region

(v) Religion

(vi) Marital Status

(vii) Educational Qualifications

(viii) Methodology

(ix) Locality

(x) Father's Occupation

(xi) Mother's Occupation

b **Personality Factors**

Cattell's 16 personality factors

TOOLS USED

For the purpose of the study, the following tools were used:

- Scale to assess the attitudes towards values of B.Ed. students. The investigator developed the tool.
- Questionnaire to assess the value practices of B.Ed. students. The investigator developed the tool.
- Cattell's 16 Personality Factor Questionnaire Form-C to assess the personality of the B.Ed. students.

SAMPLE FRAME

The state of Andhra Pradesh consists of 3 regions namely Rayalaseema, Telengana and Coastal Regions. All the three regions were included in the study. Out of the different B.Ed. Colleges existing in the regions, a sample of three colleges was randomly chosen. All the B.Ed. students studying in the respective colleges were included in the sample. Thus, the sample of the study consisted of 960 B.Ed. Students. The sample frame for the study is 2x4x2 factorial design with two divisions in gender (Male/Female), four divisions in methodologies (Mathematics/Physical Sciences/Biological Sciences/Social Studies) and two divisions in locality (Urban/Rural).

COLLECTION OF DATA

The instruments *viz.*, Rating Scale to measure B.Ed. Students' Attitudes towards Values, Questionnaire Schedule to measure Value Practices of the B.Ed. Students, 16 Personality Factor Questionnaire and the personal data sheet were administered to the 960 B.Ed. Students individually after establishing proper rapport with them. The B.Ed. students were explained, the purpose and significance of the study and the method in which they had to answer the different items under different instruments or tools used in the study. Sufficient time was given to them to respond to the items. Care was taken to see that the respondents answered all the items in all the data gathering tools.

ANALYSIS OF THE DATA

The data collected thus was analyzed by using relevant statistical techniques like descriptive statistical measures, 't' test, ANOVA (F-Ratio) to find out whether differences in the independent variables accounted for significant differences in the dependent variables. Multiple correlation coefficient 'R' was calculated by carrying out step-wise Regression analysis to find out whether it was possible to predict the two dependent variables *viz.*, Attitudes towards Values and Value Practices with the help of the independent variables. The usual levels of significance *viz.*, 0.05 and 0.01 were employed to test the significance of the values obtained. The obtained results were also represented graphically wherever necessary.

CONCLUSION OF STUDY

From the statistical analysis of the investigation, the following conclusion were drawn:

Section—I

- In general, the attitudes of B.Ed. Students were positive on all the values.
- The attitudes of B.Ed. Students towards various values were different.
- The first and foremost important value as perceived by the B.Ed. Students where the attitudes were high was the Health value. The next three values Democratic, Knowledge and Hedonistic Values were more or less equally perceived. The fifth place is for Social Value and the next place comes to Aesthetic Value. The last but one place is for Power Value and the last place regarding the forming of attitudes is the Religious value.
- The practices of B.Ed. Student regarding any value were less than their attitudes, except for the religious value.
- It is quite natural that even though the B.Ed. Students' attitudes are high regarding their values, they may not practice them as per their attitudes.

- The practices of various values of B.Ed. students were different.
- The B.Ed. students possess high practice of democratic value and the second highly practiced value is Hedonistic value. The third and fourth highly practiced values are Social and Knowledge values respectively. They exhibited more or less equal practice regarding Health, Aesthetic Values. The next level in their practice was given to the Religious value. The last but one place goes to Power value, the least practiced value by the B.Ed. students was the Economic Value.
- It was found that there was a gap between the attitudes towards values and value practices of the B.Ed. Students.
- The value, which has highest attitude, is the health value and it is placed fifth regarding practice. The second higher value regarding attitude is democratic value and that is the most practiced value. There is negligible difference between attitudes and practices of the Democratic Value. The third value regarding attitude is knowledge, but it is placed fourth regarding the practice.
- The fourth and fifth place goes to Hedonistic and Social values regarding attitudes and they are placed second and third respectively regarding practice. The sixth place goes to Aesthetic value regarding both attitudes and practices.
- The next successive value, which has high attitude, is the Economic value but this is the least practiced value. The eighth place goes to Power value regarding attitudes and practices. The value, which has lowest attitude, is the Religious value and it is placed seventh regarding practice.

Section—II

1. In general, the attitudes of B.Ed. students were positive on all values. The variables Methodology, age, region could bring significant variation in general in the formation of attitudes towards values among B.Ed. Students. The other variables *viz.,* gender, marital status, caste, religion and educational qualification could bring significant variation on the specific individual values only. The variables locality and parent's occupation could not bring any significant variation in the attitudes towards values of B.Ed. Students.
2. The variables region, religion, marital status, locality, parent's occupation and educational qualification could bring significant variation in general in the value practices among B.Ed. Students. The other variables *viz.,* gender, age, caste, methodology could bring significant variation on the specific individual values only

3. *a.* ***Gender:*** The attitudes towards values of female B.Ed. Students are more favorable than male B.Ed. students

   b. The female B.Ed. Students practice values better than male B.Ed. students

4. *a.* ***Age:*** The B.Ed. Students who are 22 years and below have more positive attitudes towards values than the B.Ed. Students who are above 22 years.

   b. The B.Ed. Students who are above 22 years have better value practices than the B.Ed. Students who are 22 years and below.

5. *a.* ***Caste:*** In case of Caste, the B.Ed. Students belonging to Scheduled Caste have more favourable attitudes towards values when compared to the B.Ed. Students belonging to Backward and Forward Castes.

   b. The B.Ed. Students belonging to Backward Caste have better value practices when compared to the B.Ed. Students belonging to Forward Caste and Scheduled Caste.

6. *a.* ***Region*:** In case of region, the B.Ed. Students belonging to Coastal region have more positive attitudes towards values when compared to the B.Ed. Students belonging to Telengana and Rayalaseema regions.

   b. The B.Ed. Students belonging to Rayalaseema region have better value practices than the B.Ed. Students belonging to Coastal and Telengana regions.

7. *a.* ***Religion:*** The B.Ed. Students belonging to Muslim religion have more positive attitudes towards values than B.Ed. Students belonging to Christian and Hindu religions.

   b. The B.Ed. Students belonging to Hindu religion have better value practices than the B.Ed. Students belonging to Muslim and Christian religions.

8. *a.* ***Marital Status*:** The unmarried B.Ed. Students have more positive attitudes towards values than married B.Ed. Students.

   b. The unmarried B.Ed. Students have better value practices than married B.Ed. Students.

9. *a.* ***Educational Qualifications:*** The graduate B.Ed. Students have more positive attitudes towards values than B.Ed students who completed their post-graduation.

   b. The graduate B.Ed. Students have better value practices than B.Ed students who completed their post-graduation.

10. *a.* ***Methodologies:*** The B.Ed. students who belong to Biological sciences methodology have more positive attitudes towards values than the B.Ed. students who belong to Social Studies, Physical sciences and Mathematics methodologies.

    b. The B.Ed. students who belong to Mathematics methodology have better value practices than the B.Ed. students who belong to Physical sciences, Biological sciences and Social Studies methodologies.

11. *a.* ***Locality:*** The B.Ed. Students belonging to urban locality have more positive attitudes towards values than the B.Ed. students belonging to rural locality.

    b. The B.Ed. Students belonging to rural locality have better value practices than the B.Ed. students belonging to rural locality.

12. *a.* ***Father's Occupation:*** The B.Ed. Students whose fathers are unskilled have more positive attitudes towards values than the B.Ed. Students whose fathers have professional jobs and skilled work.

    b. The B.Ed. Students whose fathers have skilled work have better value practices than the B.Ed. Students whose fathers have unskilled work and professional jobs.

13. a. ***Mother's Occupation:*** The B.Ed. Students whose fathers are professionals have more positive attitudes towards values than the B.Ed. Students whose fathers have skilled and unskilled work.

    b. The B.Ed. Students whose fathers are professionals have better value practices than the B.Ed. Students whose fathers have unskilled and skilled work.

Section—III

1. There is relationship between personality traits and attitude towards values of B.Ed. students and of all factors, Factor—A is better related.
2. There is relationship between personality traits and value practices of B.Ed. students, except for Factor—B.
3. *a.* **Factor—A:** Attitudes towards values of B.Ed. Students were affected by their reservedness. The outgoing B.Ed. Students possess high attitudes towards economic, power, hedonistic and aesthetic values than reserved B.Ed. Students.

    b. The more outgoing B.Ed. Students practice their values at greater level than reserved B.Ed. Students, except for social, religious and knowledge values.

4 *a.* **Factor—B:** Attitudes towards social, knowledge and health values of B.Ed. Students were partially affected by their intelligence.

b. Intelligence does not have any relationship with value practices of the B.Ed. Students.

5. a. **Factor—C:** The emotionally stable or emotionally less stable B.Ed. Students do not have high attitudes towards values, except on the aesthetic value.

b. The emotionally stable B.Ed. Students practice values very well than the less emotionally stable B.Ed. Students.

6. a. **Factor—E:** B.Ed. Students whether dominant or submissive, do not vary with their attitudes towards values, except for Economic and Knowledge values.

b. B.Ed. students with submissive nature practice values more than dominant B.Ed. students, except for aesthetic value.

7. a. **Factor—F:** The sober or enthusiastic nature of the B.Ed. students has nothing to do with the attitudes of values but have more concern with their economic and aesthetic values.

b. The enthusiastic B.Ed. students practice values more than sober B.Ed. students, except for economic, power and hedonistic values.

8. a. **Factor—G:** B.Ed. students whether persistent or expedient do not possess any relationship with their attitudes towards values, except regarding social, religious and economic values.

b. The B.Ed. students who have persistent nature practice values more than B.Ed. students who are expedient, except for the aesthetic value.

9. *a.* **Factor—H:** Shyness or venturesome B.Ed. Students do not possess any relationship with their attitudes towards values except for economic, knowledge and aesthetic values.

b. B.Ed. Students who are shy natured practice values better than adventurous students, except for economic, aesthetic and health values.

10. *a.* **Factor—I:** B.Ed. Students whether tough-minded or tender-minded they do not vary in their attitudes towards values, except for aesthetic value.

b. The tough-minded B.Ed. students practice values more than tender-minded students, except for religious and economic values.

11. *a.* **Factor—L:** Whether the B.Ed. Students has trusting or suspecting nature they do not vary in their attitudes towards values, except for democratic value.

b. B.Ed. Students with trusting nature practice social, religious and hedonistic values better than B.Ed. students with suspecting nature.

12. a. **Factor—M:** B.Ed. Students whether practical or imaginative do not vary in their attitudes towards values, except for aesthetic value.

b. The B.Ed. Students with imaginative nature practice social, democratic, aesthetic and health values better than practical minded B.Ed. students

13. a. **Factor—N:** B.Ed. Students whether forthright or polished do not vary in their attitudes towards values, except for economic and aesthetic value.

b. The forthright B.Ed. Students practice religious, economic, democratic, knowledge and aesthetic values better than B.Ed. students of polished nature.

14. a. **Factor—O:** B.Ed. students whether secure or insecure do not vary in their attitudes towards values, except for democratic and power values.

b. The unsecured B.Ed. students practice values better than the secured B.Ed. students, except for economic value.

15. a. **Factor—Q1:** B.Ed. Students with conservative or experimenting nature do not vary in their attitudes towards values, except for democratic value.

b. The B.Ed. students with experimenting nature practices aesthetic and health values better than the conservative B.Ed. Students.

16. a. **Factor—Q2:** Attitudes towards values do not vary whether the B.Ed. Students are dependent or self-sufficient, except for economic and aesthetic values.

b. The B.Ed. Students with dependent nature practice social, religious and health values better than the students who are self-sufficient.

17. a. **Factor—Q3:** Attitudes towards values of B.Ed. Students do not vary whether the B.Ed. students are uncontrolled or controlled, except for social, religious and economic values.

b. Value Practices of B.Ed. Students do not vary whether the B.Ed. students are uncontrolled or controlled, except for economic, democratic, power, hedonistic and health values.

18. a. **Factor—Q4:** Attitudes towards values of B.Ed. Students do not vary whether the B.Ed. students are relaxed or tense, except for economic, knowledge and power values.

b. Value Practices of B.Ed. Students do not vary whether the B.Ed. students are relaxed or tense, except for economic and power values.

Section—IV

1. Only 2.6 per cent of variance in ATV (attitudes towards values) of B.Ed. students could be explained with the help of the three independent variables namely Methodology, Factor—A and Region. That means Methodology, Factor—A and Region were found to be the significant factors which have strong association with the ATV (attitudes towards values).
2. Only 15 per cent of variance in POV (practices of values) was predicted significantly by the variables Region, Factor—F, Factor—E and Marital Status. That means Region, Factor—F, Factor—E and Marital Status were found to be the significant factors which have strong association with the POV (practices of values).

SUGGESTIONS FOR FURTHER RESEARCH

- The study is limited to Andhra Pradesh; it can be extended to other states in India.
- The present study is confined to B.Ed. students. The same study can be done on the DIET students, M.Ed. students and Research Scholars in Education and students of other general courses.
- Studies, which can probe into the reasons for different levels of attitudes towards values and value practices among students, can be attempted.
- The values are limited to 9 dimensions; the other dimensions can also be taken in the study.
- Attempts can be made for the construction of standardized tools to assess the attitudes towards values and their practices of B.Ed. students in covering different value dimensions separately.
- In this study only one Form of Personality is used and future researchers can go for more than one form.

EDUCATIONAL IMPLICATIONS OF THE STUDY

- Values are eternal in nature and any amount of negligence of promoting values from childhood onwards is likely to have its impact on the individual and society at large. Indian tradition is deeply rooted for value system and the values, which require the attention of the school system.
- Since the promotion of values among students depends upon teachers, it is suggested that the different teacher training institutions like B.Ed.,

DIET, IASE, Academic staff colleges should devote sufficient time to disseminate different aspects of values.

- As part of the in-service training programme teachers should be given training in practicing values and in inculcation of the same in the students.
- Moreover, teachers should try to create interest among the students through their method of teaching and co-curricular activities.
- The teaching methods which are practicable in nature should be included in the curriculum of teacher training course and the teachers should be trained properly in those methods during pre-service training.
- The present B.Ed. syllabus is covering only one unit of the paper philosophical foundations on value education, which is not sufficient. It is suggested to include a few more units in the syllabus on value education. Value education need not be limited to curricular aspects but should also find a place in co-curricular and extra curricular activities of B.Ed. students.
- There is a great need to educate the parents and society on values, which goes a long way in moulding the children to be value-oriented. So, Parent Teacher Associations must be organized regularly to involve the parents and to make them support in shaping the personality of the students.
- Training in Guidance and Counselling should be given to the teachers to assist the pupils whenever and wherever needed.
- Teachers' traditional and conservative attitudes should be changed by involving them in social activities and arranging the Citizenship Training Camp during the pre-service training period.
- Teacher should realize the importance of value based teachings.
- Teacher's dairy and Student's dairy should be maintained for the smooth work of daily activities.
- Seminars and workshops should be conducted regularly under the supervision of the higher officials.
- B.Ed. students are would be teachers and they should know widely about values. Then only they will be able to practice and inculcate among others. The following suggestions are offered to foster each of the values
- To increase the social value among B.Ed. students, the following activities are suggested:

(i) Providing opportunities for group activities;

(ii) Life histories of social reformers should be made known to students;

(iii) N.S.S. and N.C.C. units should be established in B.Ed. colleges;

(iv) Social awareness camps on various issues should be conducted;

(v) Guest lectures by eminent personalities should be arranged to foster the social values among B.Ed. Students;

- To boost the religious value of the students:

(i) Teachers and administrators have to act as role models in their day-to-day dealings with the students;

(ii) Birthday celebrations of great leaders who are known for their sacrifice, honesty in their personal life may be celebrated;

(iii) The biographies of great religious leaders should be included in the curriculum;

(iv) All religions common principles should be made known to B.Ed. students;

(v) The contribution of religious leaders to the development of society can be highlighted by special lectures by inviting people of eminence.

- To foster economic value of the students:

(i) Small savings for students may be started in colleges in collaboration with near by post office and banks;

(ii) The accounts may be maintained by students;

- For the development of democratic value, the following activities are suggested:

(i) Students should be encouraged to read literature, books and articles, two periods per week can be allotted for library work under the teachers supervision;

(ii) Important days be celebrated by the students themselves only;

(iii) Organization of seminars, debates, sharing the work, providing collective responsibilities and duties to the individuals should be encouraged to increase the democratic values among the B.Ed. students;

- To increase the knowledge value among B.Ed. students, the following activities are suggested:

(i) Assignments, project works should be given;

(ii) Making a hobby to read good books;

(iii) Providing opportunities in problem solving skills;

- To develop power value in students, the following activities are suggested:

(i) Elimination of negative usage of power;

(ii) To build up leadership qualities;

(iii) Organization of seminars, functions, tours, field trips by students.

- To develop hedonistic value:

(i) seminars, workshops, group discussions and symposium may be arranged in B.Ed. colleges.

- To foster the aesthetic value of the students:

(i) Campus should be neat and clean with beautiful trees maintained by B.Ed. students:

(ii) B.Ed. students may be encouraged to take part in decoration of the college during celebrations:

(iii) B.Ed. college managements can arrange picnics and tours to the place of aesthetic interest also, drawing and painting competitions may be organized.

- To increase the health value among B.Ed. students, the following activities are to be promoted:

(i) playing games, participation in sports should be compulsory:

(ii) Practicing yoga, meditation should be included in curriculum:

(iii) For physical fitness—good food habits, morning jagging, drill should be included.

BIBLIOGRAPHY

Adaval (1979): In the Article "A Comparative Study of the Personality Traits of Effective and Less Effective Secondary School Teachers" by Kamala Chopra, *National Journal of Education,* Vol. 6, No. 1, p. 35.

Adhikari G.S. (1986): 'A Study of Values in Relation to SES of Rural Students', *Indian Psychological Abstract,* 249 (1), 39 (Full Article in Asian *Journal of Psychological and Education*, 179 (1), 15-18.

Aggarwal K.G. (1979): *Comprehensive Values Scale*, Agra, National Psychological Corporation.

Aggarwal, Rekha Rani (1986): *'Differential Values Questionnaire' (D.V.Q)* Lucknow, Ankur Psychological Agency.

Aggarwall, L. (1960): 'Value System and Dimensions of University Students of U.P.', In M.B.Buch (Ed.) Second Survey of Research in Education (1972-1978).

Ahluwalia, S.P. (1997): *Teacher Values Inventory,* Agra, National Psychological Corporation.

Alexander, P.J., (1975); 'Teacher Characteristics as Perceived by B.Ed. Trainees', Unpublished M.Ed. Dissertation, University of Kerala.

Ali S.F. and Krunanidhi S. (1998): *A Study of Religiosity and Values*, Indian Education Abstract, 4, 43.

Allport G.W. (1961): Pattern and Growth in Personality, Henry, Holt and Co., Inc., New York.

Allport G.W., Vernon P.E and Lindzey G (1951): 'A Manual of Study of Values', Houghton Mifflin Co. Boston.

Allport, G.W. (1937): Personality—A Psychological Interpretation, Henry, Holt and Co., Inc., New York.

Aluja Fabregat (1996): Personality Measured by EPQ and 16 PF and Their *Relationship to Attitudes Towards Social Values* , Peer Reviewed Journal, Vol 16(5): 48-54.

Anantharaman R.N. (1981): 'The Effect of Sex, Social Class and Rural Urban Locality of Values', *Indian Psychological Abstracts*, 18(1), 51, Full Article in Journal of Psychological Researches, 1680, 24, 112-114.

Anderson, H.H and Brewer, E.H.M. (1965): Studies of Teacher's Classroom Personalities, *Applied Psychology*, Monographs, 6, p. 157.

Annamma, A.K. (1985): 'Values Aspirations and Adjustments of College Students', In M.B.Buch (Ed.) Fourth Survey of Research in Education, *NCERT*, New Delhi.

Arokiasamy, S. (1993): 'Value Perception of the First Degree Students in Colleges Affiliated to Madurai Kamraj University in Relation to Certain Personality and Environmental Factors', *Ph.D Thesis*, M.K. University, Madurai.

Arun K.Gupta Renu Gangal (1989): 'Value Emphasis as Perceived by Pupils of Primary, Middle and High School Stage in Different Institutions', *Indian Educational Review*, Vol. XXIV, No. 1, January 1989.

Assor, Avi (2000): Value Accessibility and Teacher's Ability to Encourage Independent and Critical Thought in Students', *Journal Social Psychology of Education*, 1999, Vol. 2 (3-4): pp. 315-338.

Bajpai, Sunil (1998): 'Sex Difference in Value Patterns of Tribal Students', *Journal of Educational Research and Extension* Vol. 35(4), October December 1998.

Bansal, Saroj (1986): *Culture Values Inventory,* Agra, National Psychological Corporation.

Barbara, Sherman, R. and Robert Blackburn, T. (1975): Personal Characteristics and Teaching Effectiveness of College Faculty, *Journal of Educational Psychology,* Vol. 67, No.1, pp. 124-131.

Barone, Thomas Nicholas (1998): 'A Comparative Study of Value Perceptions and Normalize Rule Compliance of Malaysian and American School students' Dissertation *Abstracts International*, Vol. 59, No.9, March 1999.

Barone, Thomas. N (2004): "Moral Dimensions of Teacher Student Interactions in Malaysian Secondary Schools".

Baythi. J (1987): 'Values in Relation to Religious and Moral Education', *Journal of Indian Education,* 13(2), 15-17.

Berman, Alan, M., (2001): "The Process of Exploration in Identity Formation", *Journal of Adolescence*, August 2001; Vol 24 (4): 513-528.

Bertera, Francis John (1979): 'Value Change in Graduate School' *Dissertation Abstracts International*, Vol. 46, No.4, October 1985.

Bhagavathy, G.P.K. (1977): 'Analytical Study of the Personality, Intelligence, Values and Problem of Adolescent Girls', In M.B.Buch (Ed.) *Third Survey of Research in Education 1978–1983, NCERT*, New Delhi.

Bhagoliwal, S. (1982): "A Study of Personality Characteristics Associated with Teaching Effectiveness as Seen Through Rorschach Technique, Ph.D., Edn, Aligarh University, in *"Third Survey of Educational Research"* by Buch, M.B. (1983), Abst. No. 1083, p. 759.

Bhargava, M. (1997): 'Modern Psychological Testing and Measurement', Agra, Har Prasad Bhargava.

Bhatnagar, J.N. (1979): 'Investigation into the Values, Aspirations and Personality Traits of Adolescents of Rajasthan", In M.B.Buch (Ed.) *Third Survey of Research in Education 1978–1983, NCERT*, New Delhi.

Broadly, Carl Amos (1998): 'Values, Knowledge and Competence is that are Important to your Envelopments Professionals', *Dissertation Abstracts International*, Vol. 59, No. 12, June 1999.

Cattell, R.B. (1946): "The Description and Measurement of Personality", *World Book*, New York.

Cattell, R.B. (1950): "The Main Personality Factors in a Questionnaire, Self-Estimated Material", *Journal of Social Psychology*, Vol. 31, pp.3-38.

Cattell, R.B. (1957): Personality and Motivation Structure and Measurement, New York, *World Book*.

Cattell, R.B. (1962): "16 PF Questionnaire, Form—C", Institute of Personality and Ability Testing, Illinois.

Cattell, R.B. (1964): Validity and Reliability: A Proposed More Basic Set of Concepts, *Journal of Educational Psychology*, 55, pp.1-22.

Chand S.K. (1992): 'A Study of Personal Values of Adolescent Boys and Girls in Relations to Socio-economic Status and Academic Achievement'.

Chandrakumar P.S. and Arokiasamy S. (1974): 'Gender Differences in the Value Orientation Among the College Students', *Journal of Community Guidance and Research* Vol. 11 (3), 187-193.

Chaplin, J.P. (1975): "Dictionary of Psychology", New York, Dell Publishing Co. Inc., p. 398.

Chaturvedi, Archana (2001): 'Personality Pattern: Moral Values and Natural Awakening Among Students Studying in Schools of Different Cultural Associations', *Indian Journal of Educational Research*, Vol. (2002) 45- 51.

Chauhan S.S. (1978): Advanced Educational Psychology, Vikas Publishing House Private Limited, New Delhi, p. 7.

Chauhan, N.S. and Aurora, S. et.al. (1981): 'Value-orientation Scale', Agra Manovigynan Anusandhan Peeth.

Chetty, K.M., (2003): Perspectives of Value-oriented Education, p. 16.

Chhaganlal, Nandani Man Sukhbai (1992): 'A Study of the Value, Adjustment, Attitude Which the Teaching Profession and Academic Achievement of Researchers' Children as Compared to Non-Teachers Children'. [Ph.D. Edu. Saurashtra University.

Chhaya (1974): An Investigation into Certain Psychological Characters of Effective School Teachers (A Comparative Study of Effective and Ineffective School Teachers), Doctoral Thesis in Education, Kanpur University.

Christine J. Yeh, Robert T. Carler and Alex L. Pieterse (2004): 'Cultural Values and Racial Identity Apartheid Among Asian American Students—An Exploratory Investigation', *Journal of Counseling and Values*, January 2004, Vol. 48, pp. 82-95.

Clapp, F.L. (1977): School Effectiveness Expectations, ERIC Journal, ED 258 360, EA 017058, pp.27.

Datta B. (1992): 'Comparative Study of Needs, Values, Aspirations and Adjustments in Relation to Academic Achievements of Scheduled Castes and Other Students of Secondary Schools of Kumaon Ph.D (Edu.) Kumaon University, Nainital, Uttaranchal, India.

Dayakara Reddy, V. (1987): "A Study of Moral Judgement in Relation to Intelligence, Personality and Other Variables", *Unpublishing Ph.D. Thesis*.

De, D.K. (1974): 'A Study of Values of High School Boys and Some Schools in West Bengal', M.B.Buch (Ed) Second Survey of Research in Education 1972-1978, Society for Educational Research and Development, Baroda.

Dennis, W. (1961): 'Use's Test in Bortha, S.E. 'Some Value Differences Among Adult', *Journal of Social Psychology*, 1964, Vol. 63.

Derek Rowntree (1981): A Dictionary of Education, Harper and Row Publisher, London, pp. 2, 16, 229, 303, 315, 327.

Dewey, John (1966): 'In Arthur G with John Dewes as Education', New York; Wiley.

Diwedi, C.B. (1983): 'An Investigation into the Changing Social Values and Their Educational Implications', In M.B.Buch *Fourth Survey of Research in Education 1983-1988*, Vol. II, NCERT, New Delhi.

Dunbar, Edward (2000); Personality and Social Group Value Determinants of Out-group Bias, *Journal of Cross Cultural Psychology,* March 2000: Vol 31 (2): 267-275.

Edwards, A.L. (1969): Techniques of Attitude Scale Construction, Vakils, Feffer and Simmons Pvt. Ltd., Bombay, India.

Eysenck, H.J. (1970): "The Structure of Human Personality", Mathuen and Co, London.

Garrett, Henry, B. (1967): "Statistics in Psychology and Education, pp. 337-370.

Gaur, R.S. (1975): 'A Study of Values and Perceptions of High School Students of the State of Rajasthan, and Their Relation to Learning', In M.B.Buch (Ed) Second Survey of Research in Education 1972-1978, Society for Educational Research and Development, Baroda.

Getzels, J.W. and Jackson, P.W. (1963): The Teacher Personality and Characteristics', In N.L. Gage (Ed.), Handbook of Research on Teaching, Chicago, Rand McNally.

Good, C.V. (1973) (Ed.). "Dictionary of Education", McGraw-Hill Book Company, New Delhi, pp. 3, 7, 49, 233, 441, 464, 465, 511, 563, 564, 565, 586, 594, 613, 638.

Gordon, L.V. (1956): 'Survey of Interpersonal Values', *Cited in Journal of Educational,* Psychology. 1962.

Goyal, R.P. (1974): "A Study of Some Personality Correlates of Creativity in Secondary School Teachers under Training", Ph.D. (Education), Punjab University.

Grewal, S.S. (1976): "Intellectual and Personality Correlates of Teacher Effectiveness at the Higher Secondary School Stage", *Unpublished Doctoral Thesis in Education,* Punjab University, India.

Guilford, J.P. (1954): Psychometric Methods, Tata McGraw-Hill Publishing Company, Faridabad, Haryana, India.

Guilford, J.P. (1959): In The Text Book, *Advanced Educational Psychology,* by S.S.Chauhan (1979), Vikas Publishing House Pvt. Ltd., New Delhi, p. 316.

Gupta (1977A): "A Study of Personality Characteristics, Adjustment Level, Academic achievement and Professional Attitudes of Successful Teachers", Ph.D. (Education), Punjab University.

Gupta, K.L. (1981): Personality, Needs, Moral Judgement and Value Patterns of Secondary School Teachers — A Critical Analysis, Ph.D. Edu., Gor. University.

Gupta, R.C. (1975): "Prediction of Teacher Effectiveness Through Personality Test, *Ph.D. Thesis*, Benaras Hindu University, Benaras.

Gupta, R.C. (1976): "Prediction of Teacher Effectiveness through Personality Test, Unpublished Ph.D. Thesis, Education, Benaras Hindu University, India.

Gupta, R.N. (1977): A Study of the Personality Traits of Primary School Teachers, *Journal of Educational Research and Extension,* Vol. 14, No. 1, pp. 44-49.

Gupta, Ranjana, (1989): 'A Study of the Values and Moral Judgement of Adolescents of Two Representative Centers of Western and Eastern U.P.', Ph.D. (Edu) Agra University

Guyton, John William (1988): Ed. D. Mississipi State University—A Comparison of the Personality Traits of Secondary School Teachers in Mississipi Public Schools, *International Dissertation Abstract,* Vol. 48, No. 10, April, p. 2592-A.

Hartman, G.W., (1979): In the Text Book ,"Advanced Educational Psychology", by S.S. Chauhan (1979), Vikas Publishing House Pvt. Ltd., New Delhi, p. 315.

Hemming, James, (1969): 'Individual Morality', Nelson.

Hirst, P., (1970): 'Philosophy of Education in British Journal of Education Sociology', Vol. XVII, No.2, 1970.

Howie, George (1970): 'Teachers and Their Task in the World Today" Cited in Professional Development of Teachers, Jaipur, RUCTA, p. 51.

Huxley, Julian (1964) A: 'Essays of a Humanist', Pelican, *B*: 'The Humanist Frame'; Harper and Bro., New York.

Jayaswal, S., (1982): 'Education for Social, Moral and Spiritual Values': (Bharatiya Shiksha Shodh Patrika, 8, 5-6).

Jean D. Grambs and L.Morris McClure (1964): Foundations of Teaching: An Introduction to Modern Education, Holt, Rineharet and Winston, Inc, New York, pp. 3-11.

Kabir, Humayun (1959): Education in New India, George Allen and Unwin Ltd., Ruskin House, Museum Street, London.

Kalia, A.K. and Mathur., S.S. (1986): 'Value Preference of Adolescents Studying Schools with Different Socio-economic Environments', *Indian Psychological Abstracts,* 24(1), 43, Full Article in Asian *Journal of Psychology and Education* 1985, 15(1), 1-6.

Kamala Chopra (1983):"A Comparative Study of the Personality Traits of Effective and Less Effective Secondary School Teachers", *National Journal of Education,* Vol. VI, No.1, Sept., pp. 34-39.

Katiyar, P.C. (1976): 'A Study of Values and Vocational Preferences of the Intermediate Class Students in U.P.', In M.B.Buch (Ed) Second Survey of Research in Education 1972-1978, Society for Educational Research and Development, Baroda.

Kaul Lokesh (1972): "Personality Difference of Popular Teacher", *Journal of Educational Psychology*, Vol. 31, No. 2.

Kelly, Earl, C. (1939): "Education for What is Real", Harper and Brothers, New York.

Khanna, N. (1993): 'A Study of the Value Patterns of Students, Studying in Teacher Training and General Streams in a Denominatural Institute', *Journal of Educational Research and Extension,* 30(2), 19-24.

Kilpatrick, W.S.: From "Influence of Certain Psycho-sociological Factors on Scholastic Achievement of DIET Students" by V. Govinda Reddy (2002), *Unpublished Ph.D. Thesis*, S.V. University, Tirupati, India, p. 3.

Krishna Murthy, Jiddu (1981): 'On Education Letters to the School', 'Krishna Murthy Foundation of India', Madras.

Kulshresta, S.P. (1979): 'Emerging Value Pattern of Teachers and New Trends of Education in India", Light and Life Publishers, New Delhi.

Kulwanth pathania and Anitha Pathania (2006): An Article *'Fostering Values in Education*: Some Suggestion', University News, 44(26), June 26-July 02, 2006.

Kundu and Sanyal, N. (1984): 'A Value Profile of College Students Social Changes', 14(1), 9-12.

Leonard, Pauline Elavine (1997): 'Understanding the Dimensions of School Culture: An Investigation into Educator's Value-orientation and Conflicts', *Dissertation Abstracts International*, Vol. 59, No.7, January 1999.

Levine, L.S. (1971): "The American Teacher: A Tentative Psychological Description", ERIC, No. Ed 054 068.

Likert, R. (1932): A Technique for the Measurement of Attitudes, Archieves of Psychology, No. 140 (In) An Index of Job Satisfaction by Brayfield, A.H. and Rothe, H.F. (1951), *Journal of Applied Psychology,* Vol. 35, No. 5, pp. 307-311.

Lokesh Koul (1974):"Personality Correlates of Attitude Towards Teaching", *Journal of Educational Research and Extension*, Vol. 10, No.3, January, pp. 144-149.

Lueck, K. and William, R. (1965): 'An Introduction to Teaching", Henry, Holt and Co., Inc., New York, August, p. 23.

Macneil, Jeremiach Bernard (1991): 'Study of Life Roles and Values of Senior Undergraduate Education Student', *Dissertation Abstracts International,* Vol. 51, No. 11, May 1991.

Mahamood Ali, (1998): 'Personal Values, Career Aspirations, Academic Achievements and Socio-economic Status as Determinants of Educational Choices at Senior Secondary Level', Ph.D., Aligarh Muslim University.

Mahatma Gandhi, In the Textbook, "A First Course in Philosophical and Sociological Foundations of Education" by Bhatia, K.K. and Narang, C.L. M/s Prakash Brothers, Ludhiana, India, 1985, p. 7.

Makhija, G.K. (1973): 'Investigation Among Values, Interests and Intelligence and Impact on Scholastic Achievement'. In M.B.Buch (Ed) Second Survey of Research in Education 1972-1978, Society for Educational Research and Development, Baroda.

Malhotra, S.P. (1976): "Teacher Classroom Behaviour in Relation Presage Variables of Teacher Attitude and Adjustment and Product Variables of Students Liking and Perceived Behaviours by Peers, Principals and Self", Ph.D. Education, Maharaja Sayojirao University of Baroda, India.

Manar, R.N., (1981): 'A Study of Attitudes, Self-concepts and Values of Professional and Non-professional College Students and Relationship of These Variables with the Achievement'. Ph.D.(Edu.) Meerut University. Meerut, U.P., India.

Marx, M.H. and Hillex, W.A. (1973): Systems and Theory in Psychology, McGraw-Hill Book Company, New York.

Mathana, Santiwat (1985): 'A Study of College Student Values at Krungthep (Bangkok) University' *Dissertation Abstracts International*, Vol. 47, No. 5, November 1985.

Mathew George (1976): "Classroom Behaviour of Teachers and Its Relationship with Their Creativity and Self-concept", Ph.D. in Education, Maharaja Sayojirao University of Baroda, India.

Mathews, V.S.: From "An Evaluative Study of Primary School Teacher Education Programme in Andhra Pradesh" by K. Chandra Sekhar (2000) *Unpublished Ph.D. Thesis*, Department of Educatin, S.V. University, Tirupati, India.

McGowan, Patricia Mary (1984): 'A Study of the Multidimensional Representation of Values and Ethnic Differencesm', *Dissertation Abstracts International*, Vol. 45, No. 7, January 1985.

Meintjes, Barend Jacobas Johannes (1981): "Fundamental Pedagogical Criteria for Evaluating a Teacher", *Dissertation Abstracts International*, Vol. 42, No. 6.

Mishra, Karuna Shankar (1979): "Personality Traits of Fluent Teacher", The Indian Teacher, Vol. I, No.6.

Mitzel, H.E. (1960): "Teaching Effectiveness", in C.W. Harris (Ed.,) *Encyclopaedia of Educational Research*, 3rd Edition, New York, Macmillan.

Morris Charles (1957): 'Varieties of Human Value', University of Chicago Press, Chicago.

Moulay, George, J. (1964): The Scinece of Educational Research, American Book Company, New York, p. 3.

Murphy, G. and Likert, A. (1937): Public Opinion and the Individual, Harper, New York.

Murray, Joseph, H. Jr. (1995): 'A Study of the Moral Aspect of Leadership in an Urban School Context', *Dissertation Abstracts International,* Vol. 56, No. 10, April 1996.

Nayyar, Surindar Mohan (1989): 'Closed Mindedness, Open Mindedness and Teacher Values of Student-Teachers in Relation to Caste and Class', *Indian Educational Review,* Vol. 24 (1) 157-169.

Neeta Khanna (1993): 'A Study of the Value Patterns of Students Studying in Teacher Training and General Streams in a Denominational Institute'. *Journal of Education Research and Extension,* Vol. 30, No.2, October 1993, pp. 79-84.

Ojha, R.K. (1984): 'Study of Values', Agra, National Psychological Corporation.

Othman, Joharry (1997): 'Gender and Ethnic Relationship Between Values, Attitudes and Behaviour Among the Selected Malaysian Fourth and Fifth from Students', *Dissertation Abstracts International,* Vol. 58, No. 8, February 1998.

Padhan Gopal Chandra (1994): 'Moral Values of School Students in Relation to Different Personal Values', *Experiments in Education,* Vol. XXII (8) 173-179.

Padhan, G.C. (1993): 'Values Among Secondary School Students in Relation to Moral Judgement, Socio-economic Status and Sex', *Journal of Educational Research and Extension* 29(3) 113-126.

Padmanabha, T. (1992) : 'A Study of the Values of High School Pupils in Relation to Certain Selected Variables' Ph.D. (Edn) Annamalai University.

Pandey, P (1994): 'A Psycho-linguist Study of Democratic Values in Relation to Mono-bi and Tri-Lingualism', *Indian Psychological Abstracts and Reviews,* (1) 159, Full Article in Psycho-lingua, 1991, 21(2), 111-113.

Paradhama, Amara (1992): 'A Study on Role Expectations and Role Performance Among Science Teachers in Relation to Certain Personality Factors', *Unpublished Thesis,* Sri Venkateswara University, Tirupati.

Patel, C.K. (1979): 'A Study of Prevalent Value System of the Secondary Teachers of the High Schools of South Gujarath', In M.B.Buch (Ed) *Third Survey of Research in Education 1978-1983,* NCERT, New Delhi.

Patel, M.G. (1981): 'A Study of Prevalent Value System of the Students of South Gujarat Studying in Standards X and XI', Ph.D (Edu.) South Gujarat University, Surat, Gujarat University.

Patnaik, S.P. and Panda, K.C. (1982): "Personality and Attitude Patterns of Good and Poor Teachers Working in Secondary Schools, *Journal of Education and Psychology*, Vol. 39, No.4, January p. 232.

Peters and William, H. (1985): "Research-based Teacher Behaviours For Effective English Teaching", *ERIC*, Vol. 20, No. 9, September Ed 255926, p. 52.

Precker, J.A., (1952): 'Similarities of Valuing as a Factor in Selection of Peers and Near Authority Figures', *Journal of Abstracts Social Psychology*, 47 p. 406-414.

Preston, Rondall Wayne (1995): 'A Descriptive Study of Values Education Program in Texas Public Elementary Schools', *Dissertation Abstracts International*, Vol. 56, No. 5, November, 1995.

Pyari, S. (1980): 'Feeling of Security, Family Attachment and Values of Adolescent Girls in Relation to Their Educational Achievement, [Ph,D. Psy] Agra University., Agra U.P., India. In M.B.Buch (Ed) *Third Survey of Research in Education* p. 681, NCERT, New Delhi.

Rabindranatha Reddy, C., (2006): "Sri Sathya Sai System of Education *A Model to Follow"*, Value-oriented Education, Edited by V. Dayakara Reddy and D. Bhaskara Rao, Discovery Publishing House, p. 356-377.

Radhakrishnan, S., (1950): 'History of Philosophy', George Allen and Unwin Ltd., Speeches and Writings, Ministry of Information and Broadcasting.

Rajasekhar Reddy., (2004): 'Attitude Towards Value-oriented Eduation in Primary School Teachers', Edited by V. Dayakara Reddy and D. Bhaskara Rao, Discovery Publishing House, p: 343-348.

Rajini, M., (2004) 'Promoting Values in Teacher Trainees", Value-oriented Education, Edited by V. Dayakara Reddy and D. Bhaskara Rao, Discovery Publishing House, p. 349-355.

Rama Mishra (1984): "A Study of Professional Attitude of Teachers in Relation to Their Personality Adjustment", *The Educational Review*, Monthly, Vol. XC, No. 9, September Madras, India, pp. 139-141.

Ramachandra Reddy, B. and Manchala, C., (2006): 'Values and Teacher-Education System', Value-oriented Education, Edited by V. Dayakara Reddy and D.Bhaskara Rao, Discovery Publishing House, p. 244-252.

Ramesh, H.K., (2002): Professional Ethics for Teachers, Quality Management In Teacher Education, Sainath Graphics, *TECEF*, Bangalore.

Rangaswamy, G. (2007): 'A Study on Moral Judgement in Relation to Certain Psycho-sociological Factors', *Unpublished Thesis,* Sri Venkateswara University, Tirupati.

Ranu, Sarbjit Kaur (1995): 'Value–dimensions of Post-graduate Students in Relation to Their Levels of Aspiration and Intelligence', Ph.D., (Edu) Punjab University.

Rathna Kumari, B., (1987): 'A Study of Human Values Among High School Students in Andhra Pradesh in Relation to their Socio-economic Status and Mass Media Exposure', (Ph.D., Psy.) Osmania University, Hyderabad, A.P., India.

Robin A., Musselman (1986): 'Value Patterns of Freshman, Entering Temple University', *Dissertation Abstracts International,* Vol. 47, No. 8, February 1987.

Robinson, Michael (1987): "The Personality Traits of American Secondary School Teachers and Superintendents Who Work in the Association of American Schools of South America", Ph.D. Thesis, University of Maryland, *Dissertation Abstract International,* Vol. 47, No. 10, April, p. 3698-A.

Rocatto Michele, Gattino Silvia, Patris Elena (2001): 'A Study on Personality, Values Political Orientation, Psicologia-politica, November 2000, No. 21, 73-97.

Rogers, Carl (1969): 'Freedom to Learn', Merill, Ohio.

Rokeach, Milton (1973): 'The Nature of Human Values', The Free Press Macmillan Publishing Co., New York.

Rosenberg, Morris (1957): 'Occupation and Values', Glencoe, Illinois: The Free Press.

Rosenkranz, K. (1964): In the Article "Definition of Education", by Thiagarajan, K., Educational India, September (1975), p. 9.

Ryans, D.G. (1960); "Characteristics of Teachers", American Council of Education, Washington, p.79.

Saraswat, R., (1982): 'A Study of Self-concept in Relating to Adjustment, Values, Academic Achievement, Socio-economic Status and Sex of High School Students of Delhi', Ph.D. (Social Sciences), IIT., New Delhi. In M.B.Buch (Ed) *Fourth Survey of Research in Education,* p. 427, NCERT, New Delhi.

Sati B.D., (1992): 'Comparative Study of Needs, Values, Aspirations and Adjustments in Relation to Academic Achievement of S.C. and Other Students of Secondary Schools of Kumaun', Ph.D., Edu., Kumaun University.

Savage (1962): "Personality Factors and Academic Performance", The British *Journal of Educational Psychology*, Vol. 32, p. 25.

Saxena P.C. (1969): "Attitudes Intelligence and Personality Correlates of Competent Teachers", *Indian Psychological Review*, Vol. 115, pp. 107-112.

Scott, Evert Laurel (1986): 'A Comparative Study of Personality, Values and Background Characteristics of Artistically Talented, Academically Talented and Average 11th and `12th Grade Students', *Dissertation Abstracts International*, Vol. 47, No. 10, April, 1987.

Shamshuddin. Sk., (2005): 'A Study on Academic Achievement and Prevalent Values Among D.I.E.T. Students in Andhra Pradesh', *Unpublished Thesis,* Sri Venkateswara University, Tirupati.

Sharma, B.K. (1979): "An Exploratory Study of Certain Aspects of Classroom Behaviour of Science Teachers in the Macro and Micro Teaching Situations Using Interaction Analysis", Ph.D., in Education, Ayodhya University, India.

Sharma, G.R. (1974): "An Investigation into the Relationship Between Personality Factors and Teaching Effectiveness", *Journal of Educational Research and Extension,* Vol.11, No.2, October pp. 122-125.

Sharma, Meenu, (1992): 'A Study of Teachers Socio-economic Status and Values with Reference to then Attitude', Ph.D. (Edu.) Agra University.

Sheppard B. Clough, (1960): "Basic Values of Western Civilization" , Summary

Shukla, Shraddha, (1996): 'A Comparative Study of Values Among Literate and Illiterate, Working and Non-Working Women', *The Progress of Education,* Vol. LXX 1 (5) 118-119.

Sibia, Sukhvinder (1990): 'Value Patterns of Chidren at Piagetian Concrfete and Formal Stages of Development', Ph.D. (Edu.) Punjab University.

Simic, salvica., Soric, Izabela (2004): 'A Study on Personality Factors and Teacher Attitudes in Relation to Their Evaluative Methods, *Peer-Review Journal,* Suvvermera Psihologija, 2004, Vol. 7 (1), 109-128.

Singh S. (1994): 'A Study of Socially Accepted, Rejected and Neglected Children Regarding Their Academic Achievement, Values and Self Disclosure', Ph.D. (Edu.), B.R. Ambedkar University., Agra, U.P., India.

Singh, H.L. (1974): "Measurement of Teacher Values and Their Relationship with Teacher Attitudes and Job Satisfaction", D. Phil in Education, Banaras Hindu University.

Singh, H.M. (1978A): A Study of Leadership Behaviour of Heads of Secondary Schools in Haryana and its Correlates, Ph.D. Thesis, Kurukshetra University.

Singh, R.P., (1997): 'A Study of Values of Urban and Rural Adolescent Students', *Indian Educational Abstract*, 2, 38 (full Article in Praachi– *Journal of Psycho-Cultural Dimensions* 9 (1), 7-11.

Singh, S. (1976): Relationship Between Teachers Personality, Teaching Success and Behavioural Changes in Students, Ph.D. Education, Udaipur University.

Singh, Sudha (1974A): "A Comparative Study of the Personality Profiles of Married and Unmarried School Female Teachers, M.Ed. Dissertation, Banaras Hindu University, Banaras.

Sinha, S., (1981): 'Valuation Generation Gap in the View of Students and their Paents on Student Unrest', In M.B.Buch (Ed) *Third Survey of Research in Education*, 1978-1983, NCERT, New Delhi.

Solis Camera, R. Pedro (1999): A Study on Conceptual Analusis of Competitiveness: Its Relationship with Mexican Personalities, *Peer Reviewed Journal*, December 98, Vol. 14(2): 127-148.

Sombhi, P., (1990): 'A Study of the Value Problems and Some Personality Variables of the Students Studying in three Institutions, Sri Sathya Sai Institutions, Missionary School and Central School in A.P.', Ph.D. (Edu.) Himachal Pradesh University Simla, H.P., India.

Spaights, E., (1967): 'Students Appraise, Teacher's Methods and Attitudes Improving College and University Teaching, *British Journal of Educational Psychology*', Vol.15, pp. 15-17.

Spranger, E., (1928): 'Types of Man', (Tr. By P.J.W.Pigors) New York, Hafner Publishing House.

Srivastava, S.S., (1974): 'Level of Neuroticism Among Different Socioeconomic Categories", Proceedings of the 61st Session of Indian Science Congress, Section of Psychological and Educational Science, Part II, 100, 1974.

Stern, G.G. (1921): (In) Padmanabhaiah, S. (1984), Job Satisfaction and Teaching Effectiveness of Secondary School Teachers, Ph.D., thesis, Submitted to Sri Venkateswara University, Tirupati, India.

Sundarrajan, S., Sakthivel, S., and Ponnalagappan, P.L. (1988) : "The Attitude Towards Teaching of the B.Ed. Student Teachers in the Formal and Distance Education Programmes", *Experiments in Education*, Monthly, the SITU Council of Educational Research, Madras, India, Vol. XIII, No. 9, September pp. 193-207.

Super, D.E. and Mowry (1961): 'Social and Personal Desirability in the Assessment of Work Values', *Educational Psychology and Measurement*, Vol. 22, No. 4.

Susan, Jacob and Anupama Shah (1998): 'A Study of Selected Desirable Characterisitcs and Values of Home Science Students in the State of Gujarat', *Journal of Educational Research and Extension,* Vol.35 (1) January March, 1998.

Suthar, I.K. (1981): "A Study of Classroom Behaviour of Teacher Trainees in the Context of Some Personality Variables", Ph.D. in Education, Sardar Patel University, India.

Swami Vivekananda: In the Textbook, "A First Course in Philosophical and Sociological Foundations of Education" by Bhatia, K.K. and Narang, C.L. M/s Prakash Brothers, Ludhiana, India, 1985, pp. 6-7.

Taj, H., (1998): 'Personal Values of Hindu and Non-Hindu Students in Relation to Their Social Class and Modernization Perspectives in Education', 14(4), 245-248.

Talwar M.S., and Sheela, G., (2006): "A Study of Moral Judgement of Pre University Students in Relation to Gender, Socio-economic Status, Course of Study, Religion and Moral Judgement of their Teachers' Value-oriented Education, Edited by V.Dayakara Reddy and D.Bhaskara Rao, Discovery Publishing House, pp. 324-334.

Tarkunde, V.M. (1978): 'Education for Our People', (Citizens for Democracy, Allied Publishers Private Ltd., New Delhi.

Thakur, S.K. (1980): "Personality Characteristics of Teachers Showing Direct and Indirect Verbal Behaviour", *Unpublished Doctoral Dissertation,* Himachal Pradesh University, Simla, India.

Theodore, Alexander Philip (1986): 'A Study of Attitudes Concerning Values and Value Education Held by Students and Faculty Members at the University of South Albama', *Dissertation Abstracts International,* Vol. 47, No. 9, March, 1987.

Thurstone, L.L., (1959): 'Measurement of Values', Chicago, University of Chicago Press.

Tripathi, V.K.D. (1972): "A Comparative Study of the Personality Profiles of Working Teachers and Teacher-Trainees", M.Ed. Dissertation, B.H. University.

Tuckman, Bruce. W., (1978): "Survey Research" in Conducting Educational Research (Second Edition).

Upadhyaya, S.N., (1978): 'Value Test', Agra, National Psychological Corporation.

Varma, R.P., (1972): 'A Study of Relationship Between the Parents of Interpersonal Relations and Value of Teachers and Students in Secondary Schools', In M.B.Buch (Ed) Third Survey of Research in Education, 1978-1983, *NCERT,* New Delhi.

Vaugh, Kathryn (1998): 'Values, Beliefs and Behaviours: A Replication Comparative Study of Catholic Students and Public schools', *Dissertation Abstracts International,* Vol. 59, No. 12, June, 1999.

Vedprakash, (1994): 'A Study of Educational Aspirations, School Adjustment and Values or +2 Arts and Science Male Students in Relation to School Environment', Ph.D., Education, Punjab University.

Venukumar, S.D.C. (1971): A Study of The Role of Teachers in Secondary Schools, Unpublished M.Ed., Dissertation, University of Kerala.

Verma, B.P. and Sushila Devi Vashista (1987): "Personality Traits and Job Satisfaction of Secondary School Teachers", *Journal of Educational Research and Extension,* Vol. 23, No. 3, January.

Verma, B.P. and Tyagi. R (1988): 'A Study of Sex Differences in Values of Senior Secondary School Teachers', The Progress of Education 62 (9), 198-200.

Verma, D (1996): 'A Study of Value Patterns Among College Youth With Special Reference to Sense of Responsibility', *Indian Educational Abstract* (1) 40.

Verma, Dharmendra, (1995): 'A Study of Value Pattern Among College Youth of Rohilikand Region With Special Reference to Sense of Responsibility', Ph.D., Education, Rohilikand University.

Verma, Madhuri (1986): 'Study of Values', Agra, National Psychological Corporation.

Vernon, P.E. (1963): Personality Assessment: A Critical Survey, Methuen and Co. Ltd., London, pp. 14-15.

Warren, H.C. (1934): "Dictionary of Psychology", Mifflin Company, Houghton, Boston.

Wiron, Donglar (1982): 'The Teaching of Values in the College Classrooms, Faculty and Students Perception at the Three Contrasting', *Dissertation Abstracts International,* Vol. 43, January 1983.

Wolfradt, Uwe (2003): 'Personality, Values and Belief in a Just World', Personality and Individual Differences, December 2003, Vol. 35(8).

Yadav, S.K., (1999): 'Study of Personal Values Among Science Students', Bharatiya Adhunika Shiksha, 17(1), 32-39.

Zamen G.S., (1982): 'A Study of Social, Religious and Moral Values of Students of Class XI and Their Relationship with Moral Character Grants and Personality Adjustment', Ph.D. (Edu) Avadh University U.P., India. In M.B.Buch (Ed) *Fourth Survey of Research in Education,* Vol.1, p. 217, NCERT, New Delhi.

Zuberi I.A., (1984): 'A Study of Relationship Between Personal Values, Needs, Job Adjustment Temperament and Academic Year Career of Secondary School Lectures with Their Teaching Behaviour', Ph.D.(Edu) Aligarh Muslim University Aligarh, U.P., India.

INDEX